S0-CDQ-353

The Golden Anniversary Cookbook

Beta Sigma Phi International

© Favorite Recipes® Press/Nashville EMS MCMLXXX
P.O. Box 77, Nashville, Tennessee 37202
Library of Congress Cataloging in Publication Data
Main entry under title:

The Golden anniversary cookbook.

Includes index.
1. Cookery. I. Beta Sigma Phi. II. Favorite
Recipes Press/Nashville EMS.
TX715.G6137   641.5   80-18885
ISBN 0-87197-131-3

As many of you may know, I have always had a special love of cooking. In my own cookbook, I dedicated my work to the members of Beta Sigma Phi who not only took care of their families, but who shared in the cares and responsibilities of their communities.

These women made cooking more than merely serving meals; they gave it all the energy and creativity that they gave to every phase of their lives. In their hands cooking was an art and a gift of their love.

In this the Golden Anniversary year, I am once again sharing a collection of recipes with you, members of Beta Sigma Phi. I find that during the intervening years, you have shown as much or more dedication to your homes, your families, your careers and your communities. You are members of an International sisterhood who share the family traits of involvement and enthusiasm for all that your lives hold.

Through the years you have grown and expanded, learning many things and giving your knowledge to others. This book, I hope, will add to your growth and enhance your art of cooking. I also hope that you will share this knowledge with your friends and relatives as you have shared so many other things.

Some of my family recipes are included. It is a family tradition to hand down recipes and as members of the world's greatest sisterhood, I hand these down to you and your friends and relatives. I share with you two of my great loves; my love of cooking and my love of Beta Sigma Phi. I hope you will share yours too. Happy Golden Anniversary.

Dorothy Ross

Dorothy Ross
Wife of the Founder of
Beta Sigma Phi

Small Devil's Food Cake

1 cup flour
1 cup sugar
1 egg
½ cup sour milk or ½ cup milk
   and 1 tbsp. vinegar

½ cup boiling water
1 tsp. soda
1 tsp. vanilla
2 squares melted bitter chocolate

Combine flour, sugar, egg and sour milk in a mixing bowl. Mix thoroughly. Add water, soda and vanilla. Melt chocolate over hot water and add to mixture. Mix. The batter is very runny, so does not need beating. Pour in a square baking pan. Bake in a 350 degree over, for 35 minutes or until a silver knife comes clean when inserted in the center. Frost with Butter Cream Frosting, melt 1 square bitter chocolate and pour over top of frosting and spread.

Butter Cream Frosting

½ cup butter
1 lb. confectioner's sugar
   (about 3½ cups sifted)

Pinch of salt
4 to 5 tbsp. hot coffee
1½ tsp. vanilla

Cream butter. Add sugar gradually. Stir until well blended; add salt. Stir in coffee a little at a time, adding just enough to give a good spreading consistency. Beat until fluffy. Add vanilla.

Gumdrop Cookies

1 cup shortening
1 cup white sugar
1 cup brown sugar, packed
2 eggs
1 tsp. vanilla
1 cup coconut
1 cup gumdrops, chopped

1 cup chopped nuts
2 cups rolled oats
2 cups flour
1 tsp. soda
1 tsp. baking powder
½ tsp. salt

Mix the ingredients as listed. Drop on a greased baking sheet. Bake for 10 to 12 minutes at 350 degrees or until brown. Yield: 3 or 4 dozen.

Oxtails Braised

5 oxtails, cut in sections and
   browned in shortening
4 carrots, cut up
1 whole stalk celery, cut up
2 or 3 medium onions, cut up

½ tsp. pepper
2 tsp. salt
1 or more No. 2 cans tomato juice or
   tomato paste and water

After browning meat, add remaining ingredients and cover. Cook in oven, 350 degrees, for 5 hours. Add more liquid if necessary. Should be cooked down by the time it is done. Serves 4.

Table of Contents

Our sincere appreciation to all who submitted the hundreds of recipes for inclusion in this cookbook. We regret we were unable to incorporate all of the recipes due to similarity and lack of space.

Life Learning Friendship

The Golden Years—Years of life, learning and friendship with a flood of memories. For Beta Sigma Phis everywhere, this year is indeed special.

Since Walter and Dorothy Ross held that first "friendly venture" with a handful of women in 1931, so very much has happened. Since then thousands of women have become members of Beta Sigma Phi. The organization now touches the lives of women and their families all over the world.

After 50 years, it's good to celebrate afresh and anew the founding of Beta Sigma Phi. It's so much fun to remember the simple yet significant things that occur between celebrations—A new vista of knowledge opened at chapter meetings, the excitement of successful rush parties, the sisterhood shared through the years at chapter dinners, the gratification of service, and, of course, the anticipation of the future.

The Golden Anniversary Cookbook is another memorable part of this 50th Anniversary year and a part of Beta Sigma Phi forever. Every member should feel great pride as they share this cookbook with family, friends and community.

Happy Anniversary!

Appetizers
and
Beverages

Whether they're called antipasto, hors d'oeuvres, canapes or appetizers, entertaining is dull without them. Beta Sigma Phis have long known these tasty tidbits should tempt the appetite, not satisfy it. Their natural instinct for entertaining also tells them that planning beverages is just as important in menu building as planning appetizers. For that reason, bringing appetizers and beverages together in this chapter is only fitting.

Appetizers were first served with beverages during prohibition years. They were served to offset the bad taste of cheap, bathtub gin and bootleg liquor. Then when prohibition ended and cocktail hours flourished, appetizers gained popularity and were soon an accepted part of hospitality.

Now these foods have gained even greater importance. A cocktail party, chapter meeting, coffee, tea, dinner party or friendly gathering is rarely without appetizers and a delicious thirst-quenching beverage.

Included here are fifty years of Beta Sigma Phi's favorite appetizers and refreshing beverages, sure to whet the appetite and add to the enjoyment of any gathering.

Bourda-Berta Cheese Spread

1 3-oz. package cream cheese, softened
¼ tsp. garlic salt
¼ tsp. lemon pepper
¼ tsp. celery salt
½ tsp. parsley

Combine all ingredients; mix with fork. Refrigerate for several hours. Serve with crackers.

Alberta Moeller, Treas.
Xi Alpha Tau
Williamsville, New York

Cheese Puff Squares

¼ c. margarine
3 eggs, slightly beaten
1 c. milk
1 c. flour
1 tsp. salt
1 tsp. baking powder
1 10-oz. package frozen chopped spinach, thawed
½ lb. Cheddar cheese, shredded
½ lb. Monterey Jack cheese, shredded

Melt margarine in 9 × 13-inch pan; set aside. Combine eggs, milk, flour, salt and baking powder; beat well. Add spinach and cheese; mix well. Pour into melted margarine; mix well. Spread evenly in pan. Bake at 350 degrees for 35 minutes. Cool for 10 minutes. Cut into 1-inch squares. Serve warm. Yield: 20 servings.

Sylvia L. Beaty, Pres.
Xi Zeta Delta X2808
Worth, Illinois

Hot Cheese Balls

1 lb. Velveeta cheese, room temperature
1 lb. Old English cheese, room temperature
1 lg. package cream cheese, room temperature
1 tsp. garlic salt
½ to 1 c. chopped pecans
1 tsp. red pepper
Chili powder

Combine cheeses; mix well using hands. Add garlic salt, pecans and red pepper; mix well. Shape into balls. Roll in chili powder. Wrap in aluminum foil. Chill.

Shirley Annette Ward, Pres.
Xi Theta Phi X2502
Levelland, Texas

Confetti Cheddar Log

1 3-oz. package cream cheese, softened
2 c. shredded Cheddar cheese, at room temperature
¼ c. chopped pitted black olives
2 tbsp. chopped pimento
2 tbsp. chopped green pepper
½ tsp. Worcestershire sauce
Slivered almonds

Beat cream cheese until fluffy. Add cheese; beat well. Stir in olives, pimento, green pepper and Worcestershire sauce, blending well. Place on waxed paper; shape into roll. Coat with almonds; cover. Chill. Let stand for 30 minutes. Serve with assorted crackers.

Photograph for this recipe on page 13.

Cream Cheese-Pineapple Spread

2 8-oz. packages cream cheese, softened
1 8½-oz. can crushed pineapple, drained
¼ c. chopped green pepper
2 tbsp. chopped onion
1 tbsp. seasoned salt
2 c. chopped pecans

Combine first 5 ingredients and 1 cup pecans; mix well. Chill. Shape mixture into log. Roll in remaining pecans. Cover and chill until firm. May be kept for several weeks if tightly wrapped.

Carol Aldrich
Xi Delta Mu X3983
Hawarden, Iowa

Cheese Snacks

½ lb. butter, at room temperature
½ lb. American cheese, grated
2 c. flour
1 tbsp. sugar
½ tsp. salt
Jelly

Combine butter and cheese; cream until smooth. Add flour, sugar and salt; mix well. Shape into walnut-sized balls. Refrigerate for 24 hours. Let stand until room temperature. Roll each ball into circle. Put 1 tablespoon jelly in each circle; fold. Crease edges with tines of fork. Bake at 425 degrees for 15 minutes. Yield: 36-48 servings.

Ardith Day, Pres.
Preceptor Upsilon XP764
Portland, Oregon

Mexican Snack

2 c. grated Cheddar cheese
1 4-oz. can chopped green chilies, drained
2 eggs

Combine cheese and green chilies; mix well. Combine eggs and 2 tablespoons water; beat well. Add to cheese mixture. Pour into 8 × 8-inch baking pan. Bake at 350 degrees for 30 minutes. Yield: 6-8 servings.

JoAnne M. Hunter, Pres.
Xi Beta Eta X2062
Saginaw, Michigan

Parmesan Twists

¼ c. butter
1 c. grated Parmesan cheese
½ c. sour cream
1 c. flour
½ tsp. Italian seasoning
1 egg yolk
Caraway seed, poppy seed or coarse salt

Cream butter until smooth. Add cheese; beat until light and fluffy. Add sour cream gradually, beating well after each addition. Combine flour and seasoning; stir into creamed mixture. Roll out ½ of the dough on lightly floured surface to form 12 × 7-inch rectangle. Cut into 6 × ½-inch strips. Beat egg yolk with 1 tablespoon water; brush strips. Sprinkle with caraway seed. Twist each strip 2 or 3 times. Place on buttered cookie sheet. Repeat procedure with remaining dough. Bake at 350 degrees for 12 to 15 minutes or until lightly browned.

Photograph for this recipe on page 13.

Party Cheese Ball

2 8-oz. packages cream cheese, softened
2 c. shredded sharp Cheddar cheese
1 tbsp. chopped pimento
Dash of cayenne pepper
1 tbsp. chopped green pepper
1 tbsp. chopped onion
2 tsp. Worcestershire sauce
1 tsp. lemon juice
Dash of salt
Finely chopped pecans

Combine cheeses; cream until well blended. Add remaining ingredients except pecans; mix well. Shape into ball. Roll in pecans. Chill until firm. Serve with crackers.

Bonnie Reisig, Pres.
Beta Tau
Sardis, British Columbia, Canada

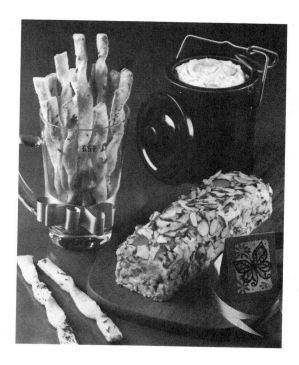

Lona's Cheese Ball

1 8-oz. package cream cheese, softened
2 oz. sharp Cheddar cheese, grated
½ sm. onion, finely chopped
2 tbsp. green relish
½ c. crushed walnuts

Combine cream cheese, Cheddar cheese, onion and relish; blend well with wooden spoon. Shape into ball. Roll in walnuts. Chill for several hours. Serve with crackers. Yield: 20 servings.

Lona A. Badcock, Pres.
Pi No. 11034
Torbay, Newfoundland, Canada

Patricia's Cheese Ball

1 8-oz. package cream cheese
1 tbsp. mayonnaise
2 tsp. Worcestershire sauce
⅛ tsp. salt
⅛ tsp. pepper
½ med. onion, grated
½ tsp. garlic powder
1 tbsp. milk
½ lb. sharp cheese, grated
Sesame seed or crushed pecans

Combine cream cheese and mayonnaise in mixer bowl; beat until smooth. Add next 7 ingredients, blending well. Refrigerate until easily shaped. Roll into ball. Roll in sesame seed. Refrigerate until firm. Yield: 10-12 servings.

Patricia S. Whitehead, Pres.
Gamma Upsilon No. 10191
Hartsville, South Carolina

Pineapple-Cheese Balls

16 oz. cream cheese, softened
1 8½-oz. can crushed pineapple, drained
¼ c. finely chopped green pepper
2 tbsp. finely chopped onion
1 tsp. seasoned salt
2 c. chopped pecans
1 tsp. chives (opt.)

Beat cream cheese until light and fluffy. Stir in pineapple. Add green pepper, onion, seasoned salt, 1 cup pecans and chives; mix well. Shape into 2 balls. Sprinkle with remaining pecans. Chill until firm.

Lee Flowers, Pres.
Sigma Gamma No. 10465
Rolla, Missouri

Potted Cheese In Sherry

½ c. butter, softened
2 c. shredded Cheddar cheese, at room
  temperature
½ c. sour cream
½ tsp. ground mace
⅛ tsp. salt
Dash of cayenne pepper
2 tbsp. dry Sherry

Cream butter until light. Add cheese; blend well. Stir in remaining ingredients; cover. Chill. Let stand for 30 minutes. Yield: 2¼ cups.

Photograph for this recipe on page 13.

Shrimp-Cheese Balls

4 3-oz. packages cream cheese, softened
3 tsp. prepared mustard
2 tsp. grated onion
2 tsp. lemon juice
Dash of cayenne pepper
1 4½-oz. can shrimp, drained
Chopped pecans

Combine first 5 ingredients; blend until smooth. Break shrimp into bite-sized pieces. Add to cream cheese mixture; stir well. Chill for 30 to 45 minutes. Form into walnut-sized balls. Roll in nuts. Chill until firm.

Jackie Haskins, City Coun. Pres.
Xi Alpha Xi X2183
Las Cruces, New Mexico

Chicken Salad Spread
(1930)

1 c. cooked chicken
½ c. celery
¼ c. olives
¼ c. walnuts
¼ c. onions
Mayonnaise

Force first 5 ingredients through food grinder. Blend ground ingredients with enough mayonnaise until of spreading consistency. Serve with bread rounds or crackers.

Betty W. Cote
Preceptor Alpha XP133
Manchester, New Hampshire

Chinese Chicken Wings

3 lb. chicken wings
Salt and pepper to taste
2 tbsp. vegetable oil
1 c. honey
½ c. soya sauce
1 tsp. garlic powder
2 tbsp. catsup
½ tsp. powdered ginger

Cut off and discard tips from chicken wings. Cut wings into 2 parts. Place in 10 × 15-inch baking pan. Sprinkle with salt, pepper and oil. Combine remaining ingredients in small saucepan; mix well. Heat just to blend. Pour over wings. Bake at 350 degrees for 1 hour, basting frequently. Serve over rice.

Rose Backs, Pres.
Preceptor Alpha Nu XP1891
Coquitlam, British Columbia, Canada

Chili Dip

1 lb. ground beef
1 tsp. chili powder
2 tbsp. catsup
¼ c. taco sauce
1 15-oz. can refried beans
Dash of pepper
1 c. grated cheese
⅓ c. chopped onion
8 to 10 green olives, sliced

Brown ground beef; drain. Add chili powder, catsup, taco sauce, beans, pepper and ½ of the cheese; mix well. Cook until cheese is melted. Pour into fondue pot. Sprinkle with onion, olives and remaining cheese; stir into melted cheese. Serve with Doritos.

Judy Cole, Sec.
Eta Iota No. 6336
Cedar Rapids, Iowa

Crab Meat Dip

1 c. mayonnaise
½ c. sour cream
1 tsp. lemon juice
1 tbsp. Sherry
1 7½-oz. can crab meat, drained and flaked
1 tbsp. chopped parsley

Combine mayonnaise, sour cream, lemon juice and Sherry; mix well. Stir in crab meat and parsley. Serve with carrot sticks or potato chips.

Joyce A. Harrahy, Pres.
Omega No. 10754
Merrimack, New Hampshire

Dill Dip

1 c. Hellmann's mayonnaise
1 c. sour cream
1 tbsp. minced dry onion
1 tbsp. parsley flakes
1 tsp. seasoned salt
1 tsp. dillweed
1 tsp. Accent
½ tsp. Worcestershire sauce

Combine all ingredients; mix well. Refrigerate overnight. Serve as dip for vegetables.

Doris Lofland, Pres.
Preceptor Alpha XP171
Milford, Delaware

Linda's Dill Dip

2 c. sour cream
2 c. mayonnaise
3 tbsp. parsley flakes
3 tsp. minced onion
3 tsp. dillweed
3 tsp. Beau Monde seasoning

Combine all ingredients; mix well. Chill until flavors blend.

Linda James
Alpha Theta No. 419
Chariton, Iowa

Hot Chipped Beef Dip

1 8-oz. package cream cheese, softened
2 tbsp. milk
2 to 4 tbsp. minced onion
2 to 4 tbsp. diced green pepper
⅛ tsp. pepper
½ c. sour cream
¾ c. finely chopped dried beef
¼ c. chopped walnuts

Combine first 7 ingredients; mix well. Place in shallow glass 9-inch pie plate. Sprinkle with walnuts. Bake at 350 degrees for 20 minutes. Serve with corn chips, potato chips or crackers. Yield: 8-10 servings.

Mary T. Dickinson, Pres.
Xi Alpha Iota X3511
Rochester, Minnesota

Mexican Olive-Avocado Dip

1 sm. can chopped ripe olives, drained
1 sm. can chopped green chilies, drained
2 tomatoes, peeled and chopped
4 lg. onions, finely chopped
1 lg. or 2 small avocados, mashed
3 tbsp. vegetable oil
1½ tbsp. vinegar
1 tsp. garlic salt

Combine all ingredients in mixing bowl; mix well. Cover. Refrigerate for 1 to 2 hours. This dip is delicious served with fresh vegetables or corn chips. Yield: 8 servings.

Susan Leggett, Pres.
Xi Delta Mu X4803
Oklahoma City, Oklahoma

Shrimp Dip

1 can cocktail shrimp, drained and chopped
1 c. grated sharp Cheddar cheese
¼ c. chopped onion
1 c. mayonnaise or salad dressing
Dash of Worcestershire sauce

Combine all ingredients; mix well. Chill to blend flavors. Serve with cauliflower, celery, chips or crackers. Yield: 8 servings.

Carolyn Abell, V.P.
Theta Xi No. 7746
Murray, Iowa

Beverly's Shrimp Dip

1 8-oz. package cream cheese, softened
½ c. catsup
3 tbsp. cream-style horseradish
1 6½-oz. can shrimp, drained and rinsed

Combine cream cheese, catsup and horseradish in mixer bowl; beat until well blended. Fold in shrimp. Chill to blend flavors. Serve with potato chips and/or assorted crackers. Yield: 2 cups.

Beverly Lennon, Treas.
Xi Alpha Nu. X5260
Rapid City, South Dakota

Brenda's Vegetable Dip

1 3-oz. package cream cheese, softened
1 c. mayonnaise
1 tbsp. tarragon vinegar
1 tsp. garlic salt
1 tsp. horseradish
1 tsp. curry powder
1 tsp. minced onion

Combine all ingredients; mix well. Chill to blend flavors. Serve with green peppers, celery, carrots, cauliflower and radishes.

Brenda D. Feller, Corr. Sec.
Nu Omega No. 6859
St. Elmo, Illinois

Broccoli Dip

1 onion, chopped
1 stick margarine
1 pkg. Kraft garlic cheese
1 can cream of mushroom soup
1 4-oz. can sliced mushrooms, drained
1 10-oz. package frozen broccoli, thawed

Saute onion in margarine. Add remaining ingredients. Cook until heated through, stirring constantly. Serve warm with tortilla chips.

Karen L. Allen
Kappa Eta No. 9578
Hugoton, Kansas

Cauliflower-Curry Dip

1 head cauliflower
1 c. mayonnaise
1 tsp. garlic salt
1 tsp. prepared horseradish
1 tsp. curry powder
⅛ tsp. sugar
1 or 2 drops of yellow food coloring (opt.)

Break cauliflower into flowerets. Cut flowerets into bite-sized pieces. Chill until serving time. Combine remaining ingredients; blend well. Serve as dip for cauliflower.

Thelma Shaw
International Honorary Mem.
Fairmont, West Virginia

Joan's Spinach Dip

1 pkg. frozen chopped spinach, thawed and
  drained
1 pkg. vegetable soup mix
1 can sliced water chestnuts, drained
1 c. mayonnaise
1 c. sour cream
1 loaf rye bread

Combine spinach, soup mix, water chestnuts, mayonnaise and sour cream; mix well. Refrigerate for 1 hour. Scoop out center of bread, reserving removed bread. Fill bread with spinach mixture. Place on serving platter. Place reserved bread around loaf. Yield: 8-10 servings.

Joan Henck, Pres.
Nu Alpha
Novelty, Ohio

Jill's Vegetable Dip

1 carton sour cream
1 c. mayonnaise
1 tbsp. onion flakes
1 tsp. parsley
1 tsp. bon appetit
1 tsp. dillweed
Dash of lemon pepper

Combine sour cream and mayonnaise; mix well. Stir in remaining ingredients; cover. Refrigerate for 2 hours. Serve with vegetables or potato chips.

Jill McDougall, Pres.
Xi Sigma X4610
Regina, Saskatchewan, Canada

Zell's Vegetable Dip

1 c. chopped spinach, drained
½ c. chopped parsley
1 tsp. salt
1 tsp. pepper
½ c. chopped onion
2 c. mayonnaise

Combine all ingredients; mix well. Refrigerate for 24 hours. Serve with carrot sticks, celery, cauliflower, zucchini sticks and cucumbers. Yield: 3 cups.

Zell Derryberry, Rec. Sec.
Alpha Upsilon
Buffalo, Wyoming

Cocktail Meatballs

2 lb. lean ground beef
2 c. herb-seasoned bread crumbs
2 eggs, slightly beaten
¾ tsp. garlic powder
¼ c. evaporated milk
½ c. chopped canned mushrooms
3 tsp. salt
½ c. chopped onion
¼ c. butter or margarine
2 tbsp. flour
1 16-oz. can tomatoes, drained
2 c. chopped green chilies

Combine ground beef, bread crumbs, eggs, ¼ teaspoon garlic powder, evaporated milk, mushrooms and 2 teaspoons salt; mix well. Shape into walnut-sized balls. Place on cookie sheet. Bake at 375 degrees for 10 minutes. Place in deep casserole; keep warm. Saute onion in margarine until tender. Add flour; stir until browned. Add tomatoes, mashing well. Add 1 cup hot water, green chilies, ½ teaspoon garlic powder and 1 teaspoon salt; mix well. Simmer for 10 to 15 minutes. Pour over meatballs; mix gently. Freezes well. Yield: 6-7 dozen.

Joanne Romero, Sec.
Alpha Tau No. 3923
Belen, New Mexico

Mini Meatballs

1 lb. ground chuck
¼ c. minced onion
1 tbsp. parsley flakes
1 tsp. salt
¼ tsp. pepper
1 tsp. Worcestershire sauce
1 c. dry bread crumbs
¼ c. milk
Butter
1 10-oz. jar grape jelly
1 10-oz. jar chili sauce

Combine first 8 ingredients; mix well. Shape into 1-inch meatballs. Brown in butter. Drain; set aside. Combine jelly and chili sauce in 3-quart saucepan. Cook over Medium heat until jelly is melted. Add meatballs; mix well. Simmer, uncovered, for 2 hours. Yield: 60 servings.

Cynthia Bevington, Pres.
Xi Iota Tau X4977
Alachua, Florida

Bacon-Oyster Roll-Ups

1 lb. bacon
1 c. herb-seasoned stuffing mix
2 5-oz. cans oyster pieces, drained

Cut bacon slices in half. Combine stuffing mix, oysters and ½ cup water; mix well. Roll into 36 balls. Wrap in bacon slices. Broil for 25 to 30 minutes.

Kathy Stamper, Sec.
Mu Rho No. 8285
Chesterfield, Missouri

Japanese Meat-On-A-Stick

½ c. soy sauce
1 c. pineapple juice
¼ c. sugar
3 to 4 cloves of garlic, crushed
1 tbsp. grated ginger
1½ to 2 lb. beef or pork

Combine first 5 ingredients; mix well. Cut meat into ½-inch wide strips. Add to pineapple juice mixture. Marinate for 24 hours. Thread strips on skewers. Place on broiler rack. Bake at 350 degrees for 4 minutes, turning skewers often.

Eros Widrig, W. and M. Chm.
Xi Nu Zeta X3068
Valencia, California

Liverwurst Spread

1 lb. liverwurst
½ tsp. leaf basil
3 tsp. onion
1 sm. clove of garlic, chopped
1 8-oz. package cream cheese, softened
1 tsp. mayonnaise
½ tsp. Tabasco sauce

Combine first 4 ingredients; mix well. Shape into ball. Combine cream cheese, mayonnaise and Tabasco sauce; mix well. Cover ball with cream cheese mixture. Garnish with parsley around base and 1 slice pimento-stuffed olive on top. Serve with crackers.

Virginia Visser, Treas.
Alpha Upsilon No. 3508
West Haven, Connecticut

Mary's Sausage Balls

1 lb. hot sausage
3 c. grated sharp cheese
3 c. Bisquick

Combine sausage and cheese; mix well. Add Bisquick; mix well. Shape into walnut-sized balls. Bake at 350 degrees for 25 minutes. Yield: 30 servings.

Mary Casteel, Pres.
Beta Nu No. 4442
Batesville, Arkansas

Party Pizza Snacks

1½ lb. pork sausage
Oregano and garlic salt to taste
Tabasco sauce and Worcestershire sauce to taste
1 tbsp. catsup
1 lb. Velveeta cheese, cubed
1 jar pizza sauce
1 1-lb. loaf party rye bread, sliced
Parmesan cheese

Brown sausages in 10-inch skillet. Add seasonings and catsup; mix well. Simmer for 15 minutes. Melt cheese in top of double boiler. Add to sausage mixture, mixing well. Spread each bread slice with 1 tablespoon pizza sauce and 1 tablespoon sausage mixture. Sprinkle with Parmesan cheese. Place on cookie sheet. Bake at 350 degrees for 8 to 10 minutes.

Christine Norris
Lambda Xi No. 7773
Mendon, Missouri

Huff 'n Puff

½ c. flour
½ c. beer
1 tbsp. cooking oil
½ tsp. salt
1 egg white
10 wieners, quartered

Combine flour, beer, oil and salt; mix well. Let stand at room temperature for 1 hour and 30 minutes to 2 hours. Beat egg white until stiff peaks form. Fold into flour mixture. Dip wiener pieces into batter. Cook in deep hot fat until lightly browned. Yield: 40 servings.

Charlotte Zimmerman, Treas.
Delta Mu No. 10009
Bellevue, Nebraska

Spiced Wieners

¼ c. chopped onion
2 tbsp. oil

½ tsp. pepper
¼ c. catsup
¼ c. vinegar
1 tsp. prepared mustard
1 tbsp. corn syrup
1 tsp. Worcestershire sauce
8 wieners, cut lengthwise

Cook onion in hot oil until tender. Combine pepper, catsup, vinegar, mustard, corn syrup and Worcestershire sauce; mix well. Add to onion; mix well. Place wieners in baking pan. Cover with sauce. Bake at 375 degrees for 30 minutes. Yield: 8 servings.

Trudy Walkup, Pres.
Phi No. 10467
Harlingen, Texas

Sticky Ham Balls

2 lb. ground ham
2 lb. ground pork
2 c. fine graham cracker crumbs
2 eggs, slightly beaten
1½ c. milk
1 can tomato soup
1½ c. (firmly packed) brown sugar
½ c. vinegar
1 tsp. dry mustard

Combine ham, pork, cracker crumbs, eggs and milk; mix well. Shape into 1-inch balls. Place in two 9 × 13-inch baking pans. Combine remaining ingredients; mix well. Pour over ham balls; cover with foil. Bake at 325 degrees for 30 minutes; uncover. Bake at 325 degrees for 1 hour longer, basting 3 times.

Joan Ackland, Pres.
Delta Omega No. 10766
Geneva, Nebraska

Quick Herb Pick-Ups

½ c. butter
2 tbsp. Parmesan cheese
1½ tsp. parsley flakes
½ tsp. dillweed
1 tbsp. onion flakes
1 10-count pkg. refrigerator biscuits, quartered

Melt butter in 8 × 12-inch casserole. Combine Parmesan cheese, parsley flakes, dillweed and onion flakes; stir into melted butter. Place biscuits in butter mixture, coating well. Bake at 425 degrees for 12 to 15 minutes.

Ronnie Graves, Pres.
Xi Phi X2150
Rogers, Arkansas

Sandwich Spread

1 env. unflavored gelatin
2 c. mayonnaise
1 tsp. salt
2 cucumbers, peeled, seeded and finely chopped
1 c. finely chopped celery
2 carrots, finely chopped
1 onion, finely chopped

Soften gelatin in ¼ cup cold water; heat to dissolve. Add remaining ingredients. Serve on slices of Arnold's or Pepperidge Farm bread. Refrigerate until serving time.

Dr. Herberta Ann Leonardy
International Honorary Mem.
Miami, Florida

Triscuit Spread

1 8-oz. package cream cheese, softened
2 tbsp. milk
½ c. sour cream
2 tbsp. minced green onion
2 tbsp. minced green pepper
⅛ tsp. pepper
1 5-oz. jar dried beef, cut into bite-sized pieces
⅓ c. sliced or chopped walnuts

Combine cream cheese and milk; blend until smooth. Add sour cream, stirring well. Add green onion, green pepper, pepper and dried beef; mix well. Spread in 9-inch glass pie plate. Sprinkle with walnuts. Bake at 350 degrees for 15 minutes. Serve with Triscuit crackers.

Edith J. Howell, Pres.
Preceptor Theta Sigma No. 1886
Glendale, California

Barbara's Crab Appetizers

1 7-oz. can crab meat, drained and flaked
1 tbsp. minced onion
1 c. shredded Swiss cheese
½ c. mayonnaise
1 tsp. lemon juice
¼ tsp. curry powder
1 12-count pkg. butterflake dinner rolls
1 5-oz. can sliced water chestnuts, drained
Dash of paprika

Combine first 6 ingredients; mix well. Separate each roll into 3 layers. Place rolls on cookie sheet. Spread with crab mixture. Top with water chestnuts and paprika. Bake at 375 degrees for 10 to 12 minutes or until lightly browned.

Barbara J. Hoffman
Xi Zeta Zeta X5338
Fort Wayne, Indiana

Clam Puffs

3 4½-oz. cans minced clams
½ c. margarine
1 c. flour
4 eggs
2 6-oz. packages cream cheese, softened
2 tbsp. minced onion flakes
Dash of salt
4 tbsp. parsley
½ tsp. Lawry's Seasoned Salt
6 drops of Tabasco sauce

Drain clams, reserving 1 cup liquid. Combine reserved liquid and margarine in saucepan. Bring to a boil. Add flour, stirring until smooth and batter holds together. Add eggs, one at a time, beating well after each addition. Drop by teaspoonfuls onto ungreased cookie sheet. Bake at 400 degrees for 10 minutes. Reduce heat. Bake at 300 degrees for 10 minutes longer. Combine remaining ingredients; mix well. Fill puffs.

Mary Ann Nordenson, Ext. Off.
Alpha Kappa No. 415
Oskaloosa, Iowa

Crab Appetizer
(1950)

1 6-oz. package cream cheese
1 10-oz. can cream of mushroom soup
1 env. unflavored gelatin
1 can crab meat
1 green onion, chopped
1 c. mayonnaise
Salt and pepper to taste
Lemon juice to taste
Tabasco sauce to taste

Combine cream cheese and soup in saucepan. Cook on Low until heated through and blended. Dissolve gelatin in 3 tablespoons cold water. Add gelatin and remaining ingredients to soup mixture; mix well. Pour into fish mold. Refrigerate overnight. Garnish with pimento, olives and parsley. Serve with Ritz crackers.

Marva Kerby, Pres.
Alpha Beta XP1931
Bonners Ferry, Idaho

Gourmet Crab Ring

1 tsp. unflavored gelatin
2 8-oz. packages cream cheese, softened
2 tbsp. cooking Sherry
¾ tsp. seasoned salt
1 2-oz. jar pimento, drained and chopped
1 6-oz. package frozen crab meat, thawed and drained

⅛ tsp. pepper
¼ c. snipped parsley

Sprinkle gelatin over ¼ cup cold water to soften. Stir over hot water until dissolved. Combine gelatin mixture and cream cheese; beat until smooth. Add Sherry, seasoned salt, pimento, crab meat, pepper and 2 tablespoons parsley; mix well. Pour into 3-cup ring mold. Chill for 4 hours or until firm. Invert on serving plate. Garnish with remaining parsley. Serve with crackers.

Carol A. Neas, Pres.
Preceptor Beta Nu XP1951
Loveland, Colorado

Salmon Party Ball

1 8-oz. package cream cheese, softened
1 tsp. lemon juice
¼ tsp. liquid smoke
1 tsp. horseradish
2 tsp. grated onion
¼ tsp. salt
1 1-lb. can salmon
½ c. chopped walnuts
3 tsp. dried parsley

Combine cream cheese, lemon juice, liquid smoke, horseradish, onion and salt; cream until smooth. Stir in salmon. Shape into ball. Roll in walnuts and parsley. Chill for 2 hours. Serve with crackers.

Pamela Reiner, Treas.
Theta No. 683
Albany, Oregon

Seafood Ball

1 8-oz. package cream cheese, softened
Milk
1 tbsp. minced onion
½ tsp. (heaping) Season All
2 stalks celery, minced
2½ to 1 c. finely chopped shrimp, clams or crab meat
Parsley flakes

Combine cream cheese and enough milk until of spreading consistency. Add remaining ingredients; mix well. Refrigerate overnight. Let stand for 1 hour. Shape into ball. Roll in parsley. Serve with crackers.

Carmen M. Kintz, Pres.
Gamma Phi No. 3753
Sarasota, Florida

Grapefruit Shrimp

3 tbsp. butter or margarine
2 lb. shrimp, peeled and deveined

½ c. chopped onion
1 tsp. dried dillweed
¼ tsp. Tabasco sauce
1 tsp. sugar
½ tsp. salt
1 tsp. grated grapefruit rind
1 c. Florida grapefruit juice

Melt butter in large skillet. Add shrimp, onion and dillweed; cook until shrimp is pink. Add Tabasco, sugar, salt, grapefruit rind and juice; mix well. Simmer for 2 minutes. Chill. Yield: 12 servings.

Photograph for this recipe on page 10.

Pickled Shrimp

2 lb. shrimp, peeled and deveined
2 med. onions, sliced
½ c. vegetable oil
1½ c. white vinegar
½ c. sugar
1½ tsp. salt
1½ tsp. celery seed
4 tbsp. capers and liquid

Cook shrimp in boiling salted water for 3 to 5 minutes or until pink and tender. Drain; rinse with cold water. Chill. Alternate layers of shrimp and onions in airtight container. Combine remaining ingredients; mix well. Pour over shrimp; seal container. Chill for 6 hours, inverting container occasionally. Remove shrimp. Yield: 6 servings.

Martha Hallman, W. and M. Chm.
Mu No. 705
Jackson, Tennessee

Shrimp Mold

1 6-oz. can tomato soup
2 8-oz. packages cream cheese
½ c. mayonnaise
1 3-oz. package lemon gelatin
1 12-oz. package frozen salad shrimp, thawed
½ to ¾ c. finely chopped onion
½ to ¾ c. finely chopped celery

Pour soup into saucepan; cook until heated through. Add cream cheese and mayonnaise. Cook over Low heat until smooth. Remove from heat. Dissolve gelatin in ½ cup hot water. Add to soup mixture. Add remaining ingredients; mix well. Pour into ring mold. Chill for 4 hours. Serve with crackers.

Mavis C. Weaver, Pres.
Xi Alpha Nu X2617
Doraville, Georgia

Shrimp Rolls

½ c. tomato juice
1 egg, beaten
½ c. dry bread crumbs
1 c. cooked rice
Pepper and garlic powder to taste
½ tsp. chopped parsley
½ tsp. celery salt
1 c. grated shrimp
Dash of curry powder
Tabasco sauce to taste
Pinch of salt
Bacon slices, halved

Combine all ingredients except bacon; mix well. Shape into walnut-sized balls. Wrap each in bacon slice. Broil, turning frequently until browned.

Mary Ruth Tasler
International Coordinator
Xi Epsilon Psi No. 1926
Port Lavaca, Texas

Shrimp Butter

2 cans med. shrimp, drained
1 tbsp. minced onion
4 tbsp. mayonnaise
1½ sticks butter, softened
1 8-oz. package cream cheese, softened
¼ tsp. garlic powder
Juice of 1 lemon

Combine all ingredients in mixer bowl. Mix at Low speed of electric mixer until well blended. Serve with snack crackers. Yield: 25-30 servings.

Virginia L. Poole
1980 Kentucky Conv. Chm.
Xi Alpha Nu X4710
Versailles, Kentucky

Mushroom Spread

1 lb. mushrooms, finely chopped
1 onion, finely minced
2 tbsp. butter
2 tbsp. lemon juice
2 hard-cooked eggs, chopped
Dash of garlic salt
¼ c. Sherry

Combine all ingredients except Sherry in skillet; mix well. Cook over Low heat for 15 minutes. Stir in Sherry. Cook over Low heat for 15 minutes longer. Serve with rye rounds.

Evelyn Berryman, Pres.
Alpha No. 10224
Italy

Grilled Stuffed Mushrooms

16 lg. mushrooms
2 tbsp. minced onion
1/3 c. deviled ham
1/4 tsp. Worcestershire sauce
1/2 tsp. salt
1/4 tsp. pepper
16 pimento strips
Cooking oil

Remove stems from mushrooms; chop stems finely. Combine chopped stems, onion, deviled ham, Worcestershire sauce, salt and pepper; mix well. Spoon into mushroom caps. Top with pimento strips. Brush with oil. Place, stuffed-side up, on broiler rack. Broil for 10 minutes. Yield: 4 servings.

Janet Lenko, Pres.
Xi Alpha Eta X3405
West Vancouver, British Columbia, Canada

Spinach Balls

2 10-oz. packages frozen chopped spinach
2 c. herb-seasoned stuffing mix
1 lg. onion, finely chopped
5 med. eggs, slightly beaten
3/4 c. melted butter
1/2 c. grated Parmesan cheese
1 tbsp. garlic salt
1 tsp. pepper
1/4 tsp. thyme

Prepare spinach according to package directions; drain. Combine spinach and remaining ingredients; mix well. Shape into nickel-sized balls. Place on cookie sheet. Bake at 350 degrees for 20 to 30 minutes.

Susan Sliney Ohrenberger
Gamma Psi No. 8135
Framingham, Massachusetts

Texas Caviar

4 c. cooked black-eyed peas, drained
1 c. vegetable oil
1 clove of garlic
1/4 c. wine vinegar
1/2 tsp. salt

Combine all ingredients; mix well. Place in jar; cover. Store in refrigerator for 24 hours; remove garlic clove. Will keep refrigerated for 2 weeks. Serve with tortilla chips or potato chips.

Martha Rebecca Beaird, Pres.
Alpha Tau Omega No. 11050
Huntsville, Texas

Water Chestnut Rumaki

1 1-lb. can water chestnuts, drained
1 lb. bacon, cut into thirds
1 c. sugar
2/3 c. catsup

Wrap each chestnut with bacon. Secure with toothpick. Place on broiler pan. Bake at 300 degrees for 1 hour; drain. Combine sugar and catsup; mix well. Dip rumaki in sugar mixture. Bake at 300 degrees for 1 hour longer. Serve in chafing dish.

Margaret Forbes, Pres.
Preceptor Delta Mu XP997
Walnut Creek, California

Zucchini Squares

3 c. thinly sliced zucchini
1 c. Bisquick
1/2 c. chopped onion
1/2 c. oil
1/2 c. Parmesan cheese
2 tbsp. parsley
1/2 tsp. salt
1/2 tsp. seasoned salt
1/2 tsp. oregano
Dash of pepper
4 eggs, beaten

Combine all ingredients; mix well. Spread on greased cookie sheet. Bake at 350 degrees for 25 minutes.

Cheryl Stiber, Pres.
Xi Epsilon Tau X4273
S. Williamsport, Pennsylvania

Curried Fruit

1 lg. can pears, drained and sliced
1 lg. can peaches, drained and sliced
1 lg. can pineapple chunks, drained
2 lg. apples, cored and sliced
1/2 c. red cherries
3/4 c. (firmly packed) brown sugar
1/2 c. butter or margarine
2 tsp. curry powder

Combine fruit in 2-quart baking dish. Sprinkle with brown sugar. Melt butter in small saucepan. Add curry powder; mix well, stirring constantly. Pour over fruit. Bake at 375 degrees for 1 hour. Serve hot. Yield: 8 servings.

Barbara K. D. Lenkey, Corr. Sec.
Xi Alpha Iota X4095
Lanham, Maryland

Honeyed Figs
(1936)

12 Mission or Kadota figs
1 c. honey
5 tbsp. wine
⅓ c. lemon juice
Few drops of vanilla extract (opt.)

Cut stems from figs. Cover figs with boiling water. Cool; drain. Cook honey and wine over Low heat until thickened. Add figs; cook until thickened. Stir in lemon juice and vanilla, stirring until syrup is very thick. Pour into hot sterilized jars; seal. Serve with meats and poultry. Yield: 4½ pints.

Mary Lou Aberasturi, Pres.
Zeta Psi XP1496
Marysville, California

Pineapple Au Gratin
(1930)

2 2-lb. cans pineapple chunks
¼ to ½ lb. Velveeta cheese, sliced
½ c. sugar
½ c. flour

Drain pineapple; reserving 1 cup juice. Layer pineapple and cheese in baking dish. Combine reserved juice, sugar and flour; mix well. Pour over pineapple and cheese. Bake at 350 degrees for 30 minutes or until thickened and lightly browned. Yield: 6-8 servings.

Juanita R. Still, Pres.
Preceptor Gamma Beta XP1825
Richmond, Missouri

Slang Jang

2 c. chopped tomatoes
1 med. onion, chopped
1 banana pepper, chopped
1 tsp. salt
1 tsp. sugar
½ tsp. pepper
½ c. white vinegar

Combine all ingredients in large bowl; toss well. Chill until serving time. May be served with peas as a relish.

Pattie Ball, Pres.
Xi Upsilon Delta No. 5210
Mt. Pleasant, Texas

Tangy Pickled Vegetables

1 c. cooking oil
¾ c. white vinegar
1 tsp. salt
Dash of red pepper
1 tsp. sugar
1 clove of garlic, minced
1 sm. cauliflower, broken into flowerets
½ lb. small mushrooms
18 black olives
1 green pepper, chopped
1 7½-oz. bottle small pickled onions, drained

Combine oil, vinegar, salt, red pepper, sugar and garlic in saucepan. Bring to a boil. Add cauliflower, mushrooms, olives and green pepper. Cook for 1 minute, stirring constantly. Remove from heat. Add onions; mix well. Refrigerate for 24 hours, stirring frequently. Drain well.

Lillian G. Barnum
International Honorary Mem.
Sparks, Nevada

Vegetable Relish

1 16-oz. can French-style green beans, drained
1 16-oz. can baby peas, drained
1 16-oz. can small kernel white corn, drained
½ c. chopped green pepper
½ c. chopped onion
1 c. chopped celery
Salt and pepper to taste
½ c. sugar
½ c. vegetable oil
½ c. vinegar

Combine first 7 ingredients; toss to mix well. Combine sugar, oil and vinegar; mix well. Pour over vegetable mixture. Refrigerate for 24 hours.

Elaine Casper, Pres.
Preceptor Alpha Epsilon XP1343
Melbourne, Iowa

Beta Bacca Beverage

2 qt. cranberry juice cocktail
2 qt. apple juice
¼ c. (firmly packed) brown sugar
10 cinnamon sticks, halved

Combine cranberry juice, apple juice and brown sugar in large saucepan or kettle; mix well. Cook over Medium heat for 1 hour or until heated through. Pour into serving cups. Add cinnamon stick to each cup.

Renee L. Kosmicki, Rec. Sec.
Alpha Sigma No. 10023
Saratoga, Wyoming

Chicha

1 c. sugar
1 stick cinnamon
4 cloves
¾ c. lime juice
1 46-oz. can unsweetened pineapple juice

Combine sugar, cinnamon, cloves and 1½ cups water in saucepan. Boil for 10 minutes. Cool. Add juices; mix well. Chill. Serve over ice. This is a Mexican punch or festive drink. Yield: 8-10 servings.

Gayle Pike, Pres.
Epsilon Omega No. 8132
Memphis, Tennessee

Homemade Kahlua

4 c. sugar
¾ c. instant coffee granules
1 pt. Brandy
6 oz. Vodka
2 vanilla beans

Combine sugar and 3¾ cups water in saucepan; bring to a boil. Boil for 5 minutes. Add coffee granules; bring to a boil. Remove from heat; cool. Add Brandy and Vodka; mix well. Pour into large glass container. Add vanilla beans. Let stand for 2 to 4 weeks. Remove vanilla beans.

Rose Marie Peterson, Treas.
Xi Beta Beta X5194
Merrill, Wisconsin

Butterscotch Benchwarmer

4 c. milk
½ c. butterscotch pieces
Colored marshmallows

Combine milk and butterscotch pieces in 2-quart saucepan. Heat until butterscotch pieces are melted, stirring occasionally. Pour into tall glasses. Top with marshmallows. Yield: 4 cups.

Photograph for this recipe on page 25.

Cheerleaders' Choice

¼ c. red cinnamon candies
¼ c. sugar
2 tbsp. whole cloves
⅛ tsp. salt
4 c. milk

Combine ½ cup water, candies, sugar, cloves and salt in 2-quart saucepan; mix well. Simmer for 5 minutes. Strain. Return liquid to saucepan. Add milk; heat to

serving temperature. Serve with cinnamon sticks. Yield: 4½ cups.

Photograph for this recipe on page 25.

Hot Buttered Rum

2 tbsp. brown sugar
1 tbsp. whole allspice
1 tbsp. whole cloves
Dash of ground nutmeg
¼ tsp. salt
1 3-in. stick cinnamon
1 qt. apple juice
1 c. rum
Butter

Combine first 7 ingredients in 3-quart saucepan; bring to a boil. Reduce heat. Simmer for 20 minutes. Stir in rum; bring to a boil. Strain. Place small amount of butter in 8 serving mugs; add rum mixture. Yield: 8 servings.

Sandra T. Walker, Pres. City Coun.
Beta Nu No. 7537
Anderson, South Carolina

Hot Grapefruit Toddy

4 6-oz. cans frozen Florida grapefruit juice
¼ c. sugar
2 sticks cinnamon
2 tsp. whole cloves

Prepare grapefruit juice according to package directions. Combine grapefruit juice and remaining ingredients in saucepan; simmer for 10 minutes. Pour into mugs. Serve with cinnamon stick muddlers. Yield: 12 servings.

Photograph for this recipe on page 10.

Kings' Coffee
(1957)

6 oz. instant coffee granules
1 tsp. cinnamon
6 oz. Brandy
¾ c. whipped cream

Combine coffee granules and 6 cups boiling water. Add cinnamon; mix well. Pour into 6 chilled glasses filled with crushed ice. Add 1 ounce Brandy to each glass. Top with whipped cream. Yield: 6 servings.

Rev. Dr. Theodora E. Renneke
International Honorary Mem.
Minneapolis, Minnesota

Percolator Punch

9 c. unsweetened pineapple juice
9 c. cranberry juice
1 c. (firmly packed) brown sugar
4½ tsp. whole cloves
4 sticks cinnamon, broken into pieces
¼ tsp. salt

Combine juices, brown sugar and 4½ cups water in 30-cup percolator. Place cloves, cinnamon and salt in percolator basket. Perk until of desired strength. Yield: 30 servings.

Minnie K. Stapleton, Pres.
Xi Alpha Tau X3313
Morristown, Tennessee

Spicy Cider Glugg

½ c. tea leaves
4 sticks cinnamon
6 whole cloves
½ c. sugar
1 c. lemon juice
1 c. orange juice
1 qt. pineapple juice
2 c. cranberry juice cocktail

2 qt. unsweetened cider
2 qt. ginger ale

Place tea leaves, cinnamon and cloves in cheesecloth bag; tie securely. Steep in 2 quarts boiling water for 10 minutes; remove bag. Add sugar, juices and cider; bring to a boil, stirring. Pour ginger ale into 2-gallon punch bowl. Add hot mixture gradually, mixing well. Yield: 30 servings.

ElDene A. Shodack, W. and M.
Preceptor Xi XP1021
Boise, Idaho

Low Calorie Spiced Tea
(1957)

1 sm. jar low calorie lemon-flavored instant tea
1 sm. jar orange breakfast drink mix
1 tbsp. cloves
1 tbsp. cinnamon

Combine all ingredients; mix well. Combine 2 teaspoons tea mixture and 1 cup boiling water per serving. Store in airtight container. Serve hot.

Shannon Rasmussen, Pres.
Eta No. 644
Providence, Utah

Russian Tea
(1950)

2 c. sugar
2 c. orange juice
¾ c. lemon juice
2 tsp. vanilla extract
1 tsp. almond extract

Combine all ingredients with 2 quarts water in large saucepan; mix well. Bring to a boil. Pour into serving cups. Yield: 28 servings.

Nancy Crouch, Soc. Comm.
Preceptor Epsilon Sigma XP1220
Fremont, California

Valerie's Russian Tea

½ c. instant tea
1½ c. sugar
2 c. Tang
1½ pkg. lemonade mix
1 tsp. ground cloves
2 tsp. cinnamon

Combine all ingredients; mix well. Combine 2 teaspoons tea mixture and 1 cup hot water per serving. Store in airtight container. Serve hot.

Valerie Rankin, V.P.
Xi Zeta Zeta X3361
Pinellas Park, Florida

Wassail
(1940)

3 sticks cinnamon
12 cloves
2 qt. orange juice
1 c. sugar
2 qt. apple juice
4 tbsp. lemon juice

Combine cinnamon, cloves and 2 cups water in saucepan; bring to a boil. Simmer for 20 minutes. Add remaining ingredients. Cook until heated through. Yield: 16 servings.

Marjorie Pack, Pres.
Psi No. 3389
Jerome, Idaho

Beta Sigma Phi Punch
(1959)

3 6-oz. cans lemonade concentrate
3 12-oz. cans apricot nectar

3 46-oz. cans unsweetened pineapple juice
1 lg. bottle ginger ale

Combine first 3 ingredients in large punch bowl; mix well. Add ice cubes. Stir in ginger ale. Yield: 60 servings.

Louella Howard, W. and M.
Zeta Lambda No. 5382
LaBelle, Florida

Can Opener Punch

2 6-oz. cans frozen lemonade, thawed
2 6-oz. cans frozen orange juice, thawed
1 6-oz. can frozen limeade, thawed
2 30-oz. cans pineapple juice
4 qt. ginger ale
1 qt. bitter lemon carbonated beverage

Combine juices; mix well. Pour over ice in large punch bowl. Add ginger ale and bitter lemon carbonated beverage; mix well. Decorate with lemon curls or slices. Yield: 60 servings.

Sandy Smith, Treas.
Upsilon Iota No. 5498
Shamrock, Texas

Cranberry Christmas Punch

1 3-oz. package cherry gelatin
1 6-oz. can frozen lemonade or orange juice
1 qt. cranberry juice, chilled
1 12-oz. bottle ginger ale

Dissolve gelatin in 1 cup boiling water. Stir in lemonade. Add cranberry juice and 3 cups cold water. Pour into punch bowl. Add ice cubes or molded ice ring. Add ginger ale gradually. Fruit flavored sherbet may be added, if desired. Yield: 25 servings.

Rosalie VanRosendale
Xi Xi No. 2525
Tioga, North Dakota

Dorothy's Fruit Punch

1½ c. orange juice
2 6-oz. cans unsweetened pineapple juice
1 12-oz. can papaya nectar
1 12-oz. can guava nectar
2 12-oz. cans mango tropical fruit drink

Combine all ingredients; mix well. Serve over crushed ice. Rum may be added to individual servings, if desired. Yield: 16-18 servings.

Dorothy B. Dunsmore, Pres.
Preceptor Delta Omicron XP1507
Alice, Texas

Fruit Punch

3 c. sugar
1 lg. can pineapple-grapefruit juice
1 12-oz. can frozen orange juice
4 bananas, mashed
1 qt. club soda

Combine sugar and 1½ quarts water; mix well. Add juices; mix well. Add bananas; mix well. Freeze for 6 hours. Let stand for 1 hour. Add club soda; mix well. Yield: 30 servings.

Judy Furr, Treas.
Gamma Eta XP1198
Denison, Texas

Fruit Slush

2 6-oz. cans frozen orange juice, thawed
1½ c. sugar
4 bananas, mashed
1 lg. can crushed pineapple
2 pkg. frozen strawberries, thawed
4 to 6 cling peaches, chopped

Combine orange juice and 4 orange juice cans of water; mix well. Add sugar and 2 cups water; mix well. Add remaining ingredients; mix well. Pour into large container. Freeze. Yield: 20 servings.

Sandy Burris
Omega No. 8568
Grand Island, Nebraska

Frozen Party Slush

1 12-oz. can frozen fruit punch
1 6-oz. can frozen limeade, thawed
4 oz. rum

Prepare fruit punch according to package directions. Add lemonade; mix well. Stir in rum. Pour into airtight container. Freeze for 24 hours. Let stand for 30 minutes before serving.

Debora J. Wittig, Treas.
Xi Theta Eta X5281
Lee's Summit, Missouri

Glori's Slush

4 c. sugar
Juice of 2 lemons
Juice of 2 oranges
1 8-oz. bottle lemon juice
2 bananas, mashed
1 48-oz. can unsweetened grapefruit juice

26 oz. Gin or Vodka
Ginger ale

Combine sugar and 4 cups water in large saucepan. Bring to a boil. Cool. Add remaining ingredients except ginger ale; mix well. Pour into plastic containers. Freeze. Spoon 2 ounces of slush into 8-ounce glass; fill with ginger ale. Yield: 1 gallon.

Glori Bardua, Corr. Sec.
Delta Theta No. 9249
North Vancouver, British Columbia, Canada

Grapefruit Spritzer

2 6-oz. cans frozen Florida grapefruit juice,
    thawed
1 qt. carbonated water, chilled

Pour grapefruit juice into large pitcher. Add carbonated water; mix well. Garnish pitcher with strip of grapefruit rind. Yield: 1½ quarts.

Photograph for this recipe on page 10.

It's-The-Berries Punch

2 16-oz. cans pitted dark sweet cherries
1 12-oz. can pineapple juice
½ c. Brandy
¼ c. lemon juice
2 ⁴/₅-qt. bottles Champagne, chilled

Drain cherries, reserving 2 tablespoons syrup. Combine cherries, reserved syrup, pineapple juice, Brandy and lemon juice; mix well. Chill. Pour into punch bowl. Pour Champagne slowly down side of bowl. Yield: 20 servings.

Willie Mai Coffman, Pres.
Laureate Upsilon PL476
New Braunfels, Texas

Orange Slush

1½ c. sugar
1 12-oz. can frozen orange juice
1 12-oz. can frozen limeade
3 c. Vodka
1 bottle 7-Up

Combine sugar and 9 cups water in saucepan; bring to a boil. Boil for 5 minutes. Cool. Stir in orange juice, limeade and Vodka. Pour into plastic or glass container. Freeze. Stir; spoon into glasses. Top with 1 ounce 7-Up. Yield: 30 servings.

Herma Colwell, Sec.
Preceptor Epsilon Zeta No. 1136
Merced, California

Salads

When Beta Sigma Phis prepared salads a half century ago, it was a tossed salad, fruit salad or potato salad and was served as a side dish—often reserved for summer.

Over the years, Beta Sigma Phi sisters began experimenting with salads, realizing they were not only delicious accompaniments to enjoy year around, but could be a meal in themselves. Exciting new recipes for congealed salads, molds, frozen salads and elegant main dishes were soon created.

As the world became more weight and nutrition conscious, salads took on still another dimension in meal planning.

Whether salads are light, hearty, hot, cold, sweet or tangy, they're always delicious.

Here's your collection . . . from attractive side dishes of fruit and vegetables . . . to appetizers . . . to healthy main dishes. You may never think "lettuce and tomato" again!

Boiled Salad Dressing
(1940)

⅔ c. sugar
¼ tsp. salt
1 tbsp. flour
⅔ c. vinegar
2 eggs, beaten
4 tsp. prepared mustard
¾ c. evaporated milk

Combine sugar, salt, flour and vinegar in top of double boiler; mix well. Stir in eggs and mustard gradually. Place over boiling water. Cook for 3 minutes, stirring constantly. Remove from heat. Add evaporated milk; mix well. Cool. Delicious for potato and fruit salads.

Christy Gailey, Pres.
Alpha Phi No. 5058
Woods Cross, Utah

Calico Rice Salad

½ c. long grain rice
1 10-oz. package frozen mixed vegetables
½ c. mayonnaise or salad dressing
½ c. milk
2 tbsp. catsup
1 tbsp. ranch-style salad dressing mix
Leaf lettuce

Prepare rice according to package directions. Place mixed vegetables in saucepan with small amount of boiling water. Cook for 5 minutes or until vegetables are just tender; drain. Combine rice and vegetables; mix well. Combine mayonnaise, milk, catsup and salad dressing mix; mix well. Mixture will be thin. Stir into rice mixture; cover. Chill. Serve in lettuce-lined bowl.

Carol Scheidres, Pres.
Alpha Pi No. 8865
Hastings, Nebraska

Chicken-Stuffed Eggs
(1959)

6 hard-cooked eggs
1 c. diced cooked chicken
½ c. chopped celery
½ tsp. dry mustard
½ tsp. salt
¼ c. salad dressing
Paprika to taste

Cut eggs in half lengthwise. Remove yolks; mash. Combine egg yolks, chicken, celery, mustard, salt and salad dressing; mix well. Fill egg whites with chicken

mixture. Sprinkle with paprika. Serve on salad greens. Yield: 6 servings.

Elvia Mae Warren
Preceptor Nu XP1760
Oxford, Alabama

Clam Salad

2 cans minced clams, drained
¾ c. chopped green onions and tops
¾ c. chopped celery
½ c. chopped parsley
½ c. mayonnaise
2 tbsp. lemon juice
Salt and pepper to taste
1 head lettuce, shredded
1 c. alfalfa sprouts
1 tomato, cut into wedges
1 hard-boiled egg, chopped
1 avocado, chopped

Combine clams, green onions, celery, parsley, mayonnaise, lemon juice, salt and pepper in bowl; mix well. Cover with plastic wrap. Refrigerate overnight. Combine lettuce and alfalfa sprouts in serving bowl. Add clam mixture; toss well. Top with tomato, egg and avocado. Yield: 6 servings.

Sally Giulieri
Preceptor Theta Pi XP1961
Stockton, California

Corned Beef Mold

1 env. unflavored gelatin
1 c. mayonnaise
2 tbsp. lemon juice
1 4-oz. car sliced mushrooms, drained
1 sm. onion, grated
2 c. chopped celery
1 can corned beef, chopped
4 hard-cooked eggs, chopped

Soften gelatin in small amount of cold water. Dissolve gelatin in 1½ cups hot water; cool. Add remaining ingredients; mix well. Pour into mold. Chill overnight. Garnish with parsley.

Donna M. Stoddard
International Honorary Mem.
Xi Theta Pi
Lakeland, Florida

Apricot Salad
(1958)

1 lg. can crushed pineapple
2 3-oz. packages apricot gelatin

⅔ c. sugar
2 jars strained apricot baby food
1 lg. can evaporated milk, chilled
1 8-oz. package cream cheese, softened
½ c. chopped nuts

Drain pineapple, reserving liquid. Combine reserved liquid, gelatin and sugar in saucepan. Bring to a boil. Remove from heat. Add baby food and pineapple. Cool. Combine evaporated milk and cream cheese; beat until smooth. Add cooled pineapple mixture; mix well. Stir in nuts. Pour into serving dish. Freeze until firm. Yield: 20 servings.

Marie Stephenson, Soc. Chm.
Xi Gamma Iota X5084
Chattanooga, Tennessee

Banana Salad

4 bananas, mashed
1 c. sugar
1 c. chopped walnuts
1½ c. buttermilk
9 oz. Cool Whip
1 tsp. vanilla extract

Combine all ingredients; mix well. Pour into 9 × 13-inch pan. Freeze. Cut into squares. Serve on lettuce leaf. Yield: 15-20 servings.

Joan Woods, Pres.
Alpha Phi No. 9533
Hamilton, Montana

Freezer Coleslaw

1 c. vinegar
2 c. sugar
1 tsp. mustard seed
1 tsp. celery seed
1 med. cabbage, shredded
1 tsp. salt
1 carrot, grated
1 green pepper, chopped

Combine vinegar, sugar, mustard seed, celery seed and ¼ cup water in saucepan; bring to a boil. Boil for 1 minute; cool. Combine cabbage and salt; mix well. Let stand for 1 hour. Drain well, pressing out excess liquid. Combine vinegar mixture, cabbage mixture, carrot and green pepper; mix well. Pour into freezer container. Freeze.

Shirley Andrzejewski
Xi Beta Pi X2478
Livonia, Michigan

Banana Cream Salad
(1939)

1 8-oz. package cream cheese, softened
2 tbsp. mayonnaise
Lemon juice
1¼ tsp. salt
½ c. crushed pineapple
¼ c. chopped maraschino cherries
3 med. bananas, diced
¼ c. chopped walnuts
1¾ c. heavy whipping cream, whipped
¼ c. sugar
2 tbsp. cornstarch
Dash of celery salt
1½ c. unsweetened pineapple juice
4 eggs, slightly beaten

Combine cream cheese, mayonnaise, 2 tablespoons lemon juice and 1 teaspoon salt; beat until smooth. Add pineapple, maraschino cherries, bananas and walnuts; mix well. Fold in ¾ cup whipped cream. Pour into large mold. Chill for 3 hours or until firm. Combine sugar, cornstarch, celery salt and ¼ teaspoon salt in top of double boiler; mix well. Stir in pineapple juice. Cook until mixture thickens, stirring constantly. Cover. Cook for 10 minutes longer, stirring occasionally. Add small amount of hot mixture to eggs. Stir eggs into hot mixture. Cook for 3 minutes longer. Stir in ¼ cup lemon juice. Cool. Fold in remaining, whipped cream. Slice congealed mixture. Serve on lettuce leaf. Spoon on cooled mixture. Yield: 6-8 servings.

Betty J. Miller, Pres.
Preceptor Alpha XP183
Lincoln, Nebraska

Brewery Salad
(1930)

1 c. sugar
2 tbsp. flour
1 c. half and half
1 can sour red cherries, drained
3 lg. bananas, sliced
1 sm. can coconut

Combine sugar and flour in saucepan. Add half and half gradually, mixing well. Cook over Medium heat until thickened, stirring constantly. Cool. Combine cherries and bananas in glass bowl. Add cooled mixture; mix well. Cover with coconut. Chill for 2 hours. Yield: 6 servings.

Carolyn J. Fribley
Xi Epsilon Phi X2729
Pana, Illinois

Fruit Cottage Delight

1 env. unflavored gelatin
4 c. creamed cottage cheese
¼ c. honey
2 tbsp. lemon juice
¼ tsp. dry mustard
Assorted fruits

Soften gelatin in ½ cup cold water in saucepan; place over Low heat to dissolve. Cool. Combine gelatin mixture and remaining ingredients; mix well. Pour into oiled 5-cup mold or individual molds. Chill until firm. Arrange assorted fresh fruits around cheese mold. Top with whipped cream and grated rind, if desired. Yield: 6-8 servings.

Photograph for this recipe on page 33.

Marie's Holiday Salad
(1945)

3 eggs, beaten
1 c. pineapple juice
Juice of 1 lemon
4 tbsp. flour
¾ c. sugar
1 lg. bottle maraschino cherries, drained
1 c. chopped nuts
1 can pineapple chunks, drained
6 lg. bananas, sliced
2 c. miniature marshmallows
1 c. whipping cream

Combine eggs, pineapple juice, lemon juice, flour and ½ cup sugar in top of double boiler; cook until thickened. Cool. Stir in cherries, nuts, pineapple, bananas and marshmallows. Combine whipping cream and ¼ cup sugar; beat until stiff peaks form. Fold into fruit mixture. Chill for 1 hour.

Marie Duke, Pres.
Preceptor Psi XP1332
Clovis, New Mexico

Orange-Avocado Salad

2 California avocados, peeled, seeded and
  sliced
3 oranges, peeled and sliced
Iceberg lettuce
¾ c. mayonnaise
¼ c. orange juice
½ tsp. paprika
½ tsp. salt

Alternate slices of avocado and orange on lettuce leaves. Combine remaining ingredients; mix well. Drizzle over salad. Yield: 6 servings.

Photograph for this recipe on page 28.

Ruth's Fruit Salad

1 3-oz. package vanilla pudding mix
3 tbsp. minute tapioca
2 11-oz. cans mandarin oranges
2 20-oz. cans pineapple chunks
1 6-oz. can frozen orange juice
2 pts. strawberries
6 bananas, sliced

Combine pudding mix and tapioca in saucepan. Drain oranges and pineapple chunks, reserving juice. Combine orange juice and reserved juices with enough water to measure 3 cups liquid. Add to pudding mixture. Bring to a boil over Medium heat. Cool. Add fruits; mix well. Pour into serving dish. Refrigerate for 4 hours. Yield: 10-12 servings.

Marjorie Parks, V.P.
Delta Chi No. 9868
Casa Grande, Arizona

Xi Eta Nu Sinful Salad

1 pkg. miniature marshmallows
1 lg. can crushed pineapple, drained
1 can cherry pie filling
1 can sweetened condensed milk
1 c. chopped pecans
1 carton Cool Whip

Place marshmallows in large bowl. Add pineapple, pie filling, condensed milk, and pecans; mix well. Chill for several hours. Fold in Cool Whip. Yield: 8-10 servings.

Rose Watson, Pres.
Xi Eta Nu X2237
Bryan, Texas

Appy Happy Salad

2 3-oz. packages lemon gelatin
2 c. diced peeled apples
1 c. drained crushed pineapple
1 c. grated longhorn or Colby cheese
½ lb. miniature marshmallows
½ c. mayonnaise
½ pt. whipping cream, whipped

Prepare gelatin according to package directions; cool. Chill until partially congealed. Stir in apples, pineapple, cheese, marshmallows and mayonnaise. Fold in whipped cream. Pour into 8 × 10 × 2-inch pan. Chill for 24 hours or until firm. Yield: 16-20 servings.

Barbara R. Dickerson, V.P.
Preceptor Delta Psi XP1659
Harker Heights, Texas

Apricot-Nut Salad

1 3-oz. package orange gelatin
¼ c. salad dressing
¼ c. sour cream
1 can apricots, drained
¼ c. chopped nuts
¼ c. chopped celery

Dissolve gelatin in 1½ cups boiling water. Cool. Pour cooled gelatin, salad dressing and sour cream into blender container; blend well. Add apricots; process to blend quickly. Fold in nuts and celery. Pour into mold. Chill until firm. Yield: 6-8 servings.

Eleanor Payne
Laureate Gamma PL346
Rome, Georgia

Autumn Ring Mold

2 env. unflavored gelatin
½ c. sugar
2 tbsp. lemon juice
3 c. hot cider
1 c. cored diced red apples
¼ c. finely diced celery
1 c. mincemeat
Apple wedges

Combine gelatin and sugar in saucepan; add lemon juice and 2 tablespoons water, mixing well. Cook over Low heat until gelatin is dissolved, stirring. Add hot cider. Chill until partially congealed. Add diced apples and celery. Fold in mincemeat. Pour into 6-cup ring mold. Chill until firm. Serve on lettuce leaves. Fill center with apple wedges.

Susan Elizabeth McIntire, Pres.
Iota Psi No. 9349
Paola, Kansas

Heavenly Pineapple Salad
(1940)

1 3-oz. package lemon gelatin
¾ c. pineapple juice
1 tbsp. lemon juice
1¼ c. drained crushed pineapple
1 c. shredded sharp cheese
1 c. Cool Whip

Dissolve gelatin in 1 cup boiling water in mixing bowl. Add juices; mix well. Chill until partially congealed. Fold in remaining ingredients. Pour into 1½-quart mold. Chill until firm.

Virginia Headapohl, Past Pres.
Laureate Eta PL290
Lima, Ohio

Avocado Salad
(1943)

1 No. 1 can crushed pineapple
1 3-oz. package lemon gelatin
½ tsp. salt
2 tbsp. lemon juice
½ c. mayonnaise
½ c. whipping cream, whipped
1 avocado, diced

Drain pineapple, reserving ½ cup juice. Set aside. Dissolve gelatin in 1 cup hot water. Add reserved pineapple juice; mix well. Chill until partially congealed. Add pineapple, salt and lemon juice; mix well. Fold in mayonnaise and whipped cream. Stir in avocado. Pour into serving dish. Chill until firm.

Barbara Sherfey, Corr. Sec.
Preceptor Alpha Phi XP1176
Auburn, Washington

Emerald Salad

1 15-oz. can crushed pineapple
2 sm. packages lime gelatin
1 sm. package lemon gelatin
1 3-oz. package cream cheese
½ pt. whipping cream

Drain pineapple, reserving juice. Place pineapple in 11 × 14-inch pan. Dissolve lime gelatin in 2 cups boiling water. Add enough cold water to reserved pineapple juice to measure 2 cups; add to dissolved lime gelatin. Chill until firm. Dissolve lemon gelatin and cream cheese in 1 cup boiling water. Add 1 cup cold water; mix well. Chill until partially congealed. Whip cream; fold into lemon gelatin mixture. Pour over lime gelatin mixture. Chill until firm.

Phyllis A. Cooper, Pres.
Preceptor Laureate Alpha PL133
Huntsville, Alabama

Frosted Pineapple Salad
(1958)

1 No. 2 can crushed pineapple
2 3-oz. packages lemon gelatin
2 c. 7-Up
4 med. bananas, sliced
1 c. miniature marshmallows
2 tbsp. flour
1 egg, slightly beaten
2 tbsp. butter
½ c. sugar
1 c. whipping cream, whipped
¼ c. shredded American cheese
3 tbsp. Parmesan cheese

Drain pineapple, reserving 1 cup juice. Dissolve gelatin in 2 cups boiling water. Add 7-Up; mix well. Combine bananas, marshmallows and pineapple; stir into gelatin mixture. Chill until firm. Combine reserved juice, flour, egg, butter and sugar in saucepan; cook until thickened. Cool. Fold into whipped cream. Spread evenly over congealed mixture. Sprinkle with cheeses. Yield: 12-15 servings.

Faye Boles
Beta Preceptor Iota
Jay, Florida

Golden Cream Waldorf

1 6-oz. package lemon gelatin
¼ tsp. salt
3 golden apples
Lemon juice
½ c. mayonnaise
1 c. heavy cream, whipped
1 c. finely chopped celery
½ c. finely chopped walnuts
Seedless green grapes

Dissolve gelatin in 1½ cups hot water. Add 2 ice cubes; stir until ice is melted. Add salt; stir until salt is dissolved. Chill until partially congealed. Peel 2 apples partially, leaving small amount of peel for color; core and dice. Sprinkle with lemon juice. Slice remaining apple; arrange slices, peel side down, in 8-cup ring mold. Sprinkle with lemon juice. Refrigerate. Add mayonnaise to gelatin mixture; mix well. Fold in whipped cream. Stir in diced apples, celery and walnuts. Spoon over apple slices. Chill until firm. Fill center with grapes. Yield: 8 servings.

M. Sue Burton, Corr. Sec.
Xi Iota Xi X4799
Danville, Illinois

Jell-O Salad

12 oz. strawberry Jell-O
4 c. canned applesauce
4 bananas, mashed
1 lg. package Cool Whip

Combine Jell-O, 4 cups boiling water, applesauce and bananas in order listed; mix well. Pour into 9 × 13-inch pan. Chill until firm. Cover with Cool Whip. Yield: 12 servings.

Sue L. Pieper, Treas.
Xi Theta Tau X5437
Memphis, Missouri

Lime Salad

2 3-oz. packages lime gelatin
1 c. chopped pecans
1 lg. can crushed pineapple
1 pkg. Dream Whip
½ c. milk
1 tsp. vanilla extract

Dissolve gelatin in 3 cups boiling water; cool. Add pecans and pineapple; mix well. Chill until partially congealed. Prepare Dream Whip according to package directions, using ½ cup milk and vanilla. Fold into gelatin mixture. Chill until firm.

Carole Pipetti
Theta Tau
Altoona, Pennsylvania

Pickled Jell-O

1 No. 3 can sliced peaches
6 cloves
1 lg. package orange Jello-O

Drain peaches, reserving juice. Arrange peaches in 9 × 13-inch pan. Combine reserved juice with enough water to measure 4 cups in saucepan. Add cloves; simmer for 5 minutes. Add Jell-O; stir until Jell-O is dissolved. Pour over peaches. Chill until firm.

Shirley Boscariol, Pres.
Xi Sigma Alpha X4240
Dinuba, California

Sherbet Salad

1 lg. package orange gelatin
1 pt. orange sherbet
4 bananas, sliced
1 lg. can pineapple chunks, drained
2 cans mandarin oranges, drained
½ pt. whipping cream, whipped

Dissolve gelatin in 2 cups boiling water in large bowl. Add sherbet, stirring until melted. Cool. Add bananas, pineapple and oranges; mix well. Fold in whipped cream. Pour into mold. Chill until firm.

Martha Post, Pres.
Xi Beta Pi X2646
Pilot Rock, Oregon

Steinard Salad
(1940)

1 8-oz. can crushed pineapple
1 sm. package cherry Jell-O
1 lg. package cream cheese, softened

2 tsp. cream
1 16-oz. can cherries
1 sm. package orange Jell-O
½ c. sliced olives

Drain pineapple, reserving juice. Combine reserved juice and 1¾ cups water. Dissolve cherry Jell-O in pineapple juice mixture. Add pineapple; mix well. Pour into 9 × 9-inch dish. Chill until firm. Combine cream cheese and cream; mix well. Spread over congealed layer. Drain cherries, reserving juice. Combine reserved cherry juice and 1¾ cups water. Dissolve orange Jell-O in cherry juice mixture. Add cherries; mix well. Pour over cream cheese layer. Chill until firm. Top with olives. Yield: 6-8 servings.

Mary Parker, Pres.
Xi Kappa Omega X2691
El Cajon, California

Catherine's Strawberry Salad
(1950)

3 pkg. strawberry gelatin
2 c. frozen strawberries
½ pt. sour cream

Dissolve gelatin in 2 cups boiling water. Add strawberries and 1 cup cold water; mix well. Chill for 30 minutes or until partially congealed. Fold in sour cream. Chill until firm.

Catherine Lewis, Pres.
Beta Omega No. 5327
Fort Smith, Arkansas

Strawberry-Pretzel Salad

Sugar
1½ sticks margarine
1½ c. crushed pretzels
1 pkg. cream cheese, softened
1 carton Cool Whip
1 6-oz. package strawberry gelatin
2 10-oz. packages frozen strawberries, thawed

Cream 3 tablespoons sugar and margarine. Add pretzels; mix well. Press into 9 × 13-inch pan. Bake at 350 degrees for 10 minutes. Cool. Combine cream cheese and 1 scant cup sugar; cream until smooth. Fold in Cool Whip. Spread over cooled pretzel crust. Dissolve gelatin in 2 cups boiling water; add ½ cup cold water. Stir in strawberries. Chill until partially congealed. Spread over cream cheese layer. Chill until firm. Yield: 20-24 servings.

Sue Pompa, Sec.
Xi Beta Epsilon X650
Peoria, Illinois

Golden Macaroni Salad
(1939)

2 c. macaroni
3 to 4 carrots, grated
3 to 4 stalks celery, finely chopped
7 to 8 med. sweet pickles, finely chopped
7 to 8 hard-boiled eggs
1 c. salad dressing
¾ c. sandwich spread
4 oz. French dressing
2 tbsp. sweet pickle juice
Paprika to taste

Prepare macaroni according to package directions. Rinse and drain. Combine macaroni, carrots and celery in large bowl. Add sweet pickles. Chop 5 eggs; add to macaroni mixture. Combine salad dressing, sandwich spread, French dressing and pickle juice; blend well. Pour over macaroni mixture; blend well. Slice remaining eggs over top of salad. Sprinkle with paprika. Yield: 10-12 servings.

Virginia A. Mullen
Xi Epsilon Phi X4353
Hummelstown, Pennsylvania

Macaroni-Kraut Salad

2 c. elbow macaroni
1 1-lb. can sauerkraut, drained
1 c. cherry tomatoes
¼ c. chopped onion
½ c. mayonnaise
⅓ c. chili sauce
½ c. chopped green pepper
1 tsp. salt
1 tsp. celery seed
¼ tsp. coarsely ground black pepper
¼ tsp. garlic salt
Salad greens

Prepare macaroni according to package directions; rinse and drain. Combine macaroni and remaining ingredients except greens; toss. Chill. Serve in bowl lined with salad greens. Yield: 4 servings.

Photograph for this recipe on page 39.

Luncheon Salad
(1930)

¼ c. tuna
1 hard-cooked egg, finely chopped
¼ c. chopped walnuts
1 c. chopped string beans
½ dill pickle, chopped
1 c. shredded cabbage

1½ tbsp. minced onion
¼ c. mayonnaise
¼ tsp. salt

Combine all ingredients; mix well. Serve on lettuce leaf. Garnish with additional mayonnaise sprinkled with capers or minced parsley. Yield: 4 servings.

Betty Bickhart, Pres.
Preceptor Alpha Mu XP470
San Jose, California

Shrimp-Rice Salad

3 c. cooked rice
1½ lb. boiled shrimp, peeled
1 7-oz. can tuna, drained
1½ c. chopped green onions
½ c. chopped sweet pickles
1½ c. chopped celery
¼ c. chopped pimento
3 hard-boiled eggs, chopped
1 c. mayonnaise
1 tbsp. lemon juice

Combine all ingredients in order listed; mix well. Serve on lettuce leaf or in small clam shells.

Margaret Stom, V.P.
Delta Iota XP1452
Silsbee, Texas

Shrimp Salad

1 can mushroom soup
6 oz. cream cheese
2 cans shrimp, drained
1 c. mayonnaise
1 c. chopped celery
1 env. unflavored gelatin
3 green onions, chopped

Heat soup in saucepan; add cream cheese, mixing well. Add shrimp, mayonnaise and celery; mix well. Soften gelatin in small amount of cold water. Dissolve in 3 tablespoons hot water. Add gelatin mixture and onions to shrimp mixture; mix well. Pour into greased mold. Chill until firm.

Joyce Haessler
Xi Upsilon Eta
El Dorado Hills, California

Ham Salad in Avocados

3 c. cubed cooked ham
4 hard-cooked eggs, sliced
2 sweet pickles, sliced
2 green onions, chopped

1½ c. diced celery
½ c. mayonnaise
1 tbsp. sweet pickle juice
2 California avocados, peeled and seeded
Iceberg lettuce
½ c. cashews
24 cherry tomatoes

Combine ham, eggs, pickles, onions and celery; mix well. Combine mayonnaise and sweet pickle juice; mix well. Add to ham mixture; mix well. Cut avocados in half; place on lettuce-lined plates. Fill avocados with ham mixture. Top with cashews and tomatoes. Yield: 4 servings.

Photograph for this recipe on page 41.

Camellia City Salad
(1950)

2 6-oz. jars marinated artichoke hearts
8 to 10 cherry tomatoes, halved
⅔ c. salad oil
⅓ c. wine vinegar
1 tsp. sugar
1 tsp. salt
6 c. torn salad greens, chilled
⅓ c. onion rings
⅓ c. pitted ripe olives

Place artichoke hearts and tomatoes in bowl. Combine next 4 ingredients in jar. Cover tightly. Shake jar vigorously. Pour over artichoke hearts and tomatoes; mix well. Chill for several hours, stirring occasionally. Toss with salad greens, onion rings and olives just before serving. Yield: 6-8 servings.

Sally McFarland, Pres.
Xi Gamma Kappa X3819
Cottage Grove, Oregon

Creamy Carrot Salad

1 6-oz. package orange Jell-O
3 oz. cream cheese, softened
1 c. finely grated carrots
1 9-oz. carton Cool Whip

Dissolve Jell-O in 2½ cups boiling water. Chill until partially congealed. Beat with electric mixer for 7 minutes or until light and fluffy. Add cream cheese gradually; beat well. Fold in carrots. Fold in Cool Whip. Pour into 3-quart mold. Chill until firm. Garnish with chopped walnuts. Yield: 20 servings.

Dianna Gulling, Pres.
Xi Alpha Beta X453
Maximo, Ohio

Italian Potato Salad
(1940)

6 c. diced potatoes
3 tomatoes, chopped
2 sm. onions, finely chopped
4 tbsp. salad oil
3 tsp. vinegar

Cook potatoes in water to cover until tender; drain. Cool. Combine potatoes, tomatoes and onions; mix well. Combine oil and vinegar; mix well. Pour over potato mixture; mix well. Cool thoroughly. Yield: 6 servings.

Frances Eafrati, Pres.
Xi Beta Iota X3347
Weirton, West Virginia

Kidney Bean Salad
(1940)

2 c. canned kidney beans
1 c. firmly chopped celery
¾ c. chopped sweet pickle
5 hard-cooked eggs, chopped
½ c. Hellmann's mayonnaise
½ c. chopped peanuts

Rinse kidney beans; drain well. Combine kidney beans with remaining ingredients; mix well. Serve in lettuce-lined bowl.

Natalie Gross, Treas.
Xi Alpha Omicron X1528
Orlando, Florida

Luscious Salad

1 head cauliflower
1 bunch broccoli
6 or 7 green onions
1 green pepper
1 c. sour cream
1 c. salad dressing
⅓ c. sugar
1 tbsp. wine vinegar
Dash of Tabasco sauce
Dash of Worcestershire sauce

Cut vegetables in bite-sized pieces; place in large bowl. Combine remaining ingredients; mix well. Pour over vegetables; toss well. Yield: 10 servings.

Joan Carsrud
Xi Zeta Upsilon X3131
Carbondale, Illinois

Red White and Green Salad

5 c. broccoli flowerets
2½ c. cauliflowerets
1 onion, chopped
2 c. halved cherry tomatoes
1 c. mayonnaise
½ c. sour cream
1 tbsp. vinegar
2 tbsp. sugar
Salt and pepper to taste

Combine broccoli, cauliflowerets, onion and cherry tomatoes in large bowl. Combine mayonnaise, sour cream, vinegar and sugar; mix well. Pour over vegetables; toss. Sprinkle with salt and pepper. Chill for 3 to 4 hours. Yield: 8-10 servings.

Linda L. Isbell, Soc. Chm.
Xi Gamma Nu X4269
Alva, Oklahoma

Spinach Salad

1 lb. spinach
½ sm. head lettuce
1 green onion and top, sliced
⅓ c. olive oil
3 tbsp. lemon juice
1 tbsp. honey
1 tbsp. toasted sesame seed

Rinse spinach; pat dry with paper towel. Tear spinach and lettuce into bite-sized pieces; place in salad bowl. Add onion; toss well. Combine olive oil, lemon juice and honey in jar; shake well. Pour dressing over salad; toss to coat. Sprinkle with sesame seed. Yield: 6 servings.

Mary Frances Sowle, Pres.
Xi Beta Omega X2762
Mt. Pleasant, Michigan

Taco Salad

1 can kidney beans
1 head lettuce, shredded
2 to 3 tomatoes, diced
2 onions, diced
½ lb. sharp cheese, shredded
1 to 2 sm. packages Fritos, crushed
Italian dressing to taste

Rinse and drain kidney beans. Add lettuce, tomatoes, onions, cheese and Fritos; mix well. Toss with Italian dressing. Yield: 6 servings.

Dale Twining, Treas.
Delta No. 923
Pittsfield, Massachusetts

Avocado Salad

1 sm. package lime gelatin
1 sm. package cream cheese
½ c. mayonnaise
1 avocado, peeled and cubed
2 stalks celery, finely chopped
1 sm. onion, grated
Pimento to taste

Dissolve gelatin in 1½ cups hot water. Chill until partially congealed. Combine cream cheese and mayonnaise; cream until smooth. Add avocado; mix well. Add remaining ingredients, mixing well. Fold into gelatin mixture. Pour into individual molds or 9 × 13-inch pan. Chill until firm. Serve on lettuce leaf; top with dollop of additional mayonnaise.

Janelle Harris, Pres.
Xi Delta Theta X4713
Altus, Oklahoma

Cucumber Salad

1 3-oz. package lime gelatin
¾ c. whipping cream, whipped
⅓ c. mayonnaise
1 c. chopped cucumber
¼ tsp. salt
1 tbsp. minced onion

Dissolve gelatin in ¾ cup boiling water. Cool. Combine whipped cream and mayonnaise; fold into gelatin mixture. Combine cucumber, salt and onion; stir into gelatin mixture. Refrigerate for 24 hours.

Ealsa L. Rowe
International Honorary, Mem.
Spearfish, South Dakota

Congealed Cabbage Salad

2 env. unflavored gelatin
½ c. sugar
1 tsp. salt
¼ c. vinegar
2 tbsp. lemon juice
2 c. finely shredded cabbage
1 c. chopped celery
¼ c. chopped green pepper
¼ c. diced pimento
⅓ c. sliced green olives

Combine gelatin, sugar and salt; mix well. Add 1½ cups boiling water; stir until gelatin is dissolved. Add 1½ cups cold water, vinegar and lemon juice; mix well. Chill until partially congealed. Stir in remaining ingredients. Pour into large loaf pan. Chill until firm.

Frances Kucera, V.P.
Iota Preceptor XP413
Eugene, Oregon

Meats

During the war years, Beta Sigma Phi cooks used their ingenuity to stretch the rationed meat they were allowed into as tempting a meal as possible. But when rationing ended in 1945, Beta Sigma Phi cooks had only begun! They became masterful at creating imaginative, flavorful meat dishes to please their families and friends.

With a wide variety of meats available at the markets today, they have originated a limitless number of dishes. They have found that meat dishes run the gamut from basic pot roast to barbecued ribs and elegant lamb and veal. There is a meat dish for every budget, occasion and all tastes.

This chapter has some of the best recipes using beef, lamb; pork, and the increasingly popular veal.

Now, as always, meats make the meal!

Barbecued Frankfurters and Noodles

¼ c. chopped onion
¼ c. salad oil
Cooked noodles
1 lb. frankfurters
1 tbsp. Worcestershire sauce
¼ tsp. paprika
2 tbsp. brown sugar
½ tsp. salt
½ c. lemon juice
1 c. chili sauce

Place onion and oil in saucepan; cook for 10 minutes. Place noodles in casserole. Add frankfurters. Combine onion and remaining ingredients; mix well. Pour over frankfurters. Bake at 375 degrees for 30 minutes.

Hazel Holloran
Civic Awareness
Delta Delta Eta No. 7837
Lake Isabella, California

Beef With Wine

1 3 to 4-lb. sirloin tip roast
Flour
Salt and pepper to taste
1 tbsp. shortening
1 sm. onion, chopped
1 c. white wine
1 can cream of mushroom soup

Cut roast into serving pieces. Combine flour, salt and pepper; dredge meat in flour mixture. Brown in hot shortening in Dutch oven. Add onion; cook until tender. Stir in wine; cover. Bake at 325 degrees for 1 hour. Stir in soup. Bake for 1 hour longer.

Julia A. Coffman, Pres.
Delta Rho No. 2831
Mooresville, Indiana

Betty's Overnight Barbecued Brisket

1 6 to 8-lb. beef brisket
1½ c. beer or wine
1 lg. onion, sliced
Catsup

Place brisket in large baking dish. Add beer; cover. Refrigerate for 6 to 8 hours, turning brisket occasionally. Top with onion slices. Spread with catsup; cover. Bake at 250 degrees for 6 to 8 hours. Cool; slice thin. Yield: 14-16 servings.

Betty J. Wilson, Prog. Chm.
Sigma Sigma No. 10789
Holt Summit, Missouri

Corned Beef Hash

10 lg. potatoes, diced
1 lg. onion, diced
¼ c. oil
1 can corned beef, chopped
½ tsp. salt

Brown potatoes and onion in oil in Dutch oven. Add corned beef, salt and 1½ cups water; mix well. Simmer for 30 minutes. Yield: 6 servings.

Cherrice Smith, Rec. Sec.
Xi Pi Nu X4432
Orange, Texas

Beef Burgundy

6 slices bacon
3 lb. beef stew meat
⅓ c. flour
1 can tomato soup
1 can beef broth
1 c. Burgundy wine
2 cloves of garlic, minced
2 med. bay leaves
½ tsp. salt
Dash of pepper
1 lb. carrots, quartered
1½ lb. small white onions

Cook bacon in large skillet; crumble. Coat beef with flour; brown in drippings. Place beef in 3-quart casserole. Stir soup and broth into drippings. Add wine, garlic, bay leaves, salt, pepper and bacon; mix well. Pour over beef; cover. Bake at 350 degrees for 1 hour. Add carrots and onions; cover. Bake for 15 to 30 minutes longer. Uncover last 15 minutes of cooking time. Serve over rice or noodles.

Charlotte Cisco, Corr. Sec.
Xi Epsilon Gamma X1514
Glendora, California

Easy Sherried Beef

3 lb. lean beef stew meat
2 cans golden mushroom soup
1 env. dry onion soup mix
1 can mushrooms, drained
1 can water chestnuts, drained and sliced
1 c. Sherry

Cut beef into bite-sized pieces. Combine beef and remaining ingredients; mix well. Place in casserole; cover. Bake at 300 degrees for 4 hours. Serve over rice or noodles. Yield: 6-8 servings.

LeAnn Banski, Treas.
Sigma No. 1716
Hot Springs, Arkansas

Susan's Barbecue

3 lb. beef stew meat
1 onion, chopped
1 green pepper, chopped (opt.)
1 6-oz. can tomato paste
½ c. (firmly packed) brown sugar
¼ c. cider vinegar
1 tbsp. chili powder
2 tsp. salt
2 tsp. Worcestershire sauce
1 tsp. dry mustard

Combine all ingredients in slow cooker; mix well. Cook on Low for 8 to 10 hours or until done. Mix well with wire whisk to shred meat. Yield: 10 servings.

Susan Fleury, City Coun. Pres.
Xi Eta Beta X3176
Aurora, Illinois

Kathryn's Barbecue

1 4-lb. beef roast
2 tbsp. sugar
⅓ c. soy sauce
⅔ c. vinegar
1 1-lb. 8-oz. can tomatoes
2 onions, chopped
1 c. catsup
¼ c. Worcestershire sauce

Place roast in large baking pan. Combine sugar, soy sauce, vinegar, tomatoes, onions and ½ cup water; mix well. Pour over roast; cover tightly. Bake at 350 degrees for 5 hours. Cool. Skim off fat. Add catsup and Worcestershire sauce. Cook until heated through. Yield: 8 servings.

Kathryn Kemp
Xi Beta Psi X5400
Lavista, Nebraska

Sauerbraten

2 to 3 lb. cooked beef roast, sliced
1 bay leaf
10 peppercorns
2 tbsp. brown sugar
1 to 2 c. brown gravy
½ c. vinegar
12 to 15 gingersnaps, crushed

Combine first 6 ingredients and ½ cup water in large pan; mix well. Cook over Low heat for 1 hour or until of desired tenderness. Combine gingersnaps with small amount of hot water; mix until of paste-like consistency. Spread over meat mixture. Yield: 6 servings.

Frances Sterling, Pres.
Gamma Kappa No. 6719
Brick Town, New Jersey

Swiss Steak

1 2-lb. round steak
Flour
½ tsp. salt
⅛ tsp. pepper
2 tbsp. oil
½ c. chopped celery
½ c. diced onion
¼ c. diced green pepper
⅓ c. tomato juice

Pound steak. Combine 1 cup flour, salt and pepper; dredge steak in flour mixture. Brown in hot oil. Place steak in 2-quart casserole. Saute celery, onion and green pepper in hot oil. Add 3 tablespoons flour, tomato juice and 2 cups water; mix well. Pour over steak. Bake at 375 degrees for 1 hour and 30 minutes.

Jane Ott, Pres.
Theta Nu No. 7744
Spillville, Iowa

Stuffed Round Steak

1 2 to 2½-lb. thin round steak, cut into 5 pieces
Salt and pepper to taste
4 slices bacon, diced
1 lg. onion, chopped
1½ c. toasted bread cubes
2 tbsp. minced parsley
½ tsp. celery salt
¼ tsp. sage
1 c. bouillon
1 8-oz. can tomato sauce

Sprinkle steak with salt and pepper; set aside. Saute bacon and onion. Add bread cubes, parsley, celery salt and sage; mix well. Spread over steak pieces; roll as for jelly roll. Secure with toothpicks. Place in large skillet. Add bouillon; cover. Simmer for 1 hour. Add tomato sauce; cover. Simmer for 45 minutes or until desired doneness. Garnish with minced parsley. Yield: 5 servings.

Diane T. Walker, W. and M. Chm.
Mu Nu No. 8014
Niceville, Florida

London Broil

1 lg. flank steak
1 onion, coarsely chopped
1 green pepper, coarsely chopped
1 8-oz. bottle French dressing
1 pkg. Italian or Caesar dressing mix
½ c. honey

Combine all ingredients in order listed. Refrigerate for several days. Grill or broil until of desired doneness. Carve steak diagonally. Yield: 2 servings.

Joan Robbins
Zeta Theta No. 8900
Rutherfordton, North Carolina

Beef-Potato Roulade

3 tbsp. flour
½ tsp. salt
⅛ tsp. pepper
¼ tsp. paprika
1 beef round steak, ½-in. thick
1 1⅜-oz. envelope onion soup mix
2 med. potatoes, grated
3 tbsp. oil

Combine flour, salt, pepper and paprika; mix well. Pound flour mixture into steak. Cut steak into serving pieces. Combine onion soup mix and potatoes, mix well. Place 2 tablespoons potato mixture on each piece of steak. Roll as for jelly roll; secure with wooden picks. Brown in hot oil; drain. Add 1 cup water; cover. Cook on Low heat for 1 hour and 30 minutes to 2 hours or until steak is tender.

Photograph for this recipe on page 47.

Beef Stroganoff

1 med. onion, sliced
1 clove of garlic, chopped
6 tbsp. butter
4 tbsp. flour
4 tsp. salt
1 2-lb. sirloin or round steak, cut into ½ × 2-in. strips
1 can cream of chicken soup
¾ c. consomme
¼ tsp. Tabasco sauce
1 sm. can mushrooms, drained
1 c. sour cream

Saute onion and garlic in butter until tender. Place onion mixture in casserole. Combine flour and salt in paper bag; add beef, shaking to coat well. Brown beef in butter. Add soup, consomme, Tabasco sauce and mushrooms to onion mixture; mix well. Add beef. Bake at 350 degrees for 50 minutes. Add sour cream; mix well. Bake for 10 minutes longer. Serve over hot cooked rice. Yield: 4-6 servings.

Josephine Martin, Pres.
Xi Gamma Nu X2938
McPherson, Kansas

Chinese Pepper Steak

1 lb. beef round or sirloin, cut into thin strips
Soy sauce
1 tsp. sugar
1 tsp. ground ginger
¼ c. salad oil
1 clove of garlic, halved
2 lg. green peppers, cubed
2 med. onions, sliced
2 lg. tomatoes, cubed
½ lb. mushrooms, sliced
2 tsp. cornstarch

Place beef strips in large container. Combine ¼ cup soy sauce, sugar and ½ teaspoon ginger; mix well. Pour over beef. Marinate for several hours or overnight. Heat oil in large skillet. Add garlic and ½ teaspoon ginger. Cook on Medium heat for 1 minute; remove garlic. Add green peppers and onions. Saute for 3 minutes, stirring. Add beef and marinade. Saute for 3 minutes, stirring. Add tomatoes and mushrooms; cook until heated through. Combine cornstarch and 1 tablespoon soy sauce; mix well. Add to mixture; stir well. Cook until heated through. Serve over fluffy rice or Chinese noodles.

Wanda Reed, Pres.
Preceptor Gamma XP291
Omaha, Nebraska

Stir-Fry Beef

1 lb. beef round steak, ¼-in. thick
¼ c. chopped onion
3 tbsp. soy sauce
1 tsp. instant beef bouillon granules
1 tsp. Worcestershire sauce
1 clove of garlic, minced
½ tsp. salt
Dash of pepper
4 med. carrots, diagonally sliced
1 sm. head cauliflower, broken into flowerets
2 tbsp. cooking oil
1 c. sliced mushrooms
1 6-oz. package frozen pea pods, partially thawed
1 tbsp. cornstarch

Partially freeze beef. Cut across grain into bite-sized strips. Combine onion, soy sauce, beef bouillon granules, Worcestershire sauce, garlic, salt, pepper and ⅔ cup water; mix well. Add beef; mix well.

Refrigerate for 8 hours, stirring occasionally. Drain meat, reserving marinade. Cook carrots and cauliflower in boiling salted water for 3 minutes; drain. Brown beef in hot oil in large skillet or wok. Remove meat. Add mushrooms; cook for 1 minute, stirring. Add pea pods, carrots and cauliflower; cook for 2 minutes, stirring. Add beef. Combine reserved marinade, ¼ cup cold water and cornstarch; mix well. Pour over beef. Cook until bubbly, stirring. Serve over rice or chow mein noodles.

Melinda F. Heckler, Pres.
Sigma Nu No. 9924
Shelbyville, Illinois

Italian Meat Loaf

1 can pizza sauce
1 sm. can tomato sauce
1½ lb. ground beef
1 egg, beaten
¾ c. oats
½ c. chopped onion
1 tsp. salt
½ tsp. oregano
⅛ tsp. pepper
Parmesan cheese to taste
2 c. grated mozzarella cheese

6/29/82
Very Good
Cook 1 hr. + 15 min.

Combine pizza sauce and tomato sauce; mix well. Combine ground beef, egg, oats, onion, salt, oregano, pepper and ½ cup sauce; mix well. Place on waxed paper. Pat to 10 × 12-inch rectangle. Sprinkle with cheeses. Roll as for jelly roll; seal edges. Place in loaf pan. Bake at 350 degrees for 1 hour. Drain. Cover with remaining pizza sauce mixture. Bake for 15 minutes longer. Yield: 4-6 servings.

Constance Sue Perry
Theta Phi No. 8261
New Providence, Iowa

Prize-Winning Meat Loaf

1½ lb. ground beef
¾ c. oats
¼ c. chopped onion
1½ tsp. salt
¼ tsp. pepper
1 c. tomato juice
1 egg, beaten

Combine all ingredients; mix well. Press into loaf pan. Bake at 350 degrees for 1 hour and 15 minutes. Let stand for 5 minutes; drain.

Jane S. Cochran, Pres.
Alpha Theta No. 2781
Clyde, North Carolina

Individual Meat Loaves

3 slices bacon, finely chopped
½ c. dry bread crumbs
½ c. evaporated milk
1 egg, beaten
2 tsp. salt
4 tbsp. chopped onion
1½ lb. ground chuck
½ lb. ground pork
Pepper to taste
1 env. instant beef broth
½ c. catsup
1 tbsp. Worcestershire sauce
1 tsp. chili powder

Combine bacon, crumbs, milk, egg, salt, 2 table-spoons onion, meats and pepper; mix well. Shape into 6 to 8 small loaves. Place on greased shallow baking pan. Combine beef broth, catsup, Worcestershire sauce, chili powder and 2 tablespoons onion in saucepan; cook for 5 minutes. Pour over loaves. Bake at 350 degrees for 45 minutes. Yield: 6-8 servings.

Marilyn Beaver
Beta Sigma Phi

Irene's Meat Loaf
(1950)

1 lb. ground beef
1 lb. ground pork
1½ c. oatmeal
Salt and pepper to taste
1 c. milk
2 eggs, beaten
2 tbsp. brown sugar
1 tbsp. prepared mustard
1 tsp. paprika
2 tbsp. lemon juice (opt.)
2 tbsp. catsup
2 tbsp. Worcestershire sauce

Combine beef, pork, oatmeal, salt, pepper, milk and eggs; mix well. Place in 10-inch casserole or loaf pan. Combine remaining ingredients and ¼ cup hot water; mix well. Pour over meat mixture. Bake at 350 degrees for 1 hour or until knife blade inserted near center comes out clear. Yield: 10 servings.

Irene Palmer
Pi Pi No. 9889
Barnard, Missouri

Cranberry Meatballs

1 lb. ground beef
1 c. cooked rice
½ c. tomato juice
1 egg, slightly beaten
¼ c. chopped onion
1 tbsp. Kitchen Bouquet
1 tsp. salt
1 1-lb. can whole cranberry sauce
⅓ c. (firmly packed) brown sugar
1 tbsp. lemon juice

Combine ground beef, rice, tomato juice, egg, onion, Kitchen Bouquet and salt; mix well. Shape into meatballs. Place in greased 9 × 13-inch glass baking dish. Combine remaining ingredients; mix well. Spoon over meatballs. Bake at 350 degrees for 1 hour.

LuAnn Barr
Omicron Tau
Kimberling City, Missouri

Eileen's Baked-Barbecue Meatballs

3 lb. hamburger
1½ c. quick-cooking oatmeal
6 tbsp. chopped onion
1 tbsp. salt
1½ tbsp. pepper
2 c. milk
Cooking oil
1 lg. bottle catsup
3 tbsp. Worcestershire sauce
3 tbsp. vinegar
3 tbsp. sugar

Combine first 6 ingredients; mix well. Shape into 24 large meatballs. Brown in hot oil. Place in large casserole. Combine catsup, Worcestershire sauce, vinegar, sugar and ¾ cup water; mix well. Pour over meatballs. Bake at 350 degrees for 1 hour. Yield: 12 servings.

Eileen Schiavone, Pres.
Laureate Iota
Vero Beach, Florida

Sweet and Sour Meatballs

1 can pineapple chunks
1 lb. ground beef
1 tsp. salt
1 tbsp. chopped onion
¼ c. dry bread crumbs
1 egg, slightly beaten
⅔ c. catsup
⅔ c. cider vinegar
⅓ c. (firmly packed) brown sugar

1 tbsp. cornstarch
½ tsp. paprika

Drain pineapple, reserving juice. Combine ½ of the pineapple, ground beef, salt, onion, bread crumbs, egg and ¼ cup water; mix well. Shape into small meatballs. Combine catsup, vinegar and brown sugar in skillet. Cook over Low heat. Add remaining pineapple and reserved juice; mix well. Add cornstarch; cook until thickened, stirring. Add meatballs; sprinkle with paprika. Cook until meatballs are browned. Serve over rice. Yield: 6-8 servings.

Mary Kay Ballard, V.P.
Xi Alpha Delta X4583
Douglas, Wyoming

Beef Salami

5 lb. ground beef
¼ c. salt
4 tbsp. red wine
2 tbsp. liquid smoke
1½ tsp. garlic powder
2 tbsp. chili powder
2 tsp. crushed red pepper
1¼ tsp. ground cuminseed
2 tbsp. brown sugar

Combine ground beef, salt and wine; mix well. Add liquid smoke, garlic powder, chili powder, red pepper, cuminseed and brown sugar; mix well. Cover. Refrigerate at least 24 to 48 hours. Divide into 4 equal portions. Shape each portion into a roll. Roll in cheesecloth. Cook in smoker for about 12 hours, using hickory chips. Change hickory chips 3 times during smoking. This recipe can be frozen for 6 months or refrigerated for 3 weeks.

Sandy Smith
Mu No. 706
Roseburg, Oregon

Bacon-Wrapped Beef Patties

2 lb. ground beef
1 c. shredded Cheddar cheese
⅔ c. chopped onion
¼ c. catsup
2 tbsp. Parmesan cheese
1 tsp. salt
¼ tsp. pepper
2 eggs
12 slices bacon

Combine first 8 ingredients; mix well. Shape into

patties. Wrap bacon slice around each patty. Place on cookie sheet. Bake at 375 degrees for 40 minutes. Yield: 8 servings.

Edith A. Shirer, Pres.
Preceptor Omega XP1154
Belmond, Iowa

Pinwheel Burgers
(1950)

1½ lb. ground beef
⅔ c. evaporated milk
1 egg, slightly beaten
½ c. fine cracker crumbs
½ c. finely chopped green pepper
¼ c. chopped onion
1 tbsp. prepared mustard
1 tsp. lemon pepper
1 15-oz. jar pimento cheese spread
6 hamburger buns

Combine first 8 ingredients; mix well. Place on waxed paper; pat to 12-inch square. Cover with pimento cheese spread. Roll as for jelly roll; seal edges. Cut into twelve 1-inch slices. Place each on bun half. Broil for 15 minutes or until done. Yield: 6 servings.

Alice P. Castaneda, Pres.
Preceptor Zeta Delta XP1924
Rio Grande City, Texas

Tavern Burgers
(1950)

1 c. chopped onions
3 tbsp. margarine
1 can tomato soup or paste
½ c. vinegar
2 tbsp. prepared mustard
2 tbsp. Worcestershire sauce
2 tbsp. brown sugar
½ tbsp. liquid smoke
2 lb. ground beef

Saute ½ cup onions in margarine. Add next 6 ingredients and ½ cup water; mix well. Simmer for 10 minutes. Brown ground beef. Add ½ cup onions; simmer for 5 minutes. Add tomato soup mixture; mix well. Simmer for 15 minutes longer. Serve over hamburger buns. Yield: 10 servings.

Jayne Titsworth
Alpha Tau Rho No. 11007
Coahoma, Texas

Pizza Burgers

1 lb. ground beef
¼ lb. grated cheese
½ c. Spam, grated
1 tsp. oregano
1 can pizza sauce
1 pkg. hamburger buns

Brown ground beef; drain. Add cheese, Spam, oregano and pizza sauce; mix well. Simmer until cheese is melted, stirring. Spoon on hamburger bun halves. Place on baking sheet. Bake at 350 degrees for 15 to 20 minutes. Yield: 18-24 servings.

LaRee Morsch, Rec. Sec.
Xi Alpha Gamma X3337
New Brighton, Minnesota

Depression Steak Casserole
(1935)

1 sm. green pepper, chopped
1 sm. onion, chopped
1 tbsp. oil
2 c. stewed tomatoes
1 c. tomato sauce
2 c. noodles
2 lb. hamburger
Salt and pepper to taste
1 tbsp. chili powder
1 tsp. Worcestershire sauce
1½ c. whole kernel corn

Saute green pepper and onion in hot oil. Add tomatoes, tomato sauce, noodles and ½ cup water. Simmer until noodles are tender. Place hamburger in skillet; add salt, pepper, chili powder and Worcestershire sauce. Cook until hamburger is browned. Add corn and noodles mixture; cook until thickened. Yield: 8 servings.

Millie Barnes
Delta Omicron
Lake Havasu City, Arizona

Everyone's Favorite Casserole
(1950)

1 lb. lean pork, cubed
1 lb. veal, cubed
¼ c. butter
2 cans cream of chicken soup
1 green pepper, finely chopped
1 sm. jar pimento
1 lg. can mushrooms, drained
1 lb. Velveeta cheese, cubed
1 10-oz. package noodles
½ tsp. Accent

½ tsp. pepper
½ tsp. celery salt
½ tsp. Lawry's Seasoned Salt
Bread crumbs

Saute pork and veal in butter. Add soup, green pepper, pimento and mushrooms; mix well. Cook until meat is tender. Add cheese, stirring until cheese is melted. Prepare noodles according to package directions. Combine noodles, seasonings and meat mixture; mix well. Pour into casserole. Sprinkle with bread crumbs. Bake at 350 degrees for 1 hour. Yield: 10-12 servings.

Kay Baggott, Sec.
Xi Alpha Eta No. 1028
Davenport, Iowa

Macaroni-Hamburger Casserole
(1940)

1 lb. hamburger
1 sm. onion, chopped
½ c. macaroni
1 can tomato soup
1 pkg. frozen vegetables
Potato chips

Brown hamburger and onion. Cook macaroni in salted water; rinse and drain. Add to hamburger mixture. Stir in soup. Prepare vegetables according to package directions. Stir into hamburger mixture. Pour into greased 9 × 13-inch casserole. Sprinkle with potato chips. Bake at 350 degrees for 25 minutes.

Barbara Croessman, Sec.
Xi Kappa Theta X5425
Du Quoin, Illinois

Mostaccioli

1½ lb. ground beef
⅛ tsp. minced garlic
1 onion, diced
4 c. tomato juice
2 8-oz. cans tomato paste
2 tsp. chopped parsley
2 tsp. salt
2 bay leaves
1 tbsp. sugar
1½ tsp. oregano
1 tbsp. chili powder
1 tsp. pepper
1 pkg. mostaccioli noodles
1 pkg. mozzarella cheese

Brown ground beef, garlic and onion in skillet until onion is tender. Combine tomato juice, tomato paste, parsley, salt, bay leaves, sugar, oregano, chili powder, pepper and 1 cup water in large saucepan; mix well. Add ground beef mixture; mix well. Simmer for 2 hours. Prepare noodles according to package directions. Add to ground beef mixture. Pour into large casserole. Top with cheese. Bake at 325 degrees for 25 minutes.

Debbie Cox
Mu Tau
Glendale Hts., Illinois

Musetti

2 lg. onions, chopped
½ lb. ground pork
1¼ lb. ground beef
2 lg. green peppers, chopped
2 10-oz. packages wide noodles
1 No. 3 can tomatoes
1 can Campbell's tomato soup
1½ lb. longhorn cheese, grated

Place onions, pork, beef and green peppers in skillet. Cook until just browned, stirring. Prepare noodles according to package directions; rinse and drain. Combine tomatoes and tomato soup in saucepan; cook until heated through. Combine meat mixture, noodles and tomato mixture in large glass baking dish; mix well. Sprinkle with cheese. Bake at 325 degrees for 1 hour or until cheese is melted. This recipe was given on radio by Dick Powell in an advertisement for Campbell's Soup.

Madalyne P. Brock, Exec. Dir.
International Honorary Mem.
Kansas City, Missouri

Pizza Casserole
(1950)

1 to 2 lb. ground beef
1 tsp. seasoned pepper
1 tsp. seasoned salt
½ tsp. Italian seasoning
Chopped onion to taste
1 4-oz. can sliced mushrooms and liquid
¼ lb. American cheese, sliced
1 c. chopped celery
1 sm. can chopped ripe olives, drained
2½ to 3 oz. fine dry noodles
2 c. tomato juice, V-8 or stewed tomatoes

Brown ground beef in 10-inch electric skillet. Add remaining ingredients in layers in order listed. Cover; bring to a boil. Simmer for 30 minutes.

Gerry Wiehe
Preceptor Alpha Zeta XP947
Leavenworth, Kansas

Swedish Chop Suey

1 med. onion, diced
4 to 5 stalks celery, diced
2 tbsp. diced green pepper
1 clove of garlic, diced
1 lb. ground beef
Salt and pepper to taste
1 16-oz. can spaghetti
1 can Chinese noodles

Saute onion, celery, green pepper and garlic in 10-inch skillet. Add ground beef; brown. Drain well. Add salt and pepper; mix well. Add spaghetti; cook over Low heat until heated through. Top with Chinese noodles. Garnish with chopped parsley.

Beatrice L. Preikschat, Ext. Off.
Preceptor Alpha Iota No. 917
St. Petersburg, Florida

Southern Goulash

1 lb. ground steak
1 onion, finely chopped
2 tbsp. shortening
1 c. beef broth
1½ c. spaghetti
1 tsp. salt
¼ tsp. pepper
1 tsp. Worcestershire sauce

Brown steak and onion in shortening in deep overproof saucepan. Add remaining ingredients; mix well. Cover. Bake at 325 degrees for 25 to 30 minutes. Canned or strained stewed tomatoes may be substituted for beef broth. Yield: 4 servings.

Carolyn Brothers, Pres.
Zeta Kappa No. 9140
Chesapeake, Virginia

Spaghetti with Love

1 lb. ground beef
½ c. chopped onion
¼ c. chopped green pepper
1 can cream of mushroom soup
1 can tomato soup
1 8-oz. package spaghetti
1 c. grated cheese

Brown ground beef. Add onion and green pepper, stirring to mix well. Add soups and 1 soup can water; mix well. Simmer for 10 minutes. Prepare spaghetti according to package directions; drain. Place spaghetti in 13×9-inch casserole. Add ½ cup cheese; mix well. Cover with hamburger mixture. Top with remaining cheese. Bake at 350 degrees for 30 minutes.

Diane Steed, Pres.
Xi Zeta Pi X4520
St. Louis, Missouri

Special Chili

3 to 4 lb. lean hamburger
1 sm. green pepper, diced
1 med. onion, diced
2 stalks celery, diced
1 lg. clove of garlic, minced
2 15-oz. cans kidney beans
1 28-oz. can tomatoes
2 15-oz. cans tomato sauce
2 to 3 tbsp. chili powder
2 tbsp. sugar
2 to 3 tsp. salt
2 to 3 tsp. Worcestershire sauce
4 oz. thin spaghetti, broken

Saute hamburger, green pepper, onion, celery and garlic. Add kidney beans, tomatoes and tomato sauce; mix well. Combine chili powder, sugar, salt, Worcestershire sauce and 2 cups water; mix well. Add to hamburger mixture; mix well. Simmer for 3 to 4 hours. Add additional water for desired consistency. Add spaghetti; mix well. Simmer for 30 minutes longer. Yield: 10-12 servings.

Linda Cottingham, Pres.
Xi Zeta Phi X3133
Charleston, Illinois

Chapter Casserole Chili

1 lb. ground chuck
½ c. chopped onion
1 c. finely chopped celery
1 can tomato soup
2½ c. kidney beans
1½ c. chopped cooked spaghetti
1 can mushrooms and liquid
½ c. grated cheese
3 tsp. Worcestershire sauce
½ tsp. chili powder
Salt and pepper to taste

Brown ground chuck in skillet. Add onion and celery; cover. Cook for 20 minutes. Place in 2-quart casserole. Add soup, beans, spaghetti, mushrooms, ½ of the cheese, Worcestershire sauce, chili powder, salt and pepper; mix well. Top with remaining cheese. Bake at 275 degrees for 1 hour. Yield: 6-8 servings.

Ruth E. Hill, Pres.
Preceptor Laureate Gamma PL218
Buffalo, New York

Picadillo Elegante

1½ lb. ground beef
½ tsp. salt
⅛ tsp. pepper
1 clove of garlic, minced
⅓ c. chopped onion
½ med. green pepper, cut in strips
⅓ c. seedless raisins
¼ c. blanched slivered almonds
¼ c. sliced pimento-stuffed green olives
¼ tsp. oregano
¼ tsp. cinnamon (opt.)
1 8-oz. can tomato sauce
¼ c. catsup

Brown ground beef; drain. Add salt, pepper, garlic, onion and green pepper; simmer for 10 minutes. Add remaining ingredients and ½ cup water; cover. Simmer for 20 minutes. Serve over cooked rice, if desired. Yield: 6 servings.

Photograph for this recipe on page 53.

Bar-Be-Cups

¾ lb. ground beef
¼ c. barbecue sauce
1 tbsp. minced onion
1 tbsp. brown sugar
1 can refrigerator biscuits
¾ c. grated cheese

Brown ground beef; drain. Add barbecue sauce, onion and brown sugar; mix well. Press biscuits into muffin tin, forming a cup. Fill with meat mixture. Top with cheese. Bake at 400 degrees for 10 to 12 minutes.

Vickie Owens
Alpha Zeta Mu No. 7733
Livingston, Texas

Continental Meat and Cheese Pie

1 lb. ground beef
½ c. bread cubes
1 tsp. salt
¼ tsp. pepper
1 pkg. frozen chopped spinach, thawed
1 8-oz. package sliced provolone cheese, chopped
1 egg
1 recipe 2-crust pie pastry
1 egg yolk, beaten
¼ lb. salami, chopped

Brown ground beef; drain. Stir in bread cubes, salt and pepper; set aside. Drain spinach; dry on paper towel. Combine spinach, cheese and egg; mix well. Place 1 pie crust in pie pan; brush lightly with egg yolk. Spoon ground beef mixture onto crust; add spinach mixture. Top with salami. Roll out remaining pie crust; cut desired shapes to vent. Place over salami. Seal edges; flute. Brush with remaining egg yolk. Bake at 375 degrees for 1 hour. Cool 10 minutes.

Jo Miller, W and M. Chm.
Xi Alpha Gamma X1589
Beckley, West Virginia

Gumbo Turnovers

1 pkg. dry yeast
1 tbsp. sugar
1 tbsp. vegetable oil
1 tsp. salt
2 to 2½ c. flour
1½ lb. hamburger
1 10¾-oz. can chicken gumbo soup
⅓ c. chili sauce
1 tbsp. minced onion

Dissolve yeast in 1 cup warm water. Add sugar, oil, ½ teaspoon salt, and enough flour for soft dough. Turn out on floured surface; knead for 5 minutes or until smooth and elastic. Place in greased bowl, turning once to grease surface. Cover; let rise for 1 hour or until doubled in bulk. Brown hamburger; drain. Add soup, chili sauce, onion and ½ teaspoon salt; mix well. Cook until heated through. Punch dough down; divide into 10 parts. Roll into 5-inch circles. Fill circles with hamburger mixture. Fold in half, sealing edges. Place, seam side down, on greased cookie sheet. Cover with damp cloth; let rise for 1 hour or until doubled in bulk. Bake at 375 degrees for 20 to 23 minutes. Yield: 10 servings.

Anita Wiley, Rec. Sec.
Eta Omega No. 6976
Halstead, Kansas

Golden Beef Quiche

1 tbsp. margarine
1 unbaked 9-in. pie crust
¾ lb. ground beef
1 med. onion, chopped
1 11-oz. can Cheddar cheese soup
6 eggs
½ c. milk
½ tsp. salt
¼ tsp. thyme
⅛ tsp. pepper

Spread margarine on pie crust. Brown ground beef and onion; drain. Spoon ground beef mixture into pie crust. Combine remaining ingredients in large bowl; beat well with wire whisk. Pour over ground beef mixture. Bake at 375 degrees for 35 to 40 minutes or until knife blade inserted in center comes out clean.

Judith Essenpreis, City Coun. Pres.
Gamma Iota No. 1143
Centralia, Illinois

Hamburger Quiche

½ lb. ground beef
½ c. mayonnaise
½ c. milk
2 eggs, beaten
1 tbsp. cornstarch
1½ c. chopped Cheddar or Swiss cheese
⅓ c. sliced green onion
Dash of pepper
1 unbaked 9-in. pastry shell

Brown ground beef over Medium heat; drain. Combine mayonnaise, milk, eggs and cornstarch; blend well. Stir in ground beef, cheese, green onion and pepper. Pour into pastry shell. Bake at 350 degrees for 35 to 40 minutes or until knife blade inserted into center comes out clean. Yield: 6-8 servings.

Myrrhl Shepherd, Tel. Comm.
Xi Alpha Sigma X12525
Oshawa, Ontario, Canada

Hamburger Pie

2 lb. hamburger
1 sm. onion, diced
½ tsp. salt
½ tsp. pepper
¼ tsp. garlic powder
1 15-oz. can spaghetti sauce
1 8-oz. package crescent dinner rolls
1 egg, beaten
2 c. grated Cheddar cheese

Brown hamburger and onion; drain. Add salt, pepper, garlic powder and spaghetti sauce; mix well. Simmer until heated through. Press rolls in 9-inch pie plate to form crust; flute edges. Combine egg and 1 cup cheese; mix well. Pour over crust. Spread with hamburger mixture. Sprinkle with remaining cheese. Bake at 350 degrees for 30 minutes. Yield: 4 servings.

Susie Gundle, Corr. Sec.
Delta Xi
Hillsboro, Oregon

Hot Tamale Pie

2 c. cornmeal
1 lb. hamburger
1 med. onion, chopped
½ green pepper, chopped
2 tbsp. cooking oil
2 c. canned tomatoes
1 tsp. salt
1 tsp. pepper
1 tbsp. chili powder

Sift cornmeal into 6 cups boiling water, stirring constantly. Cook for 15 minutes. Brown hamburger, onion and green pepper in hot oil. Add tomatoes, salt, pepper and chili powder, mix well. Simmer for 10 minutes. Alternate layers of cornmeal mixture and meat mixture in 9-inch baking pan. Bake at 400 degrees for 20 minutes. Yield: 4 servings.

Genevieve P. Slavin, Pres.
Xi Eta Phi X3521
Effingham, Illinois

Meat-Za Pie

1 lb. ground beef
1 c. evaporated milk
½ c. fine dry bread crumbs
½ tsp. garlic salt
⅓ c. tomato paste
1 2-oz. can sliced mushrooms, drained
1 c. shredded sharp cheese
¼ tsp. oregano
2 tbsp. Parmesan cheese

Place ground beef, milk, bread crumbs and garlic salt in 9-inch pie plate; mix well using fork. Press firmly into sides and bottom of pie plate. Layer with tomato paste, mushrooms and sharp cheese. Sprinkle with oregano and Parmesan cheese. Bake at 375 degrees for 25 minutes or until lightly browned. Yield: 4-6 servings.

Imogene R. Bennett, Rec. Sec.
Xi Alpha Gamma X1286
Bradenton, Florida

Picnic Pizza

1 lb. hamburger
¾ c. tomato sauce
1 c. cubed cheese
¼ c. chopped pimento-stuffed green olives
Oregano to taste
Salt and pepper to taste
¼ tsp. garlic salt
8 wiener buns

Brown hamburger; drain and cool. Add tomato sauce, cheese, olives, oregano, salt, pepper and garlic salt; mix well. Fill buns with hamburger mixture. Wrap in aluminum foil. Heat on grill. Yield: 8 servings.

Dorothy Johannes, Ext. Off.
Xi Kappa X315
Rocky Ford, Colorado

Arkansas Spanish Rice

1 lb. ground beef
½ c. minced onion
¼ c. diced green pepper
1 clove of garlic, minced
2 c. tomatoes
1 6-oz. can tomato paste
2½ tsp. salt
¼ tsp. pepper
2 tsp. chili powder (opt.)
1 c. rice

Brown ground beef, onion, green pepper and garlic; drain. Stir in tomatoes, tomato paste, salt, pepper, chili powder and 1 cup water. Simmer until thickened. Soak rice in 2 cups salted water for 15 minutes; add to ground beef mixture. Cook for 5 minutes or until thickened. Yield: 6 servings.

Rita M. Walters, V.P.
Preceptor Omicron XP1740
Bentonville, Arkansas

Curried Skillet Dinner

1 lb. ground beef
1 onion, chopped
6 tomatoes, chopped
Salt and pepper to taste
Curry powder to taste
3 c. cooked rice
3 green onions, chopped
6 eggs, stir fried

Brown ground beef, onion, ½ of the tomatoes, salt, pepper and curry powder, stirring. Add rice, green onions and remaining tomatoes; mix well. Stir in eggs; cover. Simmer for 20 minutes.

Bobbie M. Alexander, V.P.
Xi Alpha Beta X3985
Aiken, South Carolina

Burger Casserole

1½ lb. ground round
1 can cream of mushroom soup
1 can Cheddar cheese soup
1 1-lb. package Tater Tots

Press ground round in 9 × 9-inch pan. Combine soups; mix well. Pour over ground round. Cover with Tater Tots. Bake at 300 degrees for 1 hour and 15 minutes.

Katherine P. McHugh
Xi Psi X1344
Toledo, Oregon

Salisburg Bourguignonne

1 can beefy mushroom soup
1½ lb. ground beef

½ c. fine dry bread crumbs
1 egg, slightly beaten
¼ tsp. salt
3 slices bacon
¼ c. Burgundy or dry red wine
1 sm. clove of garlic, minced
¼ tsp. marjoram, crushed

Combine ⅓ cup soup, ground beef, bread crumbs, egg and salt; mix well. Shape into 6 patties. Fry bacon in skillet until crisp. Remove and crumble; reserving 2 tablespoons drippings. Brown patties in drippings. Stir in remaining soup, ⅓ cup water, wine and seasonings; cover. Simmer for 20 minutes, stirring occasionally. Serve over cooked noodles. Garnish with crumbled bacon. Yield: 6 servings.

Barbara Banning
Delta Omicron No. 4295
Fort Walton Beach, Florida

Rice Delight

1 lb. ground beef
1 c. chopped celery
1 onion, chopped
1 green pepper, chopped
1 can mushroom bits and pieces
2 cans cream of chicken soup
1 c. rice

Brown ground beef in large skillet. Add celery, onion and green pepper. Cook until vegetables are tender; drain. Place in large baking dish. Add mushrooms, soup and 2 soup cans water; mix well. Stir in rice. Bake at 350 degrees for 1 hour or until rice is tender, stirring 2 or 3 times. Yield: 8-10 servings.

Dorothy Inman, V.P.
Preceptor Beta Nu
La Habra, California

Spanish Rice

1 lb. ground beef
1 sm. onion, diced
1 1-lb. can tomatoes, drained and chopped
1 5½-oz. can tomato juice
1 tsp. cuminseed
1½ tsp. garlic salt
1 tsp. salt
¼ tsp. pepper
1 c. long grain rice

Brown ground beef and onion in electric skillet; drain. Add tomatoes, tomato juice, cuminseed, garlic salt, salt, pepper and rice; mix well. Bring to a boil; cover. Reduce heat; simmer for 25 minutes. Do not stir.

Barbara Bauer
Xi Alpha Tau X3479
Lodgepole, Nebraska

Hamburger Stew

1 16-oz. can whole kernel corn
1 16-oz. can tomatoes
3 to 4 med. potatoes, sliced
3 to 4 carrots, sliced
4 c. tomato juice
1 lb. cooked ground beef, drained
1 tsp. chili powder
1 med. onion, chopped
½ tsp. celery salt
½ tsp. garlic powder
1 tsp. oregano
½ tsp. monosodium glutamate
1 bay leaf
Salt and pepper to taste

Combine all ingredients in 5-quart slow cooker. Cook on High for 4 hours. Cook on Low for 4 hours longer.

Susan E. Ristine, Pres.
Gamma No. 10366
Naples, Italy

Pate Chinois

1 lb. ground beef
2 med. onions, chopped
1 can whole kernel corn, drained
4 potatoes, cooked and mashed
Salt and pepper to taste
Paprika to taste

Brown ground beef and onions; drain. Spread in casserole. Cover with corn. Spoon on potatoes forming peaks. Sprinkle with salt, pepper and paprika. Bake at 350 degrees for 30 minutes.

Pauline Bonavire, Treas.
Preceptor Delta XP655
Natick, Massachusetts

Rio Grande Casserole

1 lb. ground beef
1 lg. onion, chopped
6 lg. corn tortillas, broken into small pieces
1 10¾-oz. can cream of chicken soup
1 15-oz. can pinto beans, drained
1 16-oz. can whole kernel corn, drained
1 10½-oz. can enchilada sauce
2 c. grated mild Cheddar cheese

Brown ground beef and onion in skillet; drain well. Add tortillas, soup, pinto beans, corn and enchilada sauce; mix well. Pour into large casserole. Top with cheese. Bake at 325 degrees for 30 minutes.

Joyce A. Shaw, Pres.
Alpha Rho Alpha No 10448
Burleson, Texas

Tally's Mexican Dish

1 lb. ground beef
1 15-oz. ranch-style beans
1 10-oz. can tomatoes and green chilies
1 10-oz. can tomato soup
1 15-oz. package Fritos corn chips
½ head lettuce, shredded
2 med. tomatoes chopped
6 green onions, chopped
½ lb. Cheddar cheese, grated

Brown ground beef in large skillet; drain. Add next 3 ingredients; mix well. Simmer for 20 minutes. Place corn chips on serving plates. Top with ground beef mixture. Sprinkle with lettuce, tomatoes, onions and cheese. Yield: 6 servings.

Melanie Clonts
International Coordinator
Alpha Zeta No. 716
Early, Texas

Tostado Casserole

1 lb. ground beef
1 15-oz. can tomato sauce
1 env. taco seasoning mix
2½ c. corn chips
1 15½-oz. can refried beans
½ c. shredded Cheddar cheese

Brown ground beef in skillet. Add 1¼ cups tomato sauce and taco seasoning mix; mix well. Line 11 × 7 × 1-inch baking dish with 2 cups corn chips. Crush remaning corn chips; set aside. Spoon ground beef mixture over corn chips. Combine refried beans and remaining tomato sauce; mix well. Spread over ground beef mixture. Bake at 375 degrees for 25 minutes or until heated through. Sprinkle with cheese and crushed corn chips. Bake at 375 degrees for 5 minutes longer or until cheese is melted. Yield: 6 servings.

Kala K. Handley, Pres.
Eta Nu No. 5255
Belton, Missouri

Trailer Stew
(1950)

1 lb. hamburger or wieners
½ c. chopped onion
1 can tomatoes
1 can red beans
1 can whole kernel corn
2½ tbsp. chili powder
Salt and pepper to taste

Brown hamburger and onion. Add tomatoes, beans, corn, chili powder, salt and pepper; mix well. Simmer for 30 minutes. If wieners are used, split lengthwise and cut into small pieces. Yield: 6 servings.

Nancy Crawford, Pres.
Sigma Omega No. 10897
Windsor, Missouri

Grand Slam Casserole
(1935)

1 lb. breast of lamb, cubed
½ c. sliced onion
1 tbsp. butter
1 c. diced carrots
1 c. diced potatoes
2 c. drained tomatoes
1½ tsp. salt
¼ tsp. pepper
3 tbsp. minute tapioca
6 to 8 unbaked baking powder biscuits, ¼-in. thick

Brown lamb and onion in butter. Add 1 cup boiling water. Pour into greased casserole; cover. Bake at 350 degrees for 1 hour or until meat is tender. Add carrots, potatoes, tomatoes, salt and pepper; cover. Bake for 30 minutes longer or until vegetables are tender. Sprinkle with tapioca; mix well. Top with biscuits. Bake for 12 to 15 minutes longer or until biscuits are browned. Yield: 6 servings.

Ruby G. Hartje
Xi Gamma Nu Exemplar No. 1437
Anna, Illinois

Grilled Leg of Lamb

1 leg of lamb, butterflied
½ c. oil
1 c. red wine
½ tsp. salt
1 tsp. pepper
¼ tsp. each thyme, oregano, rosemary and sweet basil
1 onion, finely chopped
2 cloves of garlic, minced

Place leg of lamb in large container. Combine remaining ingredients; mix well. Pour over lamb. Marinate at room temperature for 3 hours. Cook on electric or charcoal grill to desired doneness. Yield: 8 servings.

Jayne Brown
International Honorary Mem.
Xi Alpha Omicron X3878
McCall, Idaho

Cherry-Glazed Ham

1 7-lb. fully-cooked ham
Red maraschino cherries
1 c. (firmly packed) brown sugar
½ c. orange juice
½ tsp. whole cloves
2 med. oranges, sliced
1 c. finely diced celery
1 8½-oz. can pineapple tidbits, drained
⅔ c. chopped parsley

Bake ham at 325 degrees for 1 hour and 30 minutes. Drain one 8-ounce jar cherries, reserving syrup. Combine brown sugar, reserved syrup, orange juice and cloves in saucepan; cook until thickened. Score ham; decorate with cherries and orange slices. Brush with glaze. Bake at 325 degrees for 30 minutes, basting frequently. Drain and chop one 4-ounce jar cherries. Combine cherries and remaining ingredients; mix well. Chill. Serve with ham.

Photograph for this recipe on page 42.

Cherry-Sauced Ham

1 21-oz. can cherry pie filling
¼ c. red wine vinegar
1 tsp. cinnamon
½ tsp. ground cloves
1 3-lb. fully-cooked canned ham

Combine pie filling, vinegar, cinnamon and cloves in saucepan; mix well. Bring to a boil, stirring frequently. Reduce heat; simmer for 2 minutes. Place ham in baking pan. Cover with pie filling mixture. Bake at 325 degrees for 30 minutes or until heated through.

Karren Moreland
Beta Epsilon No. 4205
Roswell, New Mexico

Carole's Ham Balls

2½ lb. ground ham
1 lb. ground beef
2 lb. ground lean pork
3 eggs, beaten
3 c. finely crushed graham crackers
2 c. milk
2 cans tomato soup
2½ c. (firmly packed) brown sugar
¾ c. white vinegar
2 tsp. dry mustard

Combine first 6 ingredients; mix well. Shape into 25 balls; using ½-cup measure. Place in shallow baking dish. Combine remaining ingredients; mix well. Pour over ham balls. Bake at 350 degrees for 1 hour.

Carole Hoover, V.P.
Xi Zeta Epsilon X5259
Dallas Center, Iowa

Ham Casserole a la Betty

¼ c. chopped green onion
¼ c. chopped green pepper
2 tbsp. butter
1 tbsp. flour
Dash of pepper
1 c. milk
4 oz. grated Cheddar cheese
¼ c. mayonnaise
3 c. diced cooked potatoes
2 c. diced cooked ham

Cook onion and green pepper in butter until tender. Add flour and pepper; mix well. Add milk; bring to a boil, stirring constantly. Reduce heat. Add remaining ingredients; mix well. Pour into 2-quart glass casserole. Bake at 350 degrees for 35 minutes.

Betty Montgomery, Pres.
Xi Alpha Beta X4724
Greenwood, Mississippi

Ham Casserole Deluxe

¼ c. chopped onion
¼ c. chopped green pepper
2 tbsp. butter or margarine
3 tbsp. flour
1 can chicken and rice soup
1 c. milk
2 c. cubed cooked ham
3 hard-cooked eggs, sliced
1 6-count pkg. refrigerator biscuits

Saute onion and green pepper in butter until tender. Add flour; stir until blended. Add soup and milk; mix well. Cook until thickened and bubbly, stirring constantly. Add ham and eggs, bring to a boil. Pour into 8 × 12-inch baking dish. Cut each biscuit in half horizontally; arrange on ham mixture. Bake at 450 degrees for 10 to 12 minutes or until biscuits are golden brown. Yield: 4-5 servings.

Ruth C. Hartkopf
International Honorary Mem.
Delta No. 514
Idaho Falls, Idaho

Ham Loaf

3 lb. lean pork, ground
1½ lb. smoked ham, ground
1½ c. cracker crumbs
3 eggs, beaten
Juice of ½ lemon
1½ c. milk

Combine first 5 ingredients; mix well. Add milk; knead. Press into 2 loaf pans; place in pan of water. Cover. Bake at 350 degrees for 2 hours.

Polly J. Butler, Pres.
Preceptor Pi XP1449
Burley, Idaho

Ham Loaf With Raisin Sauce
(1946)

2 lb. ham, ground
2 lb. pork, ground
1 c. bread crumbs
1 c. milk
2 eggs, beaten
1 sm. onion, grated
1 tsp. salt
¼ tsp. pepper
1 c. (firmly packed) brown sugar
⅓ c. vinegar
1 tsp. dry mustard
1¾-oz. envelope brown gravy mix
1½ c. apple juice
½ c. seedless raisins
1 tsp. grated orange rind

Combine first 8 ingredients; mix well. Shape into 2 small loaves; place in shallow pan. Combine brown sugar, vinegar, mustard and ½ cup water in saucepan; bring to a boil. Boil for 1 minute. Pour over loaves. Bake at 350 degrees for 1 hour and 30 minutes, basting 2 or 3 times. Combine remaining ingredients in saucepan; mix well. Bring to a boil; boil until mixture thickens, stirring. Pour over ham loaves.

Dorothy Baker, Pres.
Preceptor Zeta XP270
Dearborn, Michigan

Ham Logs
(1950)

2 lb. ground ham
2 lb. hamburger
¼ c. catsup
3 tbsp. chopped bell pepper
1 med. onion, diced
1 to 1½ c. soft bread crumbs
1 can cream of mushroom soup
2 eggs, beaten
1 tsp. salt
¼ tsp. pepper
⅓ c. (firmly packed) brown sugar
⅓ c. vinegar
2 tbsp. prepared mustard
1 c. salad dressing
2 tbsp. horseradish

Combine first 12 ingredients and 1 tablespoon mustard; mix well. Roll into serving-sized logs. Bake at 350 degrees for 45 minutes to 1 hour. Combine 1 tablespoon mustard, salad dressing and horseradish; mix well. Sweeten to taste. Serve with ham logs. Yield: 12-14 servings.

Lorene Buster, Past Pres.
Xi Alpha Mu X1277
Coffeyville, Kansas

Ham-Stuffed Potatoes

4 lg. potatoes
2 c. ground ham
1 c. mayonnaise
1 tbsp. chopped green pepper
1 tbsp. chopped onion
1 tbsp. chopped pimento
½ c. grated Chedder cheese
¼ c. grated Swiss cheese

Bake potatoes; cool. Cut slice from top of potatoes. Scoop out centers; cube. Combine potato, ham, mayonnaise, green pepper, onion and pimento; toss. Fill potato shells. Combine cheeses; sprinkle over potatoes. Place on baking sheet. Bake at 450 degrees for 15 minutes or until cheese is melted.

Terelyn Garlington, Pres.
Rho Xi No. 4750
Stanton, Texas

Deviled Pork Chops

¼ c. catsup or chili sauce
2 tsp. Worcestershire sauce
1 tsp. prepared mustard
1½ tbsp. lemon juice
¼ tsp. onion powder
¼ tsp. paprika
½ tsp. salt
6 to 10 pork chops

Combine all ingredients except pork chops; mix well. Layer pork chops in large baking dish. Pour sauce over pork chops. Refrigerate for 4 hours. Add ¼ cup hot water. Bake at 400 degrees for 15 minutes. Reduce heat to 275 degrees. Bake for 1 hour and 15 minutes or until pork chops are done.

Donna Kelso, Pres.
Xi Alpha Epsilon X1372
Goulais River, Ontario, Canada

Gourmet Pork Chops

8 center-cut pork chops
Butter

1 2¼-oz. can button mushrooms
1 env. dry onion soup mix
1 c. white wine
1 c. chicken broth
2 tsp. garlic spread
1 c. sour cream

Trim fat from pork chops. Brown pork chops in butter in skillet. Remove chops. Brown mushrooms. Add soup mix, wine, broth and garlic spread, stirring until well blended. Add pork chops; cover. Simmer for 45 minutes or until tender. Stir in sour cream; cook until just heated through. Garnish with parsley. Yield: 4 servings.

Dee Mattes, Pres.
Beta Theta No. 7510
Columbia, Maryland

Forty-five Minute Pork Chop Dinner

6 pork chops
1 tbsp. shortening
4 potatoes, sliced
4 sm. onions, sliced
6 carrots, sliced
1 can peas, drained

Brown pork chops in shortening in large skillet. Remove three pork chops; add half the sliced vegetables in layers. Add remaining pork chops and sliced vegetables. Pour in peas. Add ½ cup hot water; cover. Simmer for 30 minutes.

Sandy Nease
Xi Alpha Eta X1095
Atchison, Kansas

Pork Chops Italiano

6 pork chops
3 tbsp. oil
1 19-oz. can tomatoes
½ c. tomato juice (opt.)
½ c. rice
1 c. diced onion
1 sm. green pepper, diced
1 tsp. sugar
½ tsp. salt
¼ tsp. pepper

Brown pork chops in oil in electric skillet. Combine remaining ingredients; mix well. Pour over pork chops; cover. Simmer at 200 degrees for 1 hour and 15 minutes or until tender. Yield: 6 servings.

Paulette Baumgartner
Alpha Rho No. 11060
Estevan, Saskatchewan, Canada

Orange-Glazed Pork Chops

4 1½-in. thick pork chops
⅓ c. chopped onion
½ c. chopped celery
2 tbsp. butter
1½ c. soft bread crumbs
2 tbsp. chopped parsley
1 tsp. salt
½ tsp. grated orange rind
1½ tsp. seasoned salt
Orange Juice
¼ c. (firmly packed) brown sugar
¼ c. orange marmalade
2 tbsp. cider vinegar

Cut pocket in pork chops. Saute onion and celery in butter. Add bread cubes; brown lightly. Remove from heat. Add parsley, salt, orange rind and 1 teaspoon seasoned salt. Add 3 tablespoons orange juice; toss lightly. Fill pockets with bread crumb mixture. Stand pork chops on rib bones on rack in roasting pan. Sprinkle with ½ teaspoon seasoned salt. Pour water in roasting pan ½-inch deep. Cover with aluminum foil. Bake at 375 degrees for 1 hour and 30 minutes. Combine ½ cup orange juice, brown sugar, marmalade and vinegar in saucepan; bring to a boil, stirring. Reduce heat. Simmer for 15 minutes. Remove foil from chops; pour off water. Brush chops with orange juice glaze. Bake, uncovered, for 30 minutes longer, basting every 10 minutes wih glaze.

Gail Miller
Xi Gamma Epsilon
Pennsylvania

Pork Chop-Potato Scallop

4 pork chops
1 can cream of mushroom soup
½ c. sour cream
2 tbsp. chopped parsley
4 c. thinly-sliced potatoes
Salt and pepper to taste

Brown pork chops in skillet; set aside. Combine soup, sour cream, parsley, and ¼ cup water; blend well. Alternate layers of potatoes and soup mixture in 2-quart casserole, adding salt and pepper to each layer. Top with pork chops; cover. Bake at 375 degrees for 1 hour and 15 minutes. Yield: 4 servings.

Freda G. Kirkpatrick, Pres.
Xi Delta Zeta X1708
Dayton, Ohio

Spanish Pork Chops

6 pork chops
Salt and pepper to taste
2 tbsp. oil
2 tbsp. sugar
1 tsp. dry mustard
¼ c. vinegar
¼ c. catsup

Sprinkle pork chops with salt and pepper. Brown in hot oil in 10-inch skillet. Combine sugar, dry mustard, vinegar, catsup and ½ cup water; mix well. Pour over pork chops. Simmer for 45 minutes or until tender. Yield: 6 servings.

Lily Case, V.P.
Xi Alpha Sigma X3935
Wilder, Idaho

Polynesian Pork

½ pork loin
Salt and pepper to taste
½ c. soy sauce
½ c. catsup
¼ c. honey
1 lg. clove of garlic, crushed

Place loin on rack in shallow baking pan. Sprinkle with salt and pepper. Combine remaining ingredients; mix well. Bake at 350 degrees for 2 hours to 2 hours and 30 minutes, basting frequently with catsup mixture. Yield: 6 servings.

Becky Clayton, Pres.
Xi Theta X992
Durham, North Carolina

Pork-Sauerkraut Pinwheel

2 c. canned sauerkraut
1 lb ground pork
½ c. fine dry bread crumbs
1 egg, beaten
1 tsp. salt
Dash of pepper
½ tsp. Worcestershire sauce
¼ c. chopped onion
5 slices bacon

Drain and snip sauerkraut. Combine pork, bread crumbs, egg, salt, pepper and Worcestershire sauce; mix well. Place pork mixture on waxed paper. Shape into 10 x 17-inch rectangle. Combine sauerkraut and onion; mix well. Spread over pork mixture. Roll as for jelly roll. Place in shallow baking dish. Arrange bacon slices over top. Bake at 350 degrees for 45 minutes. Yield: 6-8 servings.

Cindy Kruckenberg, Pres.
Iota Mu No. 9513
Gilbert, Iowa

Pork Tenderloin A La Freud
(1936)

8 pork tenderloin patties
Flour
Salt and pepper to taste
Bacon drippings
½ lb. mushrooms
1 clove of garlic, chopped
1 10½-oz. can consomme
Chopped parsley to taste
1 tomato, chopped

Dredge patties with seasoned flour. Brown patties in bacon drippings in skillet. Place patties in large casserole. Brown mushrooms in bacon drippings. Place over patties. Brown garlic in bacon drippings. Add consomme; bring to a boil. Pour over patties. Add parsley and tomato; cover. Bake at 300 degrees for 2 hours. Yield: 4 servings.

Verna C. Starkey, Treas.
Xi Delta Iota X5188
Sequim, Washington

Sausage Casserole

¾ lb. mild sausage
¾ lb. hot sausage
¾ c. chopped celery
1 med. onion, chopped
1 green pepper, chopped
2 pkg. chicken noodle soup mix
1 c. brown rice
½ c. slivered almonds
1 c. mushrooms

Brown sausage, celery, onion and green pepper; drain. Place in greased 2-quart casserole. Add remaining ingredients and 4½ cups boiling water; mix well. Cover. Bake at 350 degrees for 1 hour and 30 minutes. Yield: 6 servings.

Mildred Borden, Treas.
Xi Rho Phi No. 4766
Brackettville, Texas

Sweet and Sour Spareribs

3 lb. spareribs, cut in serving pieces
⅔ c. (firmly packed) brown sugar
2 tbsp. cornstarch
2 tsp. dry mustard
⅔ c. vinegar
1 c. crushed pineapple
½ c. catsup
¼ c. finely, chopped onion
2 tbsp. soy sauce
Salt and pepper to taste

Place spareribs in single layer in large shallow baking pan. Bake at 425 degrees for 20 to 30 minutes; drain. Combine brown sugar, cornstarch, dry mustard, vinegar, pineapple, catsup, onion, soy sauce and ½ cup water in saucepan; stir until smooth. Cook over Medium heat until thick and glossy, stirring constantly. Sprinkle spareribs with salt and pepper. Spoon half the sauce over spareribs. Reduce oven temperature to 350 degrees. Bake for 45 minutes. Turn spareribs; cover with remaining sauce. Bake for 30 minutes longer or until well done.

Beverly Scott, Pres.
Xi Gamma Sigma X3918
Elma, Washington

Curried Veal Stew With Poppy Seed Noodles

2 c. chopped onions
4 tbsp. butter or margarine
3 lb. lean veal, cubed
2 bay leaves, crushed
1 clove of garlic, minced
2 tbsp. curry powder
¼ tsp. dried thyme
1 tbsp. salt
4 cans beef broth
2 tbsp. tomato sauce
2 tbsp. flaked coconut
¼ c. chutney
1 green apple, pared and finely chopped
2½ tbsp. cornstarch
½ c. light cream
1 8-oz. package medium noodles
2 tbsp. poppy seed
12 sm. onions, peeled
1 pkg. frozen fordhook limas, thawed
1 1-lb. can whole carrots, drained
¾ lb. mushrooms, sliced

Brown onions in 2 tablespoons butter in Dutch oven. Stir in veal, bay leaves, garlic, curry powder and thyme. Sprinkle with salt. Add broth and tomato sauce; mix well. Bring to a boil; cover. Simmer for 1 hour and 30 minutes or until veal is tender. Add coconut, chutney and apple; mix well. Cook, covered, for 15 minutes. Combine cornstarch and ⅓ cup cold water; mix well. Stir into veal mixture. Cook until thickened, stirring. Stir in cream. Prepare noodles according to package directions. Combine noodles, poppy seed and 2 tablespoons butter; keep warm. Add onions to veal mixture; cover. Cook for 20 minutes. Add limas, carrots and mushrooms; mix well. Cook for 5 minutes. Serve with hot noodles.

Dottie Huys
Xi Delta Eta X3162
Brentwood, Missouri

Poultry
and
Seafood

Connoisseurs used to dispute which of America's seacoasts provided the best seafood; which game foul had the mot distinctive and satisfying taste. Today, no one worries, for every distinctive flavor provides us with still another new recipe idea.

Creating different ways to prepare our old standbys is a Beta Sigma Phi trademark. That's why you'll especially enjoy the versatility of recipes in this chapter.

One distinction of poultry and seafood any calorie-conscious cook loves is the delightful number of satisfying low-calorie dishes that can be prepared with simple light seasonings. Or throw caution to the wind and combine rich sauces, vegetables and herbs to make memorable warm dishes families have enjoyed for generations.

They're all here—a rich variety of poultry and seafood recipes that will continue Beta Sigma Phi's tradition of cooking creativity!

Baked Chicken Supreme

2 c. sour cream
¼ c. lemon juice
4 tsp. Worcestershire sauce
4 tsp. celery salt
2 tsp. paprika
4 cloves of garlic, finely chopped
½ tsp. pepper
4 tsp. salt
6 chicken breasts, halved
1¾ c. bread crumbs
½ c. butter or margarine
½ c. shortening

Combine first 8 ingredients in large bowl; mix well. Add chicken, coating well. Cover; refrigerate over-night. Roll chicken in bread crumbs; coating well. Arrange in single layer in shallow baking pan. Melt butter and shortening in saucepan; spoon over chicken. Bake at 350 degrees for 1 hour or until chicken is tender. Yield: 12 servings.

Margaret J. Abbot, Pres.
Xi Gamma Xi X3682
Barrie, Ontario, Canada

Chicken Breasts and Mushrooms

3 chicken breasts, split, boned and skinned
2 tbsp. lemon juice
Salt to taste
White pepper to taste
½ lb. fresh mushrooms
6 tbsp. butter or margarine
½ c. finely chopped onion
⅓ c. flour
2 tbsp. oil
½ c. dry white wine
1 bay leaf
½ tsp. tarragon, crumbled

Sprinkle breasts with lemon juice, salt and white pepper; set aside. Rinse and dry mushrooms; slice. Melt 3 tablespoons butter in large skillet. Add mushrooms and onion; saute for 5 minutes. Remove mushrooms and onion from skillet; set aside. Dredge breasts with flour. Melt remaining butter in skillet; add oil. Add breasts; brown for 10 to 15 minutes. Pour off excess fat. Add mushrooms, onion, ¾ cup water, ¼ cup wine and bay leaf; cover. Simmer for 10 to 12 minutes or until chicken is tender. Place chicken and mushrooms on serving platter; keep warm. Add ¼ cup water, remaining wine and tarragon to skillet; bring to a boil, stirring. Pour over chicken and mushrooms. Yield: 6 servings.

Donna M. Roth
Xi Gamma Kappa X3056
Marion, Iowa

Chicken Breasts Supreme

4 oz. Swiss cheese, grated
¼ c. toasted chopped almonds
4 chicken breasts, halved, skinned and boned
1 c. peach or apricot preserves
3½ tbsp. Worcestershire sauce
1¼ tsp. dry mustard

Combine cheese and almonds; mix well. Cut slits in chicken; fill slits with cheese mixture. Place in baking dish. Combine remaining ingredients; mix well. Pour over chicken. Bake at 325 degrees for 1 hour, basting often. Garnish with fruit or almonds. Yield: 8 servings.

Lillian M. Bohrer, Pres.
Preceptor Eta XP299
Medford, Oregon

Chicken Cordon Bleu

4 chicken breasts
4 slices boiled ham
4 slices Swiss cheese
1 pkg. Shake and Bake for chicken

Bone and skin chicken breasts; pound with flat side of meat mallet until thin. Place 1 ham slice and 1 cheese slice on each chicken breast. Roll as for jelly roll; secure with toothpicks. Roll in Shake and Bake. Place on shallow baking pan. Bake at 400 degrees for 40 minutes. Yield: 4 servings.

Mary Hawkins, Pres.
Xi Alpha Beta X3449
Camp Springs, Maryland

Chicken Nuggets
(1959)

4 chicken breasts
½ c. dry bread crumbs
¼ c. Parmesan cheese
1 tsp. salt
1 tsp. thyme
1 tsp. basil
½ c. margarine, melted

Skin and bone chicken; cut each breast into 12 pieces. Combine bread crumbs, Parmesan cheese, salt, thyme and basil; mix well. Dip chicken pieces in margarine; roll in crumb mixture. Place on baking sheet. Bake at 400 degrees for 10 to 15 minutes. Yield: 4 dozen.

Joyce Ann Booher
Xi Epsilon Omega X5107
Centerville, Iowa

Chicken and Rice

1¾ c. minute rice
½ stick margarine, melted
1 can cream of mushroom soup
1 can cream of chicken soup
1 can cream of celery soup
3 chicken breasts, halved

Combine first 5 ingredients and ½ soup can water; mix well. Pour into 9 × 12-inch baking pan. Arrange chicken over rice mixture; cover with aluminum foil. Bake at 400 degrees for 30 minutes; remove foil. Bake for 40 minutes longer or until rice is browned. Let stand for 10 minutes. Yield: 6 servings.

Helen McCubbins, Pres.
Theta Omega No. 6170
Salisbury, Missouri

Chicken Supreme Casserole

Flour
Salt and pepper to taste
4 chicken breasts, boned and split
Cooking oil
1 can cream of celery soup
1 tsp. celery seed
4 stalks celery, coarsely diced
1 jar tiny whole onions, drained
1 can button mushrooms, drained
1 can mushroom stems and pieces, drained
¼ tsp. white pepper
3 dashes of Worcestershire sauce
1 c. sour cream
1 green pepper, cut into rings
2 tomatoes, cut into wedges

Combine flour, salt and pepper; dredge chicken in flour mixture. Brown in hot oil. Place chicken in 10 × 10 × 2-inch casserole. Combine soup, 1 soup can water, celery seed, celery, onions, mushrooms, white pepper and Worcestershire sauce in saucepan; cook until smooth and bubbly, stirring. Remove from heat. Fold in sour cream. Pour over chicken. Top with green pepper rings; cover. Bake at 350 degrees for 1 hour. Place tomato wedge inside each green pepper ring. Bake, uncovered, for 30 minutes longer. Yield: 8 servings.

Ola Peterson, Pres.
Xi Theta Iota X3752
Dongola, Illinois

Lemon Chicken

2 lg. chicken breasts, halved
Salt and pepper to taste
½ c. Italian salad dressing
1 lemon, thinly sliced
Paprika to taste

Sprinkle chicken with salt and pepper. Heat salad dressing in Dutch oven. Add chicken; simmer for 15 minutes. Top with lemon slices. Sprinkle with paprika; cover. Simmer for 10 minutes. Yield: 4 servings.

Carrie A. Bogle, Pres.
Laureate Zeta PL492
Reno, Nevada

Chicken Loaf Supreme Mold (1950)

1½ tbsp. grated onion
½ c. finely chopped celery
1 tbsp. butter
2 c. sliced cooked chicken
¾ tsp. salt
1 c. cracker crumbs
2 eggs, beaten
¾ tsp. chili powder
¾ c. milk
¾ c. cream of chicken soup

Saute onion and celery in butter. Combine remaining ingredients; mix well. Add to onion mixture; mix well. Pour into greased 8 × 10-inch pan or ring mold. Place in pan of hot water. Bake at 350 degrees for 50 minutes. Serve with chicken gravy. Yield: 6 servings.

Mae Clauson, Past Pres.
Xi Beta Sigma X2560
Fort Dodge, Iowa

Chicken Divan

2 chicken breasts, boned and split
1 10-oz. package frozen broccoli spears
1 10-oz. can cream of chicken soup
½ c. mayonnaise
1 tsp. lemon juice
½ tsp. curry powder
½ c. grated Cheddar cheese
¼ c. buttered bread crumbs, toasted

Cook chicken breasts in water to cover until tender; drain. Prepare broccoli according to package directions; drain. Place broccoli in buttered casserole. Place chicken breasts on broccoli. Combine next 4 ingredients; mix well. Pour over chicken. Sprinkle with cheese. Top with bread crumbs. Bake at 350 degrees for 25 to 30 minutes. Yield: 4 servings.

Edith A. Alexander, Pres.
Beta Gamma XP1624
Salida, Colorado

Mom Baker's Chicken-Swiss Casserole (1938)

3 to 4 lb. chicken breasts
Salt
¼ tsp. pepper
Parsley to taste
½ green pepper, sliced
1 med. bunch celery, chopped diagonally
1 sm. onion, sliced
Butter
3 tbsp. flour
1 c. light cream
½ c. ripe olives, sliced
2 pimentos, sliced
1 4-oz. can sliced mushrooms, drained
½ c. grated Swiss cheese
½ c. slivered almonds

Place chicken, 1 tablespoon salt, pepper and parsley in large saucepan; add water to cover. Cook for 1 hour and 30 minutes to 2 hours. Cool in broth. Remove chicken, reserving 1 cup broth. Remove bones from chicken; cube. Place chicken in 9 × 12-inch casserole. Saute green pepper, celery and onion in butter in skillet until tender. Remove onion mixture; set aside. Add enough butter to skillet to measure 3 tablespoons. Stir in flour until smooth. Add reserved broth, cream and 1 teaspoon salt; cook until thickened. Add olives, pimento, mushrooms, cheese and green pepper mixture; cook until heated through. Spread over chicken evenly. Sprinkle with almonds. Bake at 375 degrees for 30 to 45 minutes or until heated through.

Doris Ann Blackmore
25 Year Member
Xi Gamma Omicron X1561
Troy, Ohio

Monterey Chicken

1 8-oz. package Monterey Jack cheese
4 chicken breasts, boned and skinned
2 eggs, beaten
¾ c. dry bread crumbs
Margarine
1 chicken bouillon cube
½ c. chopped onion
½ c. chopped green pepper
2 tbsp. flour
1 tsp. salt
¼ tsp. pepper
3 c. rice, cooked
1 can sliced mushrooms, drained
2 tbsp. chopped pimento

Cut cheese into 8 thick sticks. Split breasts; flatten to ¼-inch thickness. Roll each chicken piece around cheese stick; secure with toothpicks. Dip in eggs; coat with bread crumbs. Brown on all sides in margarine; set aside. Dissolve bouillon in 1 cup boiling water. Saute onion and green pepper in ⅓ cup margarine until tender. Add flour, salt, pepper and bouillon mixture; cook until thickened. Add rice, mushrooms and pimento; mix well. Pour into shallow casserole. Top with chicken. Bake at 400 degrees for 20 minutes. Yield: 8 servings.

Evelyn Hill
Preceptor Alpha Mu XP672
Amarillo, Texas

Sweet 'n Sour Apricot Chicken

1 17-oz. can apricot halves
½ c. vinegar
⅓ c. sugar
1 tbsp. catsup
¼ tsp. salt
Pepper to taste
2 tbsp. cornstarch
1½ c. cubed cooked chicken
1 med. green pepper, chopped
1 tomato, cut into 8 wedges

Drain apricots, reserving juice. Combine all but ¼ cup reserved juice, vinegar, sugar, catsup, salt and pepper in medium saucepan; bring to a boil, stirring. Reduce heat; simmer for 5 minutes. Combine ¼ cup reserved juice and cornstarch; stir to form smooth paste. Add cornstarch mixture to vinegar mixure; mix well. Bring to a boil over Medium heat, stirring until thickened. Add apricots, chicken, green pepper and tomato; simmer for 3 minutes. Serve with rice. Yield: 4 servings.

Photograph for this recipe on page 67.

Chicken And Broccoli Au Gratin

¼ c. chopped onion
¼ c. butter or margarine
¼ c. flour
1 tsp. salt
½ tsp. curry powder
Dash of pepper
1 4-oz. can sliced mushrooms
1 13-oz. can evaporated milk
1 10-oz. package frozen broccoli spears, cooked and drained
1 chicken, cooked and cubed
1 c. shredded Monterey Jack cheese

Saute onion in butter in skillet until onion is tender. Remove from heat. Stir in flour, salt, curry powder and pepper. Drain mushrooms, reserving liquid. Add enough water to reserved liquid to measure ½ cup liquid. Stir into flour mixture gradually. Add evaporated milk; blend until smooth. Add mushrooms; cook over Medium heat until thickened, stirring. Arrange broccoli and chicken in 13 × 9-inch baking dish. Cover with sauce. Top with cheese. Bake at 375 degrees for 20 minutes or until bubbly around edges. Let stand for 15 minutes. Yield: 6 servings.

Jowana Kay Terry, Pres.
Delta Sigma No. 7976
Greenwood, Arkansas

Chicken Alexandra

1 onion, chopped
4 c. cubed cooked chicken
1 8-oz. package noodles, cooked and drained
2 cans mushroom soup
4 tbsp. Sherry
1/3 c. toasted almonds
2 tsp. chopped parsley
2 c. sour cream
4 tbsp. melted butter
1 c. seasoned bread crumbs

Saute onion until tender. Combine onion, chicken, noodles, soup, Sherry, almonds, parsley and sour cream; mix well. Pour into greased 9 × 13-inch baking pan. Top with butter and crumbs. Bake at 350 degrees for 40 minutes. Yield: 8-10 servings.

Carol Ross, Pres.
Epsilon Rho No. 5663
Monument, Colorado

Curry Chicken Divan
(1950)

2 10-oz. packages frozen broccoli spears
3 chicken breasts, cooked, boned and
    quartered
1 10-oz. can cream of chicken soup
2/3 c. mayonnaise
1/3 c. evaporated milk
1/2 c grated process American cheese
1 tsp. lemon juice
1/2 tsp. curry powder
1/2 c. fine dry bread crumbs
1 tbsp. butter, softened

Prepare broccoli according to package directions, cooking until just tender. Place broccoli in greased 2-quart baking dish. Arrange chicken over broccoli. Combine soup, mayonnaise, evaporated milk, cheese, lemon juice and curry powder; mix well. Pour over chicken. Combine bread crumbs and butter; sprinkle over chicken. Bake at 350 degrees for 25 to 30 minutes or until heated through. Yield: 6-8 servings.

Kay Blanck, Pres.
Xi Alpha Mu X780
Midland, Texas

Chicken Chow Mein

1 onion, chopped
3 stalks celery, chopped
1 4-lb. chicken, cooked and diced
2 cans mushroom soup
1½ c. chicken broth
1 5-oz. can chow mein noodles
½ c. chopped cashews

Saute onion and celery until tender. Add soup, broth and chicken; mix well. Reserve 1 cup noodles; add remaining noodles to chicken mixture, mixing well. Pour chicken mixture into buttered casserole. Bake at 350 degrees for 35 minutes. Add remaining noodles and cashews. Bake for 10 minutes longer. Yield: 5-7 servings.

Diane Woratyla, Pres.
Xi Alpha Lambda X835
Camp Hill, Pennsylvania

Chicken Enchiladas

1 lg. frying chicken
2 tbsp. butter
1½ tbsp. flour
8 oz. mild taco sauce
12 corn tortillas
Cooking oil
1 onion, finely chopped
1 lb. longhorn cheese, grated

Cook chicken in water to cover until tender. Remove chicken, reserving broth. Cool chicken; cut meat from bones in bite-sized pieces. Add butter to broth, stirring until melted. Add flour and taco sauce; cook until gravy is thickened. Dip tortillas in hot oil; dip in gravy. Place in 9 × 13-inch glass baking dish. Place about ¼ cup chicken in tortilla. Add small amount of onion and cheese. Roll as for jelly roll. Fill remaining tortillas. Cover with gravy. Bake at 350 degrees for 20 to 30 minutes. Serve with sour cream and chives. Yield: 12 servings.

Cathy L. Wirtz, Pres.
Gamma No. 134
Topeka, Kansas

Chicken Italiano

3½ lb. boned chicken
Flour
1 egg
Italian bread crumbs
1 15-oz. jar Italian cooking sauce
½ lb. mozzarella cheese, sliced
Parmesan cheese to taste
Oregano to taste

Pound chicken. Dredge chicken with flour. Combine egg and small amount of water; beat well. Dip chicken in egg mixture. Roll in crumbs. Fry until lightly browned. Pour small amount of Italian cooking sauce in 9 × 13 × 2-inch baking dish. Layer with chicken, mozzarella cheese and sauce, ending with sauce. Sprinkle with Parmesan cheese and oregano. Cover with aluminum foil. Bake at 350 degrees for 1 hour. Yield: 6 servings.

Barbara Bishop, V.P.
Gamma Rho No. 8092
Marstons Mills, Massachusetts

Hot Chicken Salad

1 10½-oz. can cream of chicken soup
½ c. mayonnaise or salad dressing
1 chicken, cooked and diced
1 c. chopped celery
1 to 1½ c. grated Cheddar cheese
1 3-oz. can French-fried onions

Combine soup and mayonnaise in 2-quart casserole; mix well. Stir in remaining ingredients. Top with additional cheese. Bake at 350 degrees for 30 minutes. Yield: 4-6 servings.

Judith E. Antonak, Pres.
Lambda Alpha No. 8308
Auburn Heights, Michigan

Chicken Delight
(1952)

1 5 to 6-lb. chicken
1 lb. egg noodles
2½ c. cream-style corn
2½ c. chopped olives
1 8-oz. can tomato sauce
1 can mushrooms, drained
¼ lb. Cheddar cheese, cubed
1 sm. can mushroom sauce
Salt and pepper to taste

Cook chicken in boiling water to cover until tender. Remove chicken, reserving broth; cut chicken from bones. Cook noodles in reserved broth. Combine chicken, noodles and remaining ingredients; mix well. Pour into 9 × 11 × 2-inch pan. Bake at 375 degrees for 45 minutes or until browned. Yield: 8-10 servings.

Rhonda Anderson
Xi Rho Gamma X3939
Yuba City, Cailfornia

Avocado-Chicken Casserole (1939)

6 oz. broken spaghetti, cooked
1 10½-oz. can celery soup
¼ c. finely chopped pimento
2 tbsp. butter or margarine
1½ c. diced cooked chicken
1 c. avocado cubes
⅓ c. grated cheese
⅓ c. buttered bread crumbs

Combine spaghetti, soup, pimento, butter and chicken; mix well. Fold in avocado. Pour into buttered 1½-quart casserole. Sprinkle with cheese and bread crumbs. Broil for 3 minutes or until cheese is melted and browned. Yield: 6 servings.

Catherine J. Zachery, Rec. Sec.
Preceptor Delta Phi XP1039
Sonora, California

Baked Chicken-Macaroni Casserole

8 oz. elbow macaroni
1½ c. sliced cooked chicken
1 8-oz. package sliced American cheese
¼ c. butter
2 tbsp. flour
1½ c. milk
Salt and pepper to taste
Paprika to taste

Prepare macaroni according to package directions; drain. Arrange in shallow 2-quart baking dish. Top with alternating layers of chicken and cheese. Melt butter in saucepan; blend in flour. Add milk; cook until thickened, stirring. Add salt and pepper; mix well. Pour over cheese. Sprinkle with paprika. Bake at 375 degrees for 25 to 30 minutes. Yield: 4-5 servings.

Patricia A. Hockett
Zeta Chi No. 6899
Shattuck, Oklahoma

Chicken Quebec

1 4 to 5 lb. chicken, cut up
6 slices bacon
1 onion, minced
2 stalks celery, diced
4 c. chicken broth or consomme
½ lb. elbow macaroni, cooked
2 tbsp. minced parsley

Remove skin from chicken. Brown chicken, bacon, onion and celery. Place chicken mixture in 2-quart casserole. Add broth. Bake at 350 degrees for 2 hours or until chicken is tender. Place macaroni around chicken mixture. Sprinkle with parsley. Bake for 15 to 20 minutes longer.

Mary E. Barrett, Treas.
Preceptor Beta XP766
Pixcourt, Quebec, Canada

Chicken Macaroni

1 12-oz. package macaroni
4 tbsp. chicken soup base
¼ c. minced onion flakes
2 5-oz. cans chicken, chopped
1 can cream of mushroom soup
1 can cream of chicken soup
1 c. milk
½ lb. Velveeta cheese, cubed
Salt and pepper to taste

Cook macaroni and soup base in 8 cups water until macaroni is tender; drain. Combine macaroni, onion, chicken, soups, milk, cheese salt and pepper; mix well. Pour into greased casserole; cover. Bake at 350 degrees for 30 minutes; stir. Yield: 6-8 servings.

Jeanette Hunter
Xi Mu Chi
El Campo, Texas

Chicken-Almond Casserole

2 c. boned chicken
3 c. white sauce
1 tbsp. chopped onion
½ c. blanched chopped almonds
¼ lb. sharp cheese, grated
⅔ c. steamed rice
Cracker crumbs

Combine chicken, white sauce, onion, almonds, cheese and rice; mix well. Pour into greased 12 × 7-inch glass baking dish. Sprinkle with cracker crumbs. Bake at 325 degrees for 45 minutes to 1 hour. Yield: 10 servings.

Opal Minor
Xi Delta Upsilon No. 3529
Sunrise Beach, Missouri

Country Club Casserole

1 chicken
1 c. chopped onions
1 c. chopped bell pepper
1 sm. jar pimento, drained
½ c. mayonnaise
1 can cream of mushroom soup
3 c. hot cooked rice
Salt and pepper to taste
Grated Cheddar cheese

Cook chicken in water to cover until tender. Cool. Remove bones; cube. Combine chicken and remaining ingredients except cheese; mix well. Pour into greased 2½-quart casserole. Top with cheese. Bake at 325 degrees for 45 minutes. Yield: 6 servings.

Melinda Schaffer, Pres.
Epsilon Gamma No. 8838
Burns, Oregon

Mush

2 10-oz. cans mushroom soup
2 2-oz. cans mushroom pieces, drained
2 7-oz. cans chicken
2 6-oz. packages chicken-flavored instant rice

Combine soup, mushrooms, chicken and 2 soup cans water in 6-quart saucepan; bring to a boil. Add rice and flavoring; cover. Simmer until rice is tender. Serve with green salad. Yield: 8 servings.

Janet May Scott, Pres.
Laureate Alpha PL319
South River, New Jersey

Chicken Tetrazzini

12 oz. spaghetti
1 med. onion, chopped
Butter or margarine
¼ c. flour
1½ c. chicken broth
1 c. heavy cream
1 tsp. salt
⅛ tsp. pepper
½ c. dry vermouth
¾ c. grated Parmesan cheese
½ lb. mushrooms, sliced
3 c. cooked chicken pieces

Prepare spaghetti according to package directions; drain. Saute onion in ¼ cup butter. Stir in flour. Add broth and cream gradually; bring to a boil, stirring. Stir in salt, pepper, vermouth and ¼ cup cheese. Saute mushrooms in 2 tablespoons butter until browned. Combine spaghetti, mushrooms and chicken in 2½-quart casserole. Cover with broth mixture. Top with remaining cheese. Bake at 375 degrees for 20 minutes or until bubbly. Yield: 6 servings.

Photograph for this recipe on page 62.

Baked Chicken With Pecans

½ c. butter
1 c. buttermilk
1 egg, slightly beaten
1 c. flour
1 c. chopped pecans
¼ c. sesame seed
¾ tsp. salt
1 tbsp. paprika
½ tsp. pepper
1 frying chicken, cut up

Melt butter in 9 × 13 × 2-inch baking pan. Combine buttermilk and egg; mix well. Combine flour, pecans, sesame seed, salt, paprika and pepper; mix well. Dip chicken pieces in milk mixture; dip in flour mxture. Place, skin side down, in melted butter; turn, skin side up. Bake at 350 degrees for 1 hour and 30 minutes, basting 2 or 3 times. Yield: 6 servings.

Nancy L. Wood, V.P.
Xi Iota Kappa No. 9471
Washington, Illinois

Chicken Cacciatore A La Bruno
(1930)

1 clove of garlic, sliced
½ c. olive oil
1 2 to 3-lb. frying chicken, cut up
1 sm. can tomatoes, drained
1¼ tsp. salt
1 tsp. rosemary
1 tsp. chopped parsley
1 tsp. pepper
1 sm. can mushrooms, drained
1 c. white cooking wine
1 sm. jar green olives, drained and chopped

Saute garlic in oil. Add chicken, browning all sides. Add remaining ingredients; mix well. Cook over Medium heat for 15 minutes; drain. Place in 12 × 12-inch baking pan. Bake at 375 degrees for 30 minutes or until chicken is tender. Serve over rice. Yield: 4 servings.

Janis K. Bruno, Ext. Off.
Zeta Eta No. 6221
Hooker, Oklahoma

Chicken Caruso
(1950)

1 2½-lb. frying chicken, cut up
¼ c. butter
3 cloves of garlic, sliced
¼ c. minced onion
1 c. catsup
¼ c. vinegar
2 tbsp. sugar
1 tsp. salt
¼ c. Worcestershire sauce

Brown chicken in butter. Place chicken in baking dish. Combine remaining ingredients and ½ cup water; mix well. Pour over chicken. Bake at 350 degrees for 1 hour and 30 minutes. Yield: 4 servings.

Josephine Legard, Treas.
Preceptor Kappa XP1266
Superior, Wisconsin

Chicken Marengo

1 2½ to 3-lb. frying chicken, cut up
1 1½-oz. package spaghetti sauce mix
½ c. dry white wine
2 tomatoes, quartered
¼ lb. mushrooms

Place chicken pieces in slow cooker. Combine spaghetti sauce mix and wine; mix well. Pour over chicken. Cook on Low for 6 to 7 hours. Add tomatoes and mushrooms; cover. Cook on High for 30 to 40 minutes or until tomatoes are tender. Yield: 4-5 servings.

Pat Lawless, Treas.
Xi Eta Theta X1957
Van Nuys, California

Chicken Piccata

2 chickens
1 tsp. salt
½ tsp. pepper
2 tsp. poultry seasoning
2 tsp. dried basil
2 tsp. rosemary

Cut chickens in half along breastbone; remove wing tips and backs. Arrange chicken, skin side down, in single layer in large shallow baking pan. Combine remaining ingredients; mix well. Sprinkle ½ of the seasonings over chicken; cover. Bake at 425 degrees for 30 minutes. Turn chicken, skin side up; sprinkle with remaining seasonings. Bake, uncovered, for 20 to 30 minutes longer or until chicken is tender and browned. Serve with lemon wedges.

June M. Carter, Pres.
Zeta Delta No. 5158
Laurel Hill, Florida

Chicken With Sour Cream Gravy
(1949)

1 2½ to 3-lb. frying chicken, cut up
3 tbsp. salad oil
4 tsp. salt
¼ tsp. pepper
2 c. diagonally-sliced celery
2 c. diagonally-sliced carrots
1 c. long grain rice
8 oz. sour cream

Brown chicken in oil in 12-inch skillet over Medium heat. Sprinkle with salt and pepper. Add 2 cups water; bring to a boil. Cover. Reduce heat; simmer for 20 minutes. Add celery and carrots; cover. Simmer for 15 minutes or until vegetables are tender, stirring occasionally. Prepare rice according to package directions. Spoon rice onto serving platter; keep warm. Place chicken and vegetables over rice. Skim fat from drippings. Add sour cream to drippings; cook until just heated through. Serve over chicken.

M. A. Sierotowicz
Xi Delta Theta X3898
Battle Creek, Michigan

Easy Chicken And Rice Casserole

1 3½-oz. can fried onions
1½ c. rice
2 tbsp. pimento
1 tbsp. instant green pepper flakes
1 2½-lb. frying chicken, cut up
1 can cream of chicken soup
½ tsp. paprika
1 c. grated longhorn cheese

Spread onions in greased 1½-quart baking dish. Combine rice, pimento and green pepper flakes; mix well. Spread over onions. Place chicken, skin side up, over rice. Combine soup and ½ soup can water; mix well. Pour over chicken, mixing well to moisten rice. Sprinkle with paprika. Cover. Bake at 300 degrees for 1 hour and 30 minutes. Sprinkle with cheese. Bake, uncovered, for 10 minutes longer. Yield: 6 servings.

Jeanne Stilwell, V.P.
Xi Beta Omega X5247
Phoenix, Arizona

Lebanese Chicken

1 med. fryer, cut up
1 tsp. salt
½ tsp. cinnamon
½ tsp. pepper
1 15-oz. can garbanzo beans and liquid
1 med. onion, coarsely chopped

Place chicken in 2-quart saucepan. Add 1 cup water; cook over Medium heat until tender. Add salt, cinnamon, pepper and beans; cook over Low heat until beans are tender. Add onion; cook for 10 to 12 minutes or until onion is tender. Serve over rice. Yield: 4 servings.

Annie Pfaff, V.P.
Preceptor Gamma Alpha XP1638
St. Augustine, Florida

Oven Chicken Stew
(1947)

1 3-lb. frying chicken, cut up
4 med. potatoes, quartered
3 med. onions, quartered
4 carrots, cut in 2-in. pieces
3 green peppers, chopped
Salt and pepper to taste
Monosodium glutamate
Pinch of garlic powder
Soy sauce to taste

Place chicken in shallow baking pan. Arrange vegetables over chicken. Season with salt, pepper, monosodium glutamate, garlic powder and soy sauce. Cover with foil; seal edges. Punch holes in foil with tines of fork. Bake at 425 degrees for 1 hour. Yield: 4 servings.

Susan M. Davenport, Pres.
Theta No. 1615
Bath, Maine

Savory Chicken
(1959)

1 c. rice
1 env. onion soup mix
3 tbsp. butter or margarine
3 c. chicken broth
1 tsp. celery salt
1 med. fryer, cut up
1 tsp. salt
1 tsp. paprika

Brown rice and soup mix in butter. Spread in buttered 13 × 9 × 2-inch baking pan. Add broth and celery salt; mix well. Arrange chicken over rice

mixture. Sprinkle with salt and paprika. Cover tightly with aluminum foil. Bake at 350 degrees for 1 hour. Remove foil. Bake for 15 minutes longer or until chicken is tender and browned. Yield: 6 servings.

Maria C. Blount
Xi Sigma
Arden, North Carolina

Gretchen's Sweet And Sour Chicken

2 2½ to 3-lb. frying chickens, cut up
1 8-oz. bottle Russian dressing
1 1⅜-oz. envelope onion soup mix
1 10-oz. jar apricot preserves

Place chicken in large shallow 13 × 9-inch baking dish. Combine remaining ingredients; mix well. Pour over chicken. Bake at 350 degrees for 1 hour and 30 minutes, basting occasionally. Serve with rice and pan drippings. Yield: 6-8 sevings.

Gretchen L. Hogan, Corr. Sec.
Xi Alpha Mu X3140
Flagstaff, Arizona

Hot Turkey Supreme

5 c. diced cooked turkey
3 c. chopped celery
1 c. blanched chopped almonds
⅔ c. chopped green pepper
¼ c. chopped pimento
¼ c. chopped onion
2 tsp. salt
¼ c. lemon juice
1 c. mayonnaise
1 8-oz. package sliced Swiss cheese
2 c. cracker crumbs
1 stick margarine, melted

Combine turkey, celery, almonds, green pepper, pimento, onion, salt, lemon juice and mayonnaise; mix well. Pour into 9 × 13-inch baking dish. Top with cheese. Combine crumbs and margarine; mix well. Sprinkle over cheese. Bake at 350 degrees for 45 minutes. Yield: 12 servings.

Orpha Buckwalter, Serv. Chm.
Xi Epsilon Tau X2681
Savanna, Illinois

Turkey Loaf

1½ lb. cooked ground turkey
½ c. bread cubes
½ c. evaporated milk
¼ c. chopped parsley
1 egg, slightly beaten

¾ tsp. salt
¼ tsp. pepper
1 c. chopped onion
¼ c. chopped celery
1 c. stuffing mix
1 c. cranberry sauce
¼ c. corn syrup
2 tbsp. grated orange rind

Combine first 7 ingredients; mix well. Press ½ of turkey mixture firmly into loaf pan. Saute onion and celery. Prepare stuffing mix according to package directions. Add to onion and celery; mix well. Spread over loaf mixture. Top with remaining turkey mixture. Bake at 350 degrees for 50 minutes. Combine cranberry sauce, corn syrup and orange rind in saucepan; mix well. Bring to a boil. Pour over turkey loaf. Yield: 6 servings.

Genevieve Varnum, Past Pres.
Eta Nu
Boyne City, Michigan

Turkey Chop Suey
(1958)

1 1-lb. can bean sprouts
½ c. sliced onions
2 tbsp. butter or margarine
1½ to 2 c. diced cooked turkey
1 c. sliced celery
1 6-oz. can water chestnuts, drained and sliced
½ c. turkey broth
2 tbsp. cornstarch
¼ tsp. salt
¼ tsp. monosodium glutamate
2 tbsp. soy sauce
4 c. hot cooked rice
½ c. blanched slivered almonds, toasted

Drain bean sprouts, reserving liquid. Saute onions in butter until tender. Add turkey, celery, water chestnuts, broth and reserved liquid; bring to a boil. Combine cornstarch, seasonings, ¼ cup water and soy sauce; mix well. Stir into turkey mixture. Cook until thickened, stirring constantly. Add bean sprouts; cook until heated through. Serve over rice and almonds. Yield: 4-6 servings.

Betty Jean Price, Treas.
Epsilon Omega No. 8555
Sylva, North Carolina

Cod Au Gratin

1 lb. cod fillets
1½ c. milk
3 tbsp. melted butter
4 tbsp. flour

½ tsp. salt
⅛ tsp. pepper
6 tbsp. grated Cheddar cheese

Simmer fillets in milk until fish flakes easily. Drain; reserving liquid. Flake fish into 4 greased 8-ounce casseroles. Combine butter, flour, salt and pepper in saucepan; mix well. Add reserved liquid gradually; mix well. Cook until thickened, stirring constantly. Add ¼ cup sauce to each casserole. Top each with 1½ tablespoons cheese. Place in shallow pan of water. Bake at 350 degrees for 15 to 20 minutes or until cheese is melted. Yield: 4 servings.

Nellie Bridges, Rec. Sec.
Eta No. 7539
Grand Falls, Newfoundland, Canada

Fish Fillets With Shrimp Sauce
(1935)

½ c. chopped celery
½ c. chopped carrots
2 sprigs of parsley
5 peppercorns
2 whole cloves
1 bay leaf
¼ c. vinegar
2 scallions, chopped
Salt
1½ lb. fish fillets
½ c. white wine
2 lg. cloves of garlic, crushed
6 lg. mushrooms, sliced
3 tbsp. butter
6 tbsp. flour
1 c. half and half
Pepper to taste
Dash of hot pepper sauce
Pinch of dillweed
½ lb. cooked shrimp

Combine first 8 ingredients and 1 tablespoon salt with 2 quarts water in large skillet; bring to a boil. Add fish; cover. Simmer for 5 minutes. Stir in wine. Let stand for several minutes. Drain, reserving 1 cup broth. Place fish on serving platter. Saute garlic and mushrooms in butter in saucepan until tender. Blend in flour. Add reserved fish broth gradually, stirring. Cook until thickened. Stir in half and half. Add salt and pepper, hot pepper sauce and dillweed; mix well. Place ½ of the shrimp in blender container; blend until finely chopped. Add chopped shrimp and remaining shrimp to sauce; mix well. Cook until heated through. Pour over fish. Yield: 4-6 servings.

Bobbye Ruth Robins, Pres.
Xi Epsilon Chi X1689
Lynwood, California

Sunny Citrus Fillets

1 lb. frozen fish fillets, thawed
½ tsp. salt
Dash of pepper
2 tbsp. finely chopped onion
Butter
2 tbsp. orange or lemon juice
1 tsp. grated orange or lemon rind
1 orange, lemon or lime, thinly sliced
2 tbsp. chopped or slivered almonds

Place fillets in greased 8 × 8-inch baking dish. Sprinkle with salt, pepper and onion. Combine 2 tablespoons melted butter, juice and rind; pour over fillets. Bake at 450 degrees for 5 minutes. Top with citrus slices. Bake for 5 minutes longer or until fish flakes easily. Brown almonds in 1 tablespoon butter in small saucepan. Sprinkle over fillets. Yield: 3-4 servings.

Dorothy Bilton
Coordinating Coun. Chm.
Brampton, Ontario, Canada

Baked Salmon Fillets In Sour Cream
(1935)

2 2½-lb. salmon fillets
1 tsp. salt
2 c. sour cream
1 onion, finely chopped
1 tbsp. lemon juice
1 tbsp. fresh dill or tarragon
1 tsp. dried dillseed or dried tarragon
Chopped parsley

Cut fillets into serving pieces; arrange, skin side down, in buttered baking dish. Sprinkle with salt. Combine remaining ingredients except parsley; mix well. Spread over fillets. Bake at 350 degrees for 20 to 35 minutes or until fish flakes easily. Sprinkle with parsley.

Zeralla Haake, Ext. Off.
Preceptor Sigma XP1685
Green Bay, Wisconsin

Mom's Salmon Mousse
(1946)

1 3-oz. package lemon gelatin
1 tsp. salt
2 tbsp. lemon juice
Dash of pepper
⅓ c. whipping cream, whipped
1 c. flaked salmon

1 c. diced cucumbers
⅓ c. mayonnaise

Dissolve gelatin and salt in 1¾ cups hot water. Add lemon juice and pepper; mix well. Chill until partially congealed. Fold in whipped cream. Combine salmon, cucumbers and mayonnaise; mix well. Add to gelatin mixture; mix well. Pour into 1½-quart mold. Chill until firm. Yield: 6-8 servings.

Ann Sample, Pres.
Alpha Delta No. 2688
Albuquerque, New Mexico

Salmon Loaf

1 1-lb. can salmon, drained
1 c. chopped celery
1 3 oz. can tuna
1 4-oz. can chopped mushrooms, drained
¼ tsp. pepper
1 c. chopped onions
¼ c. margarine, softened
3 oz. Swiss cheese, cubed
5 oz. mild Cheddar cheese, cubed

Combine all ingredients; blend well. Pour into buttered baking dish. Bake at 375 degrees for 1 hour. Yield: 6 servings.

Coral Scott, Pres.
Laureate Gamma PL332
Pocatello, Idaho

Salmon Steaks with Blue Cheese

4 salmon steaks
Olive oil
Salt and pepper to taste
½ c. butter
2 egg yolks, sightly beaten
2 tbsp. lemon juice
½ tsp. horseradish
¼ c. crumbled blue cheese
2 tbsp. chopped cucumber
1 tsp. grated onion

Brush salmon steaks with olive oil. Sprinkle with salt and pepper. Set aside. Melt butter in top of double boiler. Add egg yolks, lemon juice and horseradish; mix well. Cook until thickened, stirring constantly. Add blue cheese, cucumber, onion and pepper; mix well. Preheat broiler pan; brush with olive oil. Broil to desired doneness. Pour sauce over steaks immediately.

Cheryl Carson, City Coun. Pres.
Phi No. 7365
Soldotna, Alaska

Salmon Steaks With Creamed Macaroni

4 salmon steaks, 1-in. thick
¼ c. melted butter
2 c. elbow macaroni
1 10½-oz. can cream of celery soup
½ c. milk
2 tbsp. Chablis or 1 tbsp. lemon juice
¼ c. chopped ripe olives
1 tsp. instant minced onion

Bake salmon in butter in 425-degree oven for 10 minutes, basting frequently. Prepare macaroni according to package directions; drain. Combine macaroni and remaining ingredients; mix well. Spoon around salmon. Bake at 350 degrees for 15 minutes, brushing with additional butter as needed. Garnish with olives, lemon slice or parsley. Yield: 4 servings.

Photograph for this recipe on page 77.

Tuna Cakes
(1950)

2 tbsp. butter
3 tbsp. flour
1 c. milk
2 egg yolks, beaten

1 12½-oz. can flaked tuna
Chopped parsley
¼ tsp. celery seed
¼ tsp. onion powder
⅛ tsp. cayenne pepper
½ c. soft bread cubes
¾ c. dry bread crumbs or crushed corn flakes
Cooking oil
2 tbsp. chopped pickle
1 tbsp. minced onion
2 tbsp. lemon juice
1 c. mayonnaise

Melt butter; add flour, stirring. Add milk; cook over Low heat, stirring until smooth and thickened. Stir small amount of hot mixture into egg yolks; stir egg yolks into hot mixture. Stir until thickened. Add tuna, dash of parsley, celery seed, onion powder, cayenne pepper and bread cubes; mix well. Shape into eight 2½-inch patties; roll in dry crumbs. Fry in hot oil, turning once. Combine pickle, onion, 1 tablespoon parsley, lemon juice and mayonnaise; mix well. Serve with tuna cakes. Yield: 4 servings.

Patricia Bowman, Pres.
Zeta No. 9101
Victoria, British Columbia, Canada

Baked Sole
(1952)

¼ lb. mushrooms, chopped
1 sm. green onion, chopped
4 sprigs of parsley, chopped
¾ lb. sole, cut into 1-in. strips
1¼ c. white wine
2 tbsp. flour
½ stick margarine or butter, softened
1 c. hot cooked white rice

Layer mushrooms, green onion and parsley in 1½-quart casserole. Fold sole strips in half; layer over vegetables in herringbone pattern. Sprinkle with additional green onion. Cover with wine. Place over Low heat; heat until mixture bubbles. Bake at 350 degrees for 20 minutes. Drain, reserving liquid. Pour reserved liquid into saucepan; cook until liquid measures 1 cup. Combine flour and butter; add to hot liquid, stirring until thickened. Place sole over rice; cover with hot sauce. Yield: 2 servings.

Laura R. Heye, Rec. Sec.
Preceptor MU XP326
Olympia, Washington

Barbecued Whitefish In Foil

2 lb. frozen whitefish fillets, thawed
2 green peppers, sliced
2 onions, sliced
2 tbsp. lemon juice
¼ c. butter or margarine, melted
2 tsp. salt
1 tsp. paprika
Pepper to taste
Lemon pepper to taste

Cut fillets into serving pieces. Cut six 12 × 12-inch pieces of heavy-duty aluminum foil; grease lightly. Place portion of fillets, skin side down, on each aluminum foil square. Top with green pepper and onion. Combine remaining ingredients; mix well. Pour sauce over fillets. Seal squares tightly. Cook on grill for 30 to 45 minutes or until fish flakes easily. Yield: 6 servings.

Bonnie Reed, Treas.
Preceptor Epsilon XP1123
Prince Albert, Saskatchewan, Canada

Seven Seas Casserole

1 10½-oz. can cream of celery soup
¼ tsp. salt
¼ c. finely chopped onion
Dash of pepper
1⅓ c. minute rice
1½ c. cooked peas
1 7-oz. can tuna, drained and flaked
½ c. grated Cheddar cheese

Combine soup, salt, onion, pepper and 1⅓ cups water in saucepan; mix well. Bring to a boil, stirring occasionally. Pour ½ of the mixture into greased 1½-quart casserole. Layer with rice, peas and tuna. Cover with remaining soup mixture. Sprinkle with cheese. Bake at 375 degrees for 10 minutes; cut though mixture with knife blade. Bake at 375 degrees for 20 minutes longer. Garnish with pimento strips. Yield: 5-6 servings.

Mary Elizabeth Kane
Xi Preceptor XP410
Baxter Springs, Kansas

Tuna-Cashew Casserole

2 c. tuna
1 c. chopped cashews
1 c. chopped celery
¼ c. chopped green onions
2 c. mushroom soup
2 c. Chinese noodles

Combine tuna, cashews, celery, onions and soup; mix well. Alternate layers of tuna mixture and noodles in 9 × 13-inch baking dish, ending with noodles. Bake at 350 degrees for 45 minutes. Yield: 12 servings.

Ardella Sykes, Pres.
Preceptor Gamma Gamma XP1839
Florissant, Missouri

Baked Seafood Salad

1 7½-oz. can crab meat, drained and flaked
1 4½-oz. can shrimp, drained
1½ c. chopped celery
¼ to ½ c. chopped green pepper
¼ to ½ c. chopped onion
¼ c. chopped pimento
¾ c. sour cream
¼ to ½ c. mayonnaise
1 tbsp. lemon juice
1 to 1½ tsp. Worcestershire sauce
½ tsp. salt
Dash of pepper
1 c. soft bread crumbs
1 tbsp. melted butter

Combine crab meat, shrimp, celery, green pepper, onion and pimento; mix well. Combine next 6 ingredients; blend well. Pour over seafood mixture; mix well. Spoon into 10 × 6 × 12-inch baking dish.

Combine bread crumbs and butter; mix well. Sprinkle over seafood mixture. Bake at 350 degrees for 20 to 25 minutes.

Nuleen Gibson, Rec. Sec.
Alpha Theta XP1091
Corvallis, Oregon

Betty A. Christianson, Sec.
Xi Xi X1499
Great Falls, Montana

Barbara's Deviled Seafood Casserole

1 can crab meat, drained
3 cans med. shrimp, drained
2 c. finely chopped celery
1 c. finely chopped green pepper
1 c. salad dressing
1 c. mayonnaise
2 tsp. dry mustard
1 to 2 tsp. curry powder
¼ c. finely chopped onion
1 tsp. (scant) salt
¼ tsp. pepper
2 tsp. Worcestershire sauce
2 c. buttered soft bread crumbs
2 hard-cooked eggs, sliced

Combine first 12 ingredients; mix well. Spoon into 8 large scallop shells. Sprinkle with bread crumbs. Top with egg slices. Bake at 350 degrees for 30 minutes. May be poured into 2-quart casserole. Bake at 350 degrees for 45 minutes. Yield: 8-10 servings.

Barbara M. Johnson, City Coun. Rep.
Xi Alpha Alpha X4558
Sidney, Montana

Crab Casserole

1 c. crab meat
1 tbsp. lemon juice
½ c. mayonnaise
1 10-oz. can cream of chicken soup
3 hard-boiled eggs, chopped
1 c. chopped celery
1 tbsp. chopped onion
½ c. slivered almonds
½ tsp. salt
Corn flake or bread crumbs

Combine crab meat, lemon juice, mayonnaise, soup, eggs, celery, onions, almonds and salt; mix well. Pour into casserole. Sprinkle with crumbs. Bake at 400 degrees for 30 minutes. Yield: 6 servings.

Tina Smith, Pres.
Beta Omicron No. 7407
Prince Rupert, British Columbia, Canada

Cannery Row Casserole

8 thick slices day-old French bread
1 med. onion, chopped
2 c. crab meat, tuna or shrimp
1 c. chopped water chestnuts
4 green onions, chopped
1 c. mayonnaise
1 tsp. dry mustard
Dash of cayenne pepper
1 c. chopped celery
1 tsp. salt
2 tbsp. Sherry
¼ tsp. curry powder
3 eggs, slightly beaten
3 c. milk
1 can mushroom soup
Paprika to taste
Grated Cheddar cheese

Cube and remove crusts from bread. Place ½ of the bread in 9 × 13-inch baking dish. Combine next 11 ingredients; mix well. Pour over bread. Top with remaining bread. Combine eggs and milk; mix well. Pour over bread. Refrigerate for 4 hours or overnight. Cover with soup. Sprinkle with paprika. Bake at 325 degrees for 1 hour and 15 minutes. Top with cheese. Bake at 325 degrees for 15 minutes longer. Yield: 8 servings.

Karen Brouhard, Pres.
Eta Phi XP1696
Watsonville, California

Alaskan Crab-Mushroom Ramekins

2 tbsp. butter
½ lb. mushrooms
1½ tbsp. flour
⅔ c. dry wine
½ c. sour cream
¾ c. shredded Swiss cheese
¾ lb. Alaskan king crab meat
Salt to taste
White pepper to taste
Slivered almonds

Melt butter in large skillet. Add mushrooms; saute over Medium heat until browned. Reserve small amount of mushrooms. Sprinkle remaining mushrooms with flour; stir until bubbly. Remove from heat. Add wine gradually. Cook until thickened, stirring. Stir in sour cream, cheese, crab meat, salt and white pepper. Spoon into individual shallow baking dishes. Top with reserved mushrooms and almonds. Bake at 350 degrees for 10 to 15 minutes.

Veva Becker, Rec. Sec.
Preceptor Alpha XP189
Fairbanks, Alaska

Crab Delight
(1938)

2 tbsp. chopped green pepper
2 tbsp. butter
2 tbsp. flour
Cayenne pepper to taste
½ tsp. mustard
¼ tsp. salt
½ tsp. Worcestershire sauce
1 c. strained tomatoes
1 c. grated cheese
1 egg, slightly beaten
⅔ c. milk, scalded
1 c. flaked crab meat

Brown green pepper in butter. Add flour; stir until smooth. Combine next 7 ingredients in top of double boiler. Add green pepper mixture; mix well. Cook over hot water for 10 minutes. Add milk gradually, stirring constantly. Add crab meat; cook until heated through. Serve in patty shells or on toast rounds. Yield: 6 servings.

Mary R. Green, Corr. Sec.
Preceptor Laureate Psi X788
Newport, Oregon

Crab Meat Pie

1 6½-oz. can crab meat, drained and flaked
½ c. mayonnaise
2 tbsp. flour
2 eggs, beaten
½ c. milk
½ c. sliced onions
8 oz. grated Swiss cheese
1 unbaked pastry shell

Combine first 7 ingredients; mix well. Pour into pastry-lined pie pan. Bake at 350 degrees for 40 to 45 minutes. Let stand for 5 minutes. Yield: 6 servings.

Ruth Lane, V.P.
Preceptor Eta XP1113
Auburn, Maine

Crab Quiche

1 c. crab meat
1 unbaked 9-in. pie shell
3 eggs, beaten
1 c. milk
⅓ c. white wine
½ c. shredded Cheddar cheese

Spread crab meat evenly in pie shell. Combine eggs and milk; mix well. Stir in wine. Pour over crab meat.

Sprinkle with cheese. Bake at 350 degrees for 40 to 45 minutes. Yield: 6 servings.

Linda J. Simpson
Xi Alpha Mu
Annapolis, Maryland

Deviled Crab Meat

3 hard-cooked eggs
5 tbsp. butter, softened
2 tbsp. flour
2½ c. milk
2 tbsp. chopped parsley
1 tsp. minced onion
2 c. diced crab meat
1¼ tsp. salt
¼ tsp. paprika
2 tbsp. Sherry or Worcestershire sauce (opt.)
⅓ c. bread crumbs

Cut eggs in half while still hot; remove yolks. Mash hot yolk; add 1½ tablespoons butter. Melt 1½ tablespoons butter in saucepan; stir in flour, blending well. Add egg yolk mixture; blend well. Add milk gradually, stirring until smooth and thickened. Chop egg whites. Add egg whites, parsley, onion, crab meat, salt, paprika and Sherry to egg yolk mixture; mix well. Pour into greased casserole. Top with bread crumbs. Dot with 2 tablespoons butter. Bake at 350 degrees for 10 minutes. Yield: 10 servings.

Honorable Marjorie S. Holt
Member of Congress
Washington, D. C.

Lobster Newburg

1 pkg. frozen patty shells
⅓ c. butter
2 tbsp. flour
2 c. cream
3 egg yolks, beaten
3 c. canned lobster
1 4-oz. can butter mushrooms, drained
¼ c. Sherry
2 tsp. lemon juice
½ tsp. salt
Dash of paprika

Prepare patty shells according to package directions; set aside. Melt butter in saucepan. Add flour; stir until smooth. Add cream gradually; cook until thickened. Stir small amount of hot mixture into egg yolks; stir egg yolks into hot mixture. Cook until thickened, stirring constantly. Add lobster, mushrooms, Sherry, lemon juice and salt; mix well.

Sprinkle with paprika. Spoon into patty shells. Yield: 6 servings.

Georgiann Trenholm, Rec. Sec.
Preceptor Alpha Lambda XP1307
Gresham, Oregon

Neptune International

1 10½-oz. can mushroom soup
1½ c. milk
¾ lb. shrimp
1 8-oz. can water chestnuts, drained
1 4½-oz. can crab meat, drained and flaked
1 8-oz. can sliced mushrooms, drained
½ c. chopped green pepper
3 tbsp. chopped onion
1½ tsp. salt
½ tsp. pepper
1 8-oz. package egg noodles, cooked
½ c. grated Cheddar cheese

Combine soup and milk; blend well. Add shrimp, water chestnuts, crab meat, mushrooms, green pepper, onion, salt and pepper; mix well. Arrange ½ of the noodles in greased 2½-quart casserole. Layer with shrimp mixture and noodles, ending with shrimp mixture. Sprinkle with cheese. Bake at 350

degrees for 35 minutes or until heated through. Yield: 8 servings.

Lee McGaughey, Corr. Sec.
Xi Alpha Pi X1367
Arvada, Colorado

Scallop Casserole

Margarine
3 tbsp. cornstarch
2½ c. milk
1 pt. scallops, halved
½ c. sliced celery
¼ c. diced pimento
¼ tsp. salt
Dash of paprika
½ c. fine dry bread crumbs

Melt ¼ cup margarine in saucepan. Add cornstarch, stirring to form smooth paste. Add milk gradually; stir until smooth. Bring to a boil over Medium heat, stirring until thickened. Simmer for 1 minute. Add scallops, celery, pimento, salt and paprika; mix well. Pour into 1½-quart casserole or 10-inch pie plate. Combine bread crumbs and 2 tablespoons melted margarine; mix well. Spoon around edge of scallop mixture. Bake at 350 degrees for 30 minutes or until heated through. Garnish with lemon slices.

Photograph for this recipe on page 81.

Scallops en Brochette
(1959)

16 med. scallops, rinsed and drained
1 20-oz. can pineapple chunks
Soy sauce
8 slices bacon, halved
2 med. green peppers, cut into 1-in. pieces
2 med. onions, cut into 1-in. pieces
16 med. mushrooms

Place scallops in bowl. Drain pineapple, reserving juice. Pour pineapple juice over scallops. Add soy sauce to cover. Refrigerate overnight; drain. Wrap each scallop in 1 bacon slice. Arrange scallops between pineapple chunks, green peppers, onions and mushrooms on skewers. Place on grill. Cook for 2 minutes on each side, turning 4 times.

Ruth D. Rabold, Pres.
Preceptor Laureate Beta PL129
Salem, Oregon

Seafood Casserole

1 lg. can lobster
1 lb. haddock fillets
1 lb. scallops
4 c. milk
½ c. flour
10 tbsp. butter
1 10-oz. can cream of mushroom soup
1½ c. cooked rice
1½ c. coarse bread crumbs

Drain lobster, reserving liquid. Cut lobster and fish into serving pieces. Place fish and scallops in large saucepan; add milk. Cook over Medium-low heat for 8 minutes. Drain, reserving milk for sauce. Blend flour and 6 tablespoons butter in saucepan; heat until smooth, stirring. Add reserved milk gradually, stirring. Add soup and reserved liquid; cook until thickened, stirring. Layer sauce, rice and seafood in large buttered casserole, ending with sauce. Brown bread crumbs in 4 tablespoons butter; sprinkle over sauce. Bake at 350 degrees for 1 hour.

Sandra L. Wood
Xi Alpha Sigma X2125
Whitby, Ontario, Canada

Seafood Creole Gumbo

1 lg. onion, chopped
1 clove of garlic, chopped
1 tbsp. corn oil
3 pkg. frozen okra
2 lg. tomatoes
2 c. tomato juice

1 tsp. file powder
1 tbsp. salt
½ tsp. sugar
1 tsp. thyme
2 bay leaves
1 whitefish fillet, chopped
1 can flaked crab meat
1 c. chopped shrimp
1½ c. cooked rice

Saute onion and garlic in oil. Add okra, tomatoes, tomato juice, file powder, salt, sugar, thyme and bay leaves; mix well. Add fish and crab meat; mix well. Cook in slow cooker on High for 2 hours. Cook on Low for 6 hours. Add shrimp and rice. Cook on High for 1 hour longer. Yield: 8 servings.

Kathy Hughes, Pres.
Xi Pi Phi X4580
Lamesa, Texas

Seafood Newburg
(1935)

½ c. butter
½ c. flour
3½ c. milk
1 8-oz. can lobster, drained
1 8-oz. can crab meat, drained
1 8-oz. can shrimp, drained
2 4-oz. cans mushrooms, drained
2 egg yolks, slightly beaten
4 hard-boiled eggs, diced
2 tbsp. lemon juice
½ c. diced ripe olives

Melt butter in saucepan over Low heat. Add flour; stir until blended. Add 3 cups milk; cook until smooth and thickened. Add lobster, crab meat, shrimp and mushrooms; mix well. Remove from heat. Combine egg yolks, ½ cup milk and hard-boiled eggs; beat well. Add to seafood mixture. Cook over Low heat for 1 minute. Add lemon juice; mix well. Fold in olives. Serve over patty shell or toast points. This recipe was my mother's. She was a silver Beta. Yield: 6 servings.

Betty Klumb
Preceptor Alpha Tau XP1518
Northglenn, Colorado

Baked Shrimp With Artichokes

1 pkg. frozen artichoke hearts
2 c. cooked rice
1 c. sliced ripe olives
2 c. cooked shrimp
2 8-oz. cans tomato sauce with mushrooms
1 tsp. salt

¼ tsp. red pepper
½ tsp. onion salt
¼ tsp. minced parsley
¾ c. grated Cheddar cheese

Prepare artichoke hearts according to package directions; drain. Combine artichoke hearts with remaining ingredients except cheese; mix well. Pour into 2-quart casserole. Sprinkle with cheese. Bake at 350 degrees for 30 minutes. Yield 4 servings

Neva J. Mansfield, V.P.
Preceptor Alpha Tau XP1524
Bend, Oregon

Microwave Shrimp Jambalaya

3 tbsp. oil
3 tbsp. flour
2 c. finely chopped onion
½ c. finely chopped green pepper
4 cloves of garlic, finely chopped
1 10-oz. can tomatoes
2 c. shrimp, peeled
2 c. diced ham
2 tsp. salt
3 c. cooked rice
1 tbsp. chopped parsley
1 tbsp. chopped green onion tops

Combine oil and flour in 4-cup glass measure. Microwave on High for 5 to 6 minutes on until lightly browned. Add onion, green pepper and garlic; mix well. Microwave on High for 3 minutes. Pour onion mixture into 3-quart glass casserole. Drain tomatoes; reserving liquid. Chop tomatoes. Add tomatoes, reserved liquid, 1½ cups hot water and shrimp to onion mixture; mix well. Microwave on High for 7 minutes or until shrimp are pink. Add ham, salt and rice; cover. Microwave on High for 3 minutes. Top with parsley and green onion. Yield: 6 servings.

Kaye Krause, Pres.
Xi Alpha Delta X930
El Dorado, Kansas

Cheese And Shrimp Fondue

1 10-oz. can cream of shrimp soup
1 10-oz. can mushrooms, drained
1 4-oz. can shrimp, drained
8 oz. Velveeta cheese, cubed
Garlic salt to taste

Combine all ingredients in saucepan; mix well. Cook over Low heat until cheese is melted. Pour into fondue pot; keep warm. Serve with breadsticks on

French bread cubes. Dip into fondue using fondue forks. Yield: 4-6 servings.

Elsie Tuckey
Preceptor Beta Theta XP1768
Exeter, Ontario, Canada

Shrimp Bisque

¼ c. butter
¼ c. flour
1 tsp. salt
Pepper to taste
5 c. chicken broth
Tabasco or cayenne pepper to taste
1 med. onion, diced
1 med. carrot, diced
1 bay leaf
2 to 3 lb. shrimp, chopped
1 c. cream

Melt butter in heavy saucepan. Blend in flour, salt and pepper; heat until bubbly. Stir in chicken broth and Tabasco. Add onion, carrot and bay leaf; cover. Simmer for 10 minutes. Add ⅔ of the shrimp; simmer for 10 minutes. Pour mixture into blender container; blend well. Pour into saucepan; simmer for 10 minutes. Add remaining shrimp and cream; cook until heated through, stirring constantly. Serve with salad and breadsticks. Yield: 6 servings.

Mickie Guadagnoli, Treas.
Preceptor Gamma XP409
Casper, Wyoming

Shrimp For Ramekin
(1952)

3 cloves of garlic, chopped
1 stick butter
1 4-oz. can mushrooms, drained
1 lb. deveined shrimp
1 c. sour cream
2 tsp. paprika
1 tsp. soy sauce
Salt and pepper to taste
¾ c. grated cheese

Saute garlic in butter. Add mushrooms; saute. Add shrimp; cook for 5 minutes. Pour sour cream in top of double boiler; bring to boiling point. Add paprika; mix well. Pour over shrimp mixture; mix well. Add soy sauce; mix well. Add salt and pepper. Pour into greased casserole. Top with cheese. Broil until cheese is melted. Serve over rice. May be served in individual ramekins.

Peggy Reeves Cook, Sec.
Eta Tau No. 10395
Toccoa, Georgia

Vegetables and Side Dishes

The famous Victory Gardens sprouted in backyards of many Beta Sigma Phis during World War II. These gardens represented their patriotic support. This loyalty not only helped America in time of need, but produced an assortment of fresh vegetables that were a welcome addition to any meal.

Beta Sigma Phis still love to prepare vegetables—from asparagus to zucchini and today's recipes are oftentimes old favorites dressed up for the 80's. Even a simple onion pie prepared during the war becomes today's popular quiche.

This collection of recipes includes the vegetables you love the most, as well as creative side dishes along with eggs, cheese, fruit, pasta and rice. Whichever you choose, Beta Sigma Phi cooks are sure to have a victory in the kitchen!

Artichoke Frito Misto

8 sm. artichokes
2 tsp. salt
3 eggs
1½ tsp. garlic salt
1½ tsp. monosodium glutamate
¼ tsp. Tabasco
3 tbsp. salad oil
1 c. milk
1½ c. flour
8 tomato wedges, floured
8 cauliflowerets, cooked and drained
½ lb. whole green beans, cooked and drained
1 lb. chicken livers, floured

Rinse artichokes; cut in half. Remove thistles. Bring 1 inch water to a boil; add salt and artichokes. Cover. Cook for 35 to 45 minutes or until tender; drain. Combine eggs, garlic salt, monosodium glutamate, Tabasco and oil; beat well. Stir in milk. Add flour; mix well. Remove outer leaves and chokes from artichokes. Dip vegetables and chicken livers in batter. Fry in deep hot oil for 3 to 8 minutes, turning to brown all sides; drain. Yield: 4-6 servings.

Photograph for this recipe on page 84.

Artichoke Medley

⅓ c. butter or margarine
1 9-oz. package frozen artichoke hearts, thawed
1 tsp. onion juice
¼ tsp. white pepper
Salt to taste
1 10-oz. package frozen tiny peas, thawed
2 c. finely shredded cabbage

Melt butter in skillet; add artichoke hearts. Cover; cook over Low heat for 10 minutes. Add remaining ingredients; mix well. Cover; cook over Low heat for 5 to 7 minutes or until cabbage is tender. Serve hot or cold. Yield: 4-6 servings.

Elizabeth Knitter, Pres.
Xi Beta Mu X838
San Bernardino, California

Asparagus Casserole

1 1-lb. package frozen asparagus, thawed
2 tsp. tapioca
1 can cream of mushroom soup
1 c. light cream
2 tbsp. chopped onion
2 tbsp. chopped green pepper
1 tbsp. lemon juice
2 tsp. parsley

4 to 6 hard-cooked eggs, sliced
1 c. sliced mushrooms
½ c. grated Parmesan or Cheddar cheese

Arrange asparagus in greased 13 × 9-inch casserole. Mix tapioca, soup, cream, onion, green pepper, lemon juice and parsley; pour over asparagus. Top with egg slices and mushrooms. Sprinkle with cheese. Bake at 350 degrees for 30 to 40 minutes. Yield: 4-6 servings.

Diane Zamudio, Soc. Chm.
Xi Nu Pi No. 3138
Victorville, California

Terry's Asparagus Casserole

Ritz cracker crumbs
1 lg. can asparagus, drained
1 med. can cream of mushroom soup
1 sm. can mushrooms, drained
2 hard-cooked eggs, sliced
¼ lb. Velveeta cheese, grated

Layer crumbs, asparagus, soup, mushrooms, eggs and cheese in buttered casserole, beginning and ending with crumbs. Bake at 300 degrees for 20 minutes or until heated through. Yield: 6 servings.

Terry Brownson
Preceptor Laureate Epsilon PL263
Pensacola, Florida

Green Bean Casserole

2 16-oz. cans French-style green beans, drained
10 oz. Cheddar cheese, cut into strips
1 3-oz. can French-fried onion rings
1 10¾-oz. can cream of mushroom soup
2 tbsp. butter or margarine
½ c. milk

Alternate layers of green beans, cheese, onion rings and soup until all ingredients are used. Dot with butter. Cover with milk. Bake at 350 degrees for 45 minutes or until bubbly. Yield: 4-6 servings.

Donna M. Furry, Pres.
Alpha Sigma No. 3059
Clifton Forge, Virginia

Green Beans With Swiss Cheese
(1948)

2 tbsp. butter
2 tbsp. flour
1 tsp. sugar
1 c. sour cream
2 cans green beans, drained

½ lb. Swiss cheese, grated
1 tsp. horseradish
½ c. buttered bread crumbs

Combine first 4 ingredients as for cream sauce. Add remaining ingredients; mix well. Pour into casserole. Sprinkle with bread crumbs. Bake at 350 degrees for 30 minutes or until bubbly. Yield: 6-8 servings.

Carol R. Newton, Pres.
Rho No. 7204
Seaford, Delaware

Pam's Green Bean Casserole

2 16-oz. cans green beans and liquid
Salt and pepper to taste
1 can cream of mushroom soup
1 can French-fried onion rings

Place green beans in saucepan; sprinkle with salt and pepper. Cook until heated through. Remove from heat; drain. Add soup; cook until heated through. Pour into 9 × 11-inch casserole. Top with onion rings. Broil until onion rings are heated through and lightly browned. Yield: 8-10 servings.

Pam Kupetz, Pres.
Delta Epsilon No. 5099
Harriman, Tennessee

Margery's Lima Beans

4 pkg. frozen lima beans
¾ c. butter or margarine
¾ c. (firmly packed) brown sugar
1 tbsp. dry mustard
Salt to taste
1 to 2 tbsp. sorghum molasses
1 c. sour cream

Prepare beans according to package directions; drain. Place in greased casserole. Add butter; mix well. Combine brown sugar, dry mustard and salt; mix well. Sprinkle over beans. Add molasses; mix well. Stir in sour cream; cover. Bake at 350 degrees for 50 minutes. Bake, uncovered, for 10 minutes longer. Yield: 8 servings.

Margery Steinmetz, Prog. Chm.
Xi Chi X384
Greenville, Ohio

Savory Lima Bean Scallop
(1930)

1½ c. dried lima beans
1 sm. onion, sliced
½ tsp. salt
1 c. diced celery

2 tbsp. chopped green pepper
1 c. canned tomato soup
2 tbsp. melted butter
⅛ tsp. pepper
¼ c. buttered bread crumbs

Soak beans in cold water for 6 to 8 hours; drain. Cook beans and onion in boiling water until tender; drain. Add salt, celery, green pepper, soup, butter, pepper and ½ cup water; mix well. Pour into greased casserole. Sprinkle with crumbs. Bake at 400 degrees for 30 minutes. Yield: 6 servings.

Rosalie Nelson, Soc. Sponsor
Xi Theta Beta X2085
Redlands, California

Three Bean Pot

1 lb. hamburger
1 c. chopped onion
¼ lb. bacon, diced
½ c. (firmly packed) brown sugar
½ c. catsup
2 tbsp. vinegar
1 tbsp. dry mustard
1 tsp. salt
1 lg. can pork and beans
1 can kidney beans
1 can lima beans
½ tsp. garlic powder

Brown hamburger, onion and bacon; drain. Combine next 5 ingredients; mix well. Combine beans, hamburger mixture and brown sugar mixture in large baking dish; mix well. Add garlic powder; mix well. Bake at 325 degrees for 1 hour.

Ruth Brace, V.P.
Preceptor Alpha Epsilon XP734
Longview, Washington

Broccoli Hot Dish

2 10-oz. packages frozen chopped broccoli
2 c. grated longhorn cheese
1 c. mayonnaise
1 onion, chopped
2 eggs, beaten
1 can mushroom soup
Ritz cracker crumbs

Prepare broccoli according to package directions; drain. Combine next 5 ingredients; mix well. Add to broccoli; mix well. Place in greased 10 × 7-inch pan. Sprinkle with cracker crumbs. Bake at 350 degrees for 30 to 45 minutes. Yield: 10 servings.

Judie LaBau, Pres.
Xi Beta Gamma X5047
Wallace, Idaho

Broccoli Quiche

1 10-oz. package chopped broccoli
2 c. grated Swiss cheese
1 unbaked 9-in. pie shell
3 eggs, beaten
1 c. milk
1 tsp. seasoned salt

Cook broccoli in boiling water until tender; drain. Spread 1 cup cheese in pie shell. Layer with broccoli and remaining cheese. Combine eggs, milk and seasoned salt; mix well. Pour over cheese. Bake at 375 degrees for 30 minutes or until firm and browned. Yield: 4 servings.

Linda Lee Kent, Pres.
Tau Xi No. 10540
Sebring, Florida

Creamy Broccoli Casserole

2 10-oz. packages frozen broccoli spears
1 can cream of mushroom soup
½ c. shredded Cheddar cheese
½ c. mayonnaise
1 tbsp. lemon juice
½ c. crushed Ritz crackers
¼ c. slivered almonds

Prepare broccoli according to package directions; drain. Place in lightly oiled 8 × 8 × 2-inch baking dish. Combine soup, cheese, mayonnaise and lemon juice; mix well. Pour over broccoli. Top with cracker crumbs. Sprinkle with almonds. Bake at 350 degrees for 30 minutes. Yield: 6-8 servings.

Pat Stromsness
Gamma Alpha No. 4901
Warrenton, Oregon

Marinated Brussels Sprouts

1 10-oz. package Brussels sprouts
½ c. Italian dressing
1½ tsp. dried dillweed
3 tbsp. sliced green onion

Prepare Brussels sprouts according to package directions; drain. Combine remaining ingredients; mix well. Pour over warm Brussels sprouts. Yield: 4 servings.

Jackie Meade
Xi Alpha Omicron X4628
Oxon Hill, Maryland

Red Cabbage With Apples

1 2½-lb. red cabbage, shredded
3 lg. apples, pared and sliced
3 tbsp. melted butter
¼ c. vinegar
1½ tsp. flour
¼ c. (firmly packed) brown sugar
2 tsp. salt
Dash of pepper

Bring ¾ cup water to a boil. Add cabbage; cover. Cook for 10 minutes or until cabbage is tender. Add apples; cover. Cook for 10 minutes or until apples are tender. Combine butter, vinegar, flour, brown sugar, salt and pepper; mix well. Add to cabbage mixture; mix well. Cook until flavors blend. Yield: 4-6 servings.

Pauline Klepper, V.P.
Xi Kappa X893
East Brunswick, New Jersey

Red Cabbage With Beer

1 head red cabbage, shredded
1 med. onion, diced
1 apple, cored
½ c. vinegar
½ c. beer
½ c. sugar
½ tsp. salt
¼ tsp. pepper
¼ c. butter, softened

Combine all ingredients with ¾ cup water in large saucepan. Simmer for 1 to 2 hours. Yield: 6 servings.

Carole Joy Wagley
Beta Sigma Phi
Cerritos, California

Carrot Croquettes

2 c. mashed cooked carrots
1 tbsp. melted butter
1 egg yolk, beaten
½ tsp. salt
Dash of nutmeg
Fine bread or cracker crumbs

Combine carrots, butter, egg yolk, salt and nutmeg; mix well. Form into carrot-shaped pyramids. Roll in crumbs. Chill for 2 hours. Fry in deep hot oil for 3 to 6 minutes or until browned; drain. Yield: 6-8 servings.

Dorothy E. Rivera
Xi Beta Lambda X4316
Chama, New Mexico

Carrot Pudding
(1943)

2 c. mashed cooked carrots from your Victory
    Garden
1 tsp. salt
½ c. sugar
½ stick margarine, softened
1 c. milk
3 eggs, well beaten
2 tsp. (heaping) flour
1 tsp. baking powder
¼ tsp. cinnamon
½ c. chopped pecans

Combine all ingredients; mix well. Pour into greased
1½-quart casserole. Bake at 350 degrees for about 1
hour. Yield: 6 servings.

Mary C. Pittman, Pres.
Preceptor Alpha Pi XP1067
DeFuniak Springs, Florida

Copper Pennies

2 1-lb. cans sliced carrots, drained
1 sm. green pepper, chopped
1 onion, chopped
1 10¾-oz. can tomato soup
½ c. salad oil
1 c. sugar
¾ c. white vinegar
1 tsp. prepared mustard
1 tsp. Worcestershire sauce
Salt and pepper to taste

Combine all ingredients in order listed in large bowl;
stir to mix. Refrigerate overnight. Serve cold. Yield:
8-10 servings.

Ruth D. Waldron, Ext. Off.
Preceptor Xi XP1501
Blackwood, New Jersey

Saucy Carrots With Water Chestnuts

1 lb. carrots
2 tbsp. butter or margarine
1 8-oz. can water chestnuts, drained and sliced
¾ tsp. dried thyme, crushed
¼ tsp. ground ginger
3 tbsp. dry white wine
1 tbsp. snipped parsley

Slice carrots diagonally, ½-inch thick. Place carrots in
small amount of boiling salted water; cover. Cook
for 15 to 20 minutes or until tender-crisp; drain. Set
aside. Melt butter in saucepan; add water chestnuts,
thyme and ginger, mixing well. Cook for 2 minutes,
stirring. Add wine, parsley and carrots; cook until
heated through, stirring. Yield: 6-8 servings.

Kathe Ingham, Pres.
Preceptor Alpha Rho XP1606
Easton, Pennsylvania

Herbed Carrots

2 lb. carrots, sliced
½ c. chopped onion
1 tsp. sugar
1 tsp. basil
½ tsp. salt

Combine all ingredients; toss well. Place in greased
2-quart casserole; add enough boiling water to
cover. Cover. Bake at 350 degrees for 50 minutes.
Yield: 8 servings.

Ruth J. Craig, Serv. Chm.
Laureate Alpha PL350
Fredericton, New Brunswick, Canada

Garnished Cauliflower Supreme
(1938)

1 lg. head cauliflower
5 carrots, cooked
2 tbsp. butter
2 tbsp. flour
Salt
1 c. milk or cream
Parsley sprigs
2 hard-cooked eggs, mashed
White pepper to taste

Place cauliflower in cheesecloth bag. Cook in salted
boiling water to cover for 20 to 30 minutes or until
tender. Place cauliflower on serving platter. Cut
carrots lengthwise; stand on end around cauliflower. Melt butter in saucepan; blend in flour and ¼
teaspoon salt, stirring. Add milk; cook until thickened, stirring constantly. Pour over cauliflower and
carrots. Garnish with sprigs of parsley. Sprinkle with
eggs. Season with white pepper and salt. Yield: 6-8
servings.

Louise L. Carter, Pres.
Alpha Rho No. 5077
Kingsville, Maryland

Carolyn's Corn Pudding
(1955)

1 12-oz. can whole kernel corn
2 tbsp. flour
1 tbsp. honey
Dash of pepper
2 eggs
1 sm. can pimento, drained and chopped
1 green pepper, chopped
¼ lb. grated Cheddar cheese
½ c. milk
2 green onions, chopped

Combine all ingredients; mix well. Pour into buttered baking dish. Bake at 350 degrees for 30 minutes. Yield: 6 servings.

> Carolyn L. Lyons, Past Pres.
> Delta Theta No. 2348
> Vicksburg, Michigan

Corn Pudding

1 16-oz. can cream-style corn
1 16-oz. can whole kernel corn
½ c. milk
2 tsp. cornstarch
3 tsp. margarine
3 eggs, beaten
½ tsp. vanilla extract
Salt and pepper to taste
¼ c. chopped onions (opt.)

Combine all ingredients; mix well. Pour into 2-quart casserole. Bake at 350 degrees for 1 hour. Yield: 6 servings.

> Candace M. Baker, Corr. Sec.
> Epsilon Chi No. 3506
> Wallace, North Carolina

Corn Souffle

1 can cream-style white corn
1 can evaporated milk
1 tbsp. sugar
½ tsp. vanilla extract
2 tbsp. cornstarch
2 eggs, beaten

Combine all ingredients; mix well. Pour into buttered casserole. Bake at 350 degrees for 30 minutes or until browned. Yield: 4-6 servings.

> Dene L. Dawes, Pres.
> Xi Alpha Beta X2119
> Rocky Mount, North Carolina

Creole Corn
(1949)

2 c. corn
¼ c. chopped onion
¼ c. sliced green pepper
3 tbsp. butter or margarine
1 c. canned tomatoes, drained
Salt and pepper to taste

Cook corn, onion and green pepper in butter for 10 minutes or until corn is tender. Add remaining ingredients; cook until heated through. Yield: 6 servings.

> Angie Mitchell, Pres.
> Preceptor Zeta XP165
> Orange, California

Beth's Corn Pudding

½ c. chopped onion
¼ c. chopped green pepper
2 tbsp. chopped pimento
¼ c. margarine
2 eggs, beaten
1 1-lb. 1-oz. can cream-style corn
⅓ c. fine dry bread crumbs
1 tsp. salt
¼ tsp. pepper

Saute onion, green pepper and pimento in margarine until tender. Combine onion mixture and remaining ingredients; mix well. Pour into 1-quart casserole. Place casserole in pan of hot water. Bake at 350 degrees for 45 minutes or until firm. Yield: 4 servings.

> Beth Foshee
> Alpha Rho Epsilon No. 10477
> Missouri City, Texas

Mexican Rarebit

1 med. onion, chopped
Butter
1 c. cream-style corn
1 c. canned tomatoes
1 c. cooked rice
1 med. green pepper, chopped
½ c. grated Cheddar cheese
2 eggs, beaten
Cracker crumbs

Saute onion in butter in large skillet. Add corn, tomatoes, rice, green pepper, cheese and eggs in order listed; mix well. Pour into large casserole.

Sprinkle with additional cheese and cracker crumbs. Bake at 325 degrees for 45 minutes. Yield: 6 servings.

Doris Gene Briggs, Pres.
Preceptor Theta XP1134
Portland, Maine

Pan de Elote

1 1-lb. can cream-style corn
1 c. biscuit mix
1 egg, beaten
2 tbsp. melted butter
½ c. milk
1 tbsp. sugar
1 4-oz. can chopped green chilies, drained
½ lb. Monterey Jack cheese, thinly sliced

Combine first 6 ingredients; mix well. Pour half the batter into greased 8 × 8-inch glass casserole. Cover with green chilies and cheese. Top with remaining batter. Bake at 400 degrees for 20 minutes.

Carol Sassin, Pres.
Alpha Sigma Epsilon No. 10627
Beeville, Texas

Baked Eggplant With Walnuts
(1939)

2 med. eggplant
½ c. walnuts, finely chopped
1 c. soft bread crumbs
1 egg, slightly beaten
1 tsp. salt
Dash of pepper
¼ tsp. poultry seasoning
½ tsp. Worcestershire sauce
2 tsp. lemon juice
½ tsp. grated onion
1 tbsp. melted butter
1 c. buttered bread crumbs

Cook eggplant in boiling water until tender; peel and dice. Add walnuts, soft bread crumbs, egg, salt, pepper, poultry seasoning, Worcestershire sauce, lemon juice, onion and melted butter; mix well. Pour into greased 2½-quart baking dish. Sprinkle with buttered bread crumbs. Bake at 400 degrees for 15 to 20 minutes or until heated through.

Shirley M. Chontos, Treas.
Xi Iota Xi X2381
Vallejo, California

Melanzane
(1930)

1 lg. eggplant, cut into ½-in. slices
Salt and pepper to taste

4 tbsp. oil
4 lg. onions, chopped
4 green peppers, chopped
2 c. sliced ripe olives
½ lb. sharp Cheddar cheese, grated
1 8-oz. can tomato sauce
1 c. bread crumbs
Butter or margarine

Sprinkle eggplant with salt and pepper. Fry in hot oil until lightly browned; drain. Alternate layers of eggplant, onions, green peppers, olives and cheese in greased 2-quart casserole until all ingredients are used. Top with tomato sauce. Sprinkle with bread crumbs. Dot with butter. Bake at 375 degrees for 45 minutes. Yield: 6 servings.

Caroline Bose, Yearbook Chm.
Xi Delta Gamma X1343
Valley Center, California

Scalloped Eggplant

1 med. eggplant, peeled and cubed
½ c. minced onion
3 tsp. salt
1½ c. cracker crumbs
Dash of pepper
1¼ c. milk
6 tbsp. melted margarine

Bring 1 inch water in saucepan to a boil. Add eggplant, onion and 2 teaspoons salt; cover. Cook for 5 minutes or until eggplant is tender; drain. Spread ½ of the cracker crumbs in greased 10 × 6 × 2-inch baking dish. Arrange eggplant and onion over crumbs. Sprinkle with 1 teaspoon salt and pepper. Top with remaining crumbs. Pour milk into corners of baking dish to cover bottom. Top with butter. Bake at 350 degrees for 45 minutes.

Jeanne Goodman, Treas.
Preceptor Zeta XP239
Carthage, Missouri

Onions And Mushrooms A La Lois

1 to 2 lg. onions, quartered
12 mushrooms, sliced
4 tbsp. butter
Salt and pepper to taste
Garlic powder to taste

Place onions in large aluminum foil square. Sprinkle with remaining ingredients. Fold aluminum foil over vegetables; seal edges securely. Cook over hot coals for 1 hour. Yield: 6-12 servings.

Susan Hunnicutt, Pres.
Gamma Xi No. 6269
Fayetteville, Arkansas

Celery And Mushroom Casserole

6 c. chopped celery
½ c. sliced mushrooms
1 10½-oz. can cream of mushroom soup
1 1-lb. can peas, drained
1 c. grated Cheddar cheese
Buttered cracker crumbs

Cook celery in salted water; drain. Saute mushrooms; add to celery. Add soup and peas; mix well. Pour half the celery mixture into greased 1-quart casserole. Sprinkle with half the cheese. Layer with remaining celery mixture and cheese. Top with cracker crumbs. Bake at 350 degrees until bubbly and browned.

Marcia L. McCuistion, Pres.
Xi Kappa Delta X5051
Ft. Lauderdale, Florida

French-Sauteed Mushrooms
(1930)

6 slices bacon
2 lb. mushrooms
¼ c. chopped onion
1 clove of garlic, chopped
1 tsp. lemon juice
Salt and pepper to taste
½ c. bread crumbs

Brown bacon in 10-inch skillet. Remove bacon, reserving drippings. Drain bacon on paper towel. Add mushrooms, onion, garlic, lemon juice, salt and pepper to drippings; mix well. Cook over Medium heat until onions and mushrooms are tender. Add bacon and bread crumbs; cook until heated through.

Alverta Miller
Tau Omicron No. 10910
Plainfield, Illinois

Marinated Mushrooms

1 lb. mushrooms, sliced
6 tbsp. olive oil
¾ c. dry white wine
1½ tsp. salt
⅛ tsp. cayenne pepper
¼ tsp. oregano
¼ c. chopped parsley
2 tbsp. chopped onion
3 tbsp. lemon juice

Place mushrooms in glass or earthenware bowl. Combine remaining ingredients in saucepan; mix well. Simmer for 15 minutes. Pour over mushrooms; cover. Chill for several hours or until flavors blend.

Photograph for this recipe on page 93.

French-Fried Onion Rings

1 c. flour
¼ tsp. salt
1 egg, slightly beaten
1 c. milk
1 tsp. oil
30 lg. onion rings

Sift flour and salt togther. Add egg, milk and oil gradually, beating well after each addition. Dip onion rings in batter. Fry in hot deep fat for 2 to 5 minutes or until lightly browned.

Claudia Traynor, Pres.
Laureate Nu No. 337
Englewood, Colorado

Holiday Peas

1 sm. package frozen peas
½ tsp. salt
1 sm. onion, sliced
1½ to 2 pimentos, chopped
2 tbsp. butter
2 tbsp. flour
1 c. milk or cream
Pepper to taste

Combine peas, salt and ½ cup water in saucepan; bring to a boil. Add onion and pimentos; cook for 7 to 10 minutes or until tender. Add butter. Combine flour and milk; blend until smooth. Add to vegetable mixture; mix well. Add pepper; cook until thickened. Yield: 6-8 servings.

Nelda June Ungerer, Pres.
Preceptor Laureate PL201
Marysville, Kansas

Peas and Radishes

1 10-oz. package frozen green peas, thawed
1 tsp. sugar
2 tbsp. butter or margarine
1 lg. lettuce leaf
1 c. sliced radishes

Place peas in 1-quart baking dish. Sprinkle with sugar. Dot with butter. Spread lettuce leaf over peas. Cover. Bake at 350 degrees for 1 hour or until peas are tender. Remove lettuce leaf; discard. Stir in radishes.

Alice Jean Lenz, Pres.
Xi Beta Epsilon X952
Fort Worth, Texas

Cottage Potatoes
(1940)

6 med. potatoes
2 tbsp. chopped pimento
¼ lb. American cheese, cubed
¼ green pepper, finely diced
1 sm. onion, finely chopped
4 slices bread, cubed
¼ to ⅓ c. butter
Milk
Crushed corn flakes

Boil potates in water to cover; peel and cube. Combine potatoes and next 5 ingredients; mix well. Spoon into greased baking dish. Add butter and enough milk to moisten; mix well. Top with corn flakes. Bake at 350 degrees for 30 minutes. Yield: 8 servings.

Diana A. Burge, City Coun. Pres.
Niles, Michigan

Grated Potato Casserole

8 to 9 potatoes
⅓ c. chopped green onion
2½ c. grated Cheddar cheese
1 can cream of mushroom soup

2 c. sour cream
¼ c. melted butter

Boil potatoes in water to cover until partially cooked; peel and grate. Add onion, 2 cups cheese, soup and sour cream; mix well. Add butter; blend well. Spoon into 3-quart casserole. Top with remaining cheese. Refrigerate overnight. Bake at 350 degrees for 45 minutes. Yield: 10-15 servings.

Cathy Walden, Pres.
Xi No. 801
Cosmopolis, Washington

Lefse

4 c. hot mashed potatoes
1 tsp. salt
2 tbsp. butter or margarine
3 c. flour

Combine potatoes, salt and butter; mix well. Cool. Add flour; mix well. Roll out 1 tablespoon mixture at a time until very thin. Place on lefse plate or griddle over Medium heat. Bake until bubbly and browned; turn. Place on cloth or linen towel; cool.

Diane Gunderson, Pres.
Alpha Omicron No. 9173
Sheridan, Wyoming

Jean's Great Potatoes

1 c. sour cream
1 can cream of chicken soup
1 tsp. salt
¼ tsp. pepper
6 med. potatoes, cooked and sliced
6 hard-cooked eggs, sliced
½ c. soft bread crumbs
½ c. shredded cheese

Combine sour cream, soup, salt and pepper; mix well. Alternate layers of potatoes, eggs and sour cream mixture in casserole, starting with potatoes and ending with sour cream mixture. Sprinkle with bread crumbs and cheese. Bake at 350 degrees for 30 minutes. Yield: 6-8 servings.

Pattie B. Meyer, Pres.
Preceptor Alpha Eta XP973
North Bend, Oregon

Marian's Potato Casserole

1 lg. package frozen hashed brown potatoes,
    thawed
1 can cream of potato soup
1 can cream of celery soup
1 pt. sour cream with chives
1 c. grated sharp Cheddar cheese

Combine all ingredients; mix well. Pour into buttered 2-quart casserole. Top with additional cheese. Bake at 325 degrees for 2 hours. Yield: 8-12 servings.

Marian Dietsch
Preceptor Omicron XP1140
Sun City, Arizona

Party Potatoes

3 tbsp. chopped green pepper
1 med. onion, finely chopped
¼ c. butter
2 tbsp. flour
1 tbsp. chopped pimento
2 c. milk
Salt and pepper to taste
3 c. cubed cooked potatoes
1 c. grated cheese

Saute green pepper and onion in butter for 5 minutes. Stir in flour, pimento and milk; cook until thickened, stirring constantly. Add seasonings. Fold in potatoes. Pour into buttered 1½-quart casserole. Sprinkle with cheese. Bake at 350 degrees for 30 minutes. Yield: 6 servings.

Shirley L. Bailey, Pres.
Lambda Gamma No. 10003
Thayer, Kansas

Sour Cream and Cheese-Potato Bake

1½ c. shredded Cheddar cheese
2 cans cream of chicken soup
6 green onions and tops, chopped
2 cartons sour cream
¾ c. milk or half and half
1 sm. jar pimentos, chopped
1 2-lb. package frozen hashed brown
    potatoes, thawed
Crushed potato chips

Combine cheese, soup, onions, sour cream, milk and pimentos in large saucepan; mix well. Cook until cheese is melted, stirring occasionally; do not boil. Place potatoes in greased 13 × 8 × 2-inch casserole. Cover with cheese mixture. Top with potato chips. Bake at 350 degrees for 1 hour. Yield: 10 servings.

Josephine Isbell, Pres.
Preceptor Beta Upsilon XP1708
Monett, Missouri

Potato Bake

4 1-lb. cans sliced potatoes, drained
½ c. chopped onions
1 c. Hellmann's mayonnaise
1 lb. American cheese, diced
Salt and pepper to taste
⅓ c. sliced olives
⅓ c. sliced mushrooms
5 slices bacon, cooked and crumbled

Combine potatoes, onions, mayonnaise, cheese, salt and pepper; mix well. Pour into 13 × 9-inch baking dish. Top with olives, mushrooms and bacon. Bake at 325 degrees for 1 hour. Yield: 10-12 servings.

Ann M. Belcher
Xi Gamma Chi X2779
Lebanon, Indiana

Potato Pie

1 lb. cottage cheese
2 c. mashed potatoes
½ c. sour cream or unflavored yogurt
2 eggs, slightly beaten
½ c. chopped onions
2 tsp. salt
⅛ tsp. cayenne pepper
1 unbaked 10-in. pie shell
Grated Cheddar cheese

Combine first 7 ingredients; mix well. Pour into pie shell. Sprinkle with cheese. Bake at 425 degrees for 50 minutes. Yield: 8-10 servings.

Carol Robins, Treas.
Xi Beta Xi X4582
Ladysmith, British Columbia, Canada

Potato Casserole

1 32-oz. package frozen hashed brown
    potatoes, thawed
Salt and pepper to taste
1 can cream of chicken soup
1 8-oz. carton sour cream
2 tsp. chives (opt.)
2 c. grated Cheddar cheese
½ c. Post Toasties crumbs

Sprinkle potatoes with salt and pepper. Add soup,
sour cream and chives; mix well. Stir in cheese. Pour
into 13 × 9 × 2-inch baking dish. Sprinkle with
crumbs. Bake at 350 degrees for 1 hour. Yield: 8
servings.

Betty Blackburn
Iota Eta No. 9458
Broken Arrow, Oklahoma

Baked Spinach
(1950)

2 pkg. frozen chopped spinach
3 slices bread, cubed
½ c. cubed sharp cheese
2 eggs
2 tbsp. sugar
2 tbsp. vinegar
½ to ¾ c. milk

Prepare spinach according to package directions;
drain. Combine spinach, bread and cheese; mix well.
Spoon into 1½-quart casserole. Combine eggs and
sugar; beat until smooth. Add vinegar; beat well.
Stir in milk. Pour over spinach mixture. Bake at 400
degrees for 30 minutes. Yield: 6 servings.

Cathryn Irwin, Pres.
Xi Zeta Epsilon X5284
Noblesville, Indiana

Jeanette's Spinach Casserole
(1959)

2 pkg. frozen spinach
1½ c. sour cream
Salt and pepper to taste
¼ c. minced onion flakes
1 tsp. garlic powder
1 c. shredded mozzarella cheese

Prepare spinach according to package directions;
drain. Combine spinach, sour cream, salt, pepper,
onion flakes and garlic powder; mix well. Pour into

ovenproof bowl; cover. Bake at 350 degrees for 45
minutes. Sprinkle with cheese; cover. Bake at 350
degrees for 5 minutes longer. Yield: 6 servings.

Jeanette Azar, W. and M. Chm.
Xi Delta Iota X3925
Mt. Clemens, Michigan

Aunt Fanny's Baked Squash

3 lb. yellow squash, sliced
½ c. chopped onion
2 eggs, slightly beaten
1 tbsp. sugar
1 tsp. salt
½ tsp. pepper
1 stick margarine, softened
½ c. cracker crumbs

Cook squash until tender; drain. Mash. Combine
squash, onion, eggs, sugar, salt, pepper and ½
stick margarine; mix well. Pour into 2-quart
baking dish. Melt remaining butter; pour over
squash mixture. Sprinkle with cracker crumbs.
Bake at 375 degrees for 1 hour or until browned.
Zucchini and eggplant may be substituted for
squash. Yield: 6 servings.

Marsha R. Garza, Pres.
Lambda Xi No. 7680
Gulf Breeze, Florida

Baked Squash And Cheese
(1948)

3 lb. yellow squash, cut into 2-in. pieces
1 lg. onion, sliced
2 tbsp. butter
2 tbsp. cornstarch
1 c. evaporated milk
¾ lb. Velveeta cheese, cubed
½ c. Ritz cracker crumbs

Cook squash and onion in salted water to cover until
tender; drain. Melt butter in heavy saucepan. Add
cornstarch; stir until smooth. Add evaporated milk
and cheese; cook over Low heat until smooth and
thickened, stirring. Pour squash mixture into buttered casserole. Cover with cheese sauce. Sprinkle
with cracker crumbs. Bake at 350 degrees for 20
minutes. Yield: 8 servings.

Nancy Lancaster, Pres.
Xi Beta Rho X2592
Lakewood, Colorado

Crunchy Yam Bake
(1957)

4 med. yams
¾ c. (firmly packed) light brown sugar
Butter
1½ tsp. cinnamon
½ tsp. allspice
¼ tsp. nutmeg
1¾ c. milk
2 eggs, slightly beaten
½ c. flour
½ c. sugar
½ c. chopped walnuts

Cook yams in boiling water until tender; drain. Mash hot yams. Add brown sugar, ¼ cup butter, 1 teaspoon cinnamon, allspice and nutmeg; mix well. Add milk and eggs; beat with electric mixer. Pour into greased 3-quart casserole. Combine flour, sugar and ¼ cup butter; mix until crumbly. Add walnuts and ½ teaspoon cinnamon; mix well. Sprinkle over yam mixture. Dot with 1 tablespoon butter. Bake at 375 degrees for 35 to 40 minutes. Yield: 6 servings.

Pam Smith, Treas.
Theta Beta No. 9772
Walsh, Colorado

Curried Louisiana Yams And Pears

1 30-oz. can pear halves
½ c. butter or margarine
½ c. (firmly packed) light brown sugar
2 to 3 tbsp. curry powder
3 16-oz. cans Louisiana yams, drained
8 stemmed red maraschino cherries

Drain pears, reserving ¼ cup liquid. Melt butter in large skillet; add brown sugar, curry powder and reserved liquid. Simmer for 5 minutes, stirring occasionally. Add pears, yams and cherries; cover. Simmer for 25 minutes, stirring occasionally. Garnish with toasted slivered almonds. Yield: 6 servings.

Photograph for this recipe on page 97.

Sweet Potato Casserole

½ c. milk
2 eggs, slightly beaten
3 c. mashed sweet potatoes
1 c. sugar
½ tsp. salt
1 tsp. vanilla extract
Margarine
1 c. chopped pecans
1 c. self-rising flour
1 c. (firmly packed) brown sugar

Combine first 6 ingredients and 1 stick margarine; mix well. Pour into greased 2-quart casserole. Melt ⅓ cup margarine. Add remaining ingredients; mix well. Spread over sweet potato mixture. Bake at 350 degrees for 35 minutes. Yield: 8 servings.

Randa H. Harper, Pres.
Xi Beta Phi X4374
Lilburn, Georgia

Sweet Potato Souffle Casserole

2 c. mashed cooked sweet potatoes
2 eggs, beaten
1 c. milk
½ tsp. cinnamon
¾ c. crushed corn flakes
¾ stick butter, melted
½ c. chopped nuts
½ c. (firmly packed) brown sugar

Combine first 4 ingredients; mix well. Pour into greased 2-quart casserole. Bake at 400 degrees for 20 minutes. Combine remaining ingredients; mix well. Spread over sweet potato mixture. Bake at 400 degrees for 10 minutes longer. Yield: 12 servings.

Marie Riley, Corr. Sec.
Xi Theta X771
Mayfield, Kentucky

Yam-Berry Bake

½ c. flour
½ c. (firmly packed) brown sugar
½ c. quick-cooking oats
1 tsp. cinnamon
⅓ c. butter or margarine
2 17-oz. cans yams, drained
2 c. cranberries
1½ c. miniature marshmallows

Combine first 4 ingredients; mix well. Cut in butter until mixture resembles coarse crumbs. Combine yams, cranberries and 1 cup crumb mixture; toss well. Place in 1½-quart casserole. Top with remaining crumb mixture. Bake at 350 degrees for 35 minutes. Top with marshmallows. Place under broiler until lightly browned.

Ruth Epright, Pres.
Alpha Iota XP1355
Parkside, Pennsylvania

Tomatoes In Foil

4 lg. tomatoes
Salt and pepper to taste
8 tsp. butter

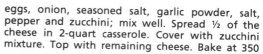

¼ c. chopped parsley
⅓ c. chopped green onions and tops
1 tsp. basil, crushed
1 tsp. tarragon, crushed
1 clove of garlic, crushed

Core tomatoes; sprinkle with salt, pepper and 2 teaspoons butter. Combine 6 teaspoons butter and remaining ingredients; mix well. Spoon onto tomatoes. Wrap each in aluminum foil; seal tightly. Grill 3 inches from hot coals for 20 minutes. May be baked at 350 degrees for 15 to 20 minutes. Yield: 4 servings.

Nan Allwine, V.P.
Xi Alpha Omicron X2678
Forest Park, Georgia

Baked Zucchini

1½ to 2 lb. zucchini, sliced
8 to 12 Ritz crackers, crushed
2 eggs, beaten
1 tbsp. minced onion
½ tsp. seasoned salt
⅛ tsp. garlic powder
Salt and pepper to taste
1 lb. mild Cheddar cheese, grated

Boil zucchini in small amount of water until just tender; drain thoroughly. Combine cracker crumbs, eggs, onion, seasoned salt, garlic powder, salt, pepper and zucchini; mix well. Spread ½ of the cheese in 2-quart casserole. Cover with zucchini mixture. Top with remaining cheese. Bake at 350 degrees for 40 minutes or until cheese is bubbly. Yield: 8 servings.

Linda S. Ross, Pres.
Xi Pi Rho No. 3860
Napa, California

Zucchy

2 sm. zucchini, sliced
1 onion, chopped
2 green peppers, chopped
1 c. chopped celery
2 c. tomato juice
Salt and pepper to taste

Combine all ingredients; mix well. Cook on Medium heat until tender. Yield: 4-6 servings.

Sandy Hawkins, V.P.
Phi Alpha Chi P2837
Ottawa, Iowa

Italian Zucchini Pie

4 c. thinly sliced zucchini
1 c. coarsely chopped onion
½ c. margarine or butter
½ c. chopped parsley
½ tsp. salt
½ tsp. pepper
¼ tsp. garlic powder
¼ tsp. sweet basil
¼ tsp. oregano
2 eggs, well beaten
2 c. shredded Muenster cheese
1 can refrigerator crescent rolls
2 tsp. Dijon or prepared mustard

Cook zucchini and onion in margarine in skillet until tender. Stir in parsley, salt, pepper, garlic powder, basil and oregano. Combine eggs and cheese in large bowl; mix well. Stir in zucchini mixture. Separate rolls into 8 triangles; press in 11-inch pie pan to form crust. Spread crust with mustard. Pour zucchini mixture into crust; spread evenly. Bake at 375 degrees for 18 to 20 minutes or until knife blade inserted near center comes out clean. Cut into wedges. Let stand for 5 minutes. Yield: 6 servings.

Betty Flynn
Laureate Alpha Gamma PL357
Hayward, California

Something Special Zucchini

2 med. zucchini, sliced
1 lg. onion, thinly sliced
2 green peppers, sliced
2 tomatoes, sliced
12 slices Old English cheese
Salt and pepper to taste
2 tbsp. butter

Arrange zucchini around sides and bottom of 2-quart baking dish. Layer with ½ of the onion, green peppers, tomatoes and 4 slices cheese. Sprinkle with salt and pepper. Dot with 1 tablespoon butter. Repeat layers. Dot with remaining butter. Cover tightly with aluminum foil. Bake at 350 degrees for 45 minutes to 1 hour. Cut remaining cheese diagonally; arrange over vegetables. Bake at 350 degrees for 2 minutes longer or until cheese begins to melt. Yield: 6-8 servings.

Judith K. Johnson, Past Pres.
Xi Delta Pi No. 3664
Columbus, Indiana

Veg-All Casserole

2 16-oz. cans Veg-All, drained
1 c. chopped celery
½ c. chopped onion
1 sm. green pepper, chopped
1 can water chestnuts, chopped
1 c. shredded Cheddar cheese
1 c. mayonnaise
1 stick margarine
3 c. bread crumbs

Combine first 7 ingredients; mix well. Place in 9 × 13-inch baking dish. Melt butter; add bread crumbs. Top casserole with buttered bread crumbs. Bake at 350 degrees for 20 minutes or until bread crumbs are browned.

Reba Bellar, Pres.
Xi Gamma Pi X5311
Lafayette, Tennessee

Trio Vegetable Casserole

1 10-oz. package frozen green peas
1 10-oz. package frozen French-style green beans
1 10-oz. package frozen baby limas
1 tbsp. Worcestershire sauce
1 tsp. prepared mustard
Juice of ½ lemon
1 sm. onion, grated
1 can water chestnuts, drained and sliced
1½ c. mayonnaise
Buttered bread crumbs

Prepare vegetables according to package directions; drain. Combine vegetables and next 6 ingredients; mix well. Pour into buttered casserole. Sprinkle with bread crumbs. Bake at 350 degrees for 30 minutes.

Jean Moss Branton, Pres.
Delta Sigma No. 6710
Shelby, North Carolina

Savory Vegetable Dish

1 10-oz. package frozen baby lima beans
1 10-oz. package frozen petite peas
1 10-oz. package frozen French-style green beans
1 c. mayonnaise
1 tsp. prepared mustard
3 dashes of Tabasco sauce
3 hard-cooked eggs, grated
½ tsp. salt
1 tsp. Worcestershire sauce
1 med. onion, chopped

Prepare vegetables according to package directions; drain. Combine remaining ingredients; mix well. Add to vegetables; mix well. Yield: 6-8 servings.

Marie N. Levy, V.P.
Laureate Iota PL300
Colorado Springs, Colorado

Vegetarian Lasagna

9 lasagna noodles
2 10-oz. packages frozen chopped spinach
1 c. grated carrots
½ c. chopped onion
2 c. sliced mushrooms
1 tbsp. vegetable oil
1 15-oz. can tomato sauce
1 6-oz. can tomato paste
½ c. chopped pitted olives
1½ tsp. oregano
1 tbsp. margarine
16 oz. cream-style cottage cheese
16 oz. Monterey Jack cheese, thinly sliced
Grated Parmesan cheese

Cook lasagna noodles in unsalted boiling water for 8 to 10 minutes or until tender; drain. Cook spinach in unsalted water according to package directions; drain. Cook carrots, onion and mushrooms in hot oil in medium saucepan until tender but not brown. Stir in tomato sauce, tomato paste, olives and oregano. Grease 13 × 9 × 2-inch baking dish with margarine. Layer ⅓ of the noodles, ⅓ of the cottage cheese, ⅓ of the spinach, ¼ of the Monterey Jack cheese and ⅓ of the sauce mixture. Repeat layers 3 times. Top with remaining cheese slices. Bake at 375 degrees for 30 minutes. Let stand for 10 minutes. Serve with additional Parmesan cheese. This recipe won first prize in the Coulee Cookbook contest.

Crystal Marschel, Ext. Off.
Xi Upsilon X2534
LaCrosse, Wisconsin

Chili-Cheese Bake

1 lb. longhorn cheese, grated
18 oz. diced green chilies
1 lb. Monterey Jack cheese, grated
4 eggs, beaten
1 pt. sour cream

Place longhorn cheese in 13 × 9-inch pan. Sprinkle with ½ of the chilies. Cover with Monterey Jack cheese. Top with remaining chilies. Combine eggs and sour cream; beat well. Pour over chilies. Bake at 325 degrees for 1 hour. Yield: 12 servings.

Jeanne Rudolph, Treas.
Preceptor Alpha Gamma XP1906
Scottsdale, Arizona

Chili-Cheese Casserole

2 7-oz. cans green chilies, drained, seeded and diced
1 lb. Monterey Jack cheese, coarsely grated

1 lb. Cheddar cheese, coarsely grated
4 eggs, separated
⅔ c. evaporated milk
1 tbsp. flour
½ tsp. salt
⅛ tsp. pepper
2 lg. tomatoes, sliced

Combine chilies and cheese; mix well. Spoon into buttered shallow 2-quart casserole; set aside. Beat egg whites until stiff peaks form; set aside. Combine egg yolks, milk, flour, salt and pepper; mix well. Fold egg whites into egg yolk mixture. Pour over cheese mixture, using a fork to press into cheese mixture. Bake at 325 degrees for 30 minutes. Arrange tomato slices on top, overlapping around edge. Bake at 325 degrees for 30 minutes longer, or until knife blade inserted into center comes out clean. Garnish with green chilies. Yield: 6-8 servings.

Judy Lakowski, Pres.
Xi Gamma Theta X1134
Redding, California

Mock Cheese Souffle

1 stick butter, melted
¾ to 1 lb. Cheddar cheese, grated
6 eggs, beaten
3 c. milk
Salt and pepper to taste
1 tbsp. chopped chives or parsley
8 slices bread

Combine first 6 ingredients; mix well. Remove crusts from bread; cut bread into 1 inch cubes. Place bread cubes in greased 3-quart casserole. Cover with cheese mixture. Refrigerate overnight. Bake at 350 degrees for 1 hour. Yield: 6 servings.

Kathy Kellogg
Beta Rho No. 1721
Hartford City, Indiana

Cheese Grits

1½ c. instant grits
1½ sticks margarine
1 lb. Velveeta cheese, cubed
3 tsp. savory salt
2 tsp. salt
Dash of Tabasco sauce
3 eggs, slightly beaten

Prepare grits according to package directions. Add remaining ingredients; stir until margarine and cheese are melted. Pour into 1 large or 2 small baking dishes. Bake at 250 degrees for 1 hour.

Ruby Smith, Pres.
Laureate Gamma PL195
Dalhart, Texas

Cheese-Grits Casserole

2½ tsp. salt
3 tsp. Lawry's Seasoned Salt
1½ c. grits
½ lb. Cheddar cheese, grated
½ c. butter or margarine
3 eggs, beaten

Bring 6 cups water to a boil. Add salt, seasoned salt and grits; cook for 6 minutes. Remove from heat. Add cheese and butter, stirring until cheese and butter are melted. Add eggs; mix well. Pour into greased 2-quart casserole. Bake at 325 degrees for 1 hour. Yield: 12 servings.

Jacque Dale, Pres.
Beta Tau No. 7894
Summerville, South Carolina

Chili-Cheese Eggs

2 8-oz. cans green chilies
½ lb. sharp Cheddar cheese, grated
9 eggs
1 pkg. taco seasoning mix

Rinse chilies; drain. Place ½ of the chilies in 8 × 8 × 2-inch baking dish. Sprinkle with ½ of the cheese. Cover with remaining chilies. Combine eggs and seasoning mix; beat well. Pour over chilies. Top with remaining cheese. Bake at 350 degrees for 30 minutes or until eggs are puffy and lightly browned. Yield: 6 servings.

Frances Dillman, Pres.
Laureate Alpha Beta PL324
Buena Park, California

Egg Casserole

6 to 8 slices bread
1 lb. sausage, cooked and drained
½ c. shredded Swiss cheese
½ c. shredded sharp cheese
1 sm. can mushrooms, drained
¾ c. light cream
1¼ c. milk
5 eggs, slightly beaten
1 tsp. Worcestershire sauce
1 tsp. prepared mustard
Salt and pepper to taste

Remove crusts from bread; cube. Place in greased 9 × 13-inch baking pan. Sprinkle sausage over bread. Add cheeses and mushrooms; mix well. Combine cream, milk and eggs; mix well. Stir in Worcestershire sauce, mustard, salt and pepper. Pour over cheese mixture; cover. Refrigerate overnight. Bake at 350 degrees for 35 minutes. Yield: 6-8 servings.

Mary Harrison, Pres.
Sigma Epsilon No. 10050
Cassville, Missouri

Egg and Cheese Bake
(1940)

1 lb. sausage
6 eggs, beaten
2 c. milk
2 slices bread, cubed
1 tsp. prepared mustard
1 c. shredded Cheddar cheese

Brown sausage; drain. Combine remaining ingredients; mix well. Stir in sausage. Pour into 9 × 13-inch baking pan. Refrigerate overnight. Bake at 350 degrees for 45 minutes. Cut into squares. Yield: 8 servings.

Carolyn Sisler, V.P.
Alpha Gamma No. 9302
Bethel, Alaska

Eggs Florentine

2 pkg. frozen spinach
2 tbsp. lemon juice
2 tbsp. minced onion
½ c. shredded Cheddar cheese
4 hard-boiled eggs, sliced
Butter or margarine
3 tbsp. flour
½ tsp. salt
½ tsp. dry mustard
¼ tsp. pepper
2¼ c. milk
½ c. dry bread crumbs

Prepare spinach according to package directions; drain. Add lemon juice and onion; mix well. Spread spinach mixture in 8 × 8 × 2-inch baking dish. Sprinkle with cheese. Top with egg slices. Melt 3 tablespoons butter in saucepan over Low heat. Blend in flour and seasonings. Cook over Low heat until smooth and bubbly, stirring constantly. Remove from heat. Stir in milk. Bring to a boil, stirring constantly. Boil for 1 minute, stirring. Pour over egg slices. Toss bread crumbs in 1 tablespoon melted butter. Sprinkle over sauce. Bake at 400 degrees for 20 minutes. Yield: 4-6 servings.

Diane E. Taylor
Omicron Chapter
Spangdahlem, Germany

Grandma Wilson's Egg Foo Yung
(1935)

2 slices bacon, chopped
½ c. chopped green onions and tops
⅓ c. thinly sliced green pepper
3 tbsp. sliced water chestnuts or mushrooms
1 c. bean sprouts
1 c. diced cooked chicken, ham or pork
4 eggs, beaten
½ tsp. salt
⅛ tsp. pepper
2 tbsp. soy sauce
1 c. cooked rice
1 c. chicken broth or pineapple juice
1 tbsp. cornstarch
1 tbsp. molasses

Fry bacon until browned. Add onions and green pepper; cook until tender. Remove from heat; cool. Combine onion mixture, water chestnuts, bean sprouts, chicken, eggs, salt, pepper, 1 tablespoon soy sauce and rice; mix well. Shape into patties. Fry in small amount of oil until brown on all sides. Combine remaining ingredients and 1 tablespoon soy sauce in saucepan; cook until thickened. Pour over patties. Yield: 4 servings.

Dorothy Peabody, Treas.
Laureate Theta PL325
Troutdale, Oregon

Jack Cheese And Egg Omelet

8 slices bacon, coarsely chopped
4 green onions, chopped
8 eggs, beaten
1 c. milk
½ tsp. seasoned salt
2½ c. grated Jack cheese

Fry bacon. Add onions; cook until tender. Combine bacon mixture, eggs, milk, seasoned salt and 2 cups cheese; stir well. Pour into 2½-quart baking pan. Bake at 350 degrees for 35 to 45 minutes. Sprinkle with remaining cheese. Bake until cheese is melted. Yield: 10-12 servings.

Fern L. Bishop, Pres.
Laureate Lambda PL254
Walla Walla, Washington

Baked Pineapple

1 c. sugar
2 tbsp. flour
½ tsp. salt
1 No. 2½ can crushed pineapple
¼ to ½ lb. grated Cheddar or longhorn cheese
Buttered bread crumbs

Combine sugar, flour and salt; mix well. Add pineapple and cheese; mix well. Pour into buttered baking dish. Cover with crumbs. Bake at 350 degrees for 40 minutes or until lightly browned. Serve with ham or chicken. Yield: 8-12 servings.

Bonnie Halligan, Treas.
Kappa Zeta No. 9920
Lenox, Iowa

Scalloped Pineapple
(1940)

½ c. butter, softened
1 c. sugar
3 eggs, slightly beaten
½ tsp. salt
½ c. milk
1 20-oz. can crushed pineapple
3 c. day-old bread cubes

Cream butter and sugar until smooth. Add eggs; beat well. Stir in salt and milk. Fold in pineapple and bread cubes. Pour into buttered 9 × 13-inch baking pan. Bake at 375 degrees for 45 minutes. Yield: 10-12 servings.

Beverly Beam
Xi Epsilon X164
Waynesboro, Pennsylvania

Gourmet Macaroni And Cheese

2 tbsp. butter
2 tbsp. chopped onions
2 tbsp. chopped celery
2 tbsp. flour
2 c. milk
1 tsp. salt
¼ tsp. pepper
2 c. cooked macaroni
½ lb. sharp Cheddar cheese, grated
¼ lb. Swiss cheese, grated
½ can olives, drained

Melt butter in skillet. Add onions and celery; cook until tender. Add flour; mix well. Add milk, salt and pepper, stirring until smooth. Cook for 2 minutes; set aside. Combine macaroni, onion mixture, cheeses and olives; mix well. Pour into buttered 1½-quart casserole. Sprinkle with additional cheese; cover. Bake at 350 degrees for 25 minutes. Bake, uncovered, for 5 minutes longer. Yield: 6 servings.

Helen M. Williams, Pres.
Xi Sigma Delta X4312
Sebastopol, California

Bavarian-Creamed Egg Noodles

1 16-oz. package egg noodles
1 10½-oz. can cream of mushroom soup
½ c. milk
½ tsp. parsley flakes
¼ tsp. salt
6 hard-cooked eggs, diced

Prepare noodles according to package directions; drain. Combine soup and milk in saucepan; mix well. Stir in noodles, parsley flakes and salt. Stir in eggs gradually. Cook over Low heat for 5 minutes, stirring. Yield: 6-8 servings.

Sally Brockmeir, Pres.
Xi Beta Xi X5085
Little Rock, Arkansas

Italian-Stuffed Shells

24 jumbo pasta shells
2 c. ricotta or cottage cheese
½ c. Parmesan cheese
8 oz. mozzarella cheese, grated
2 eggs, beaten
1 tsp. salt
Dash of pepper
1 tsp. oregano
2 c. spaghetti sauce

Prepare shells according to package directions; dry on paper towel. Combine cheeses, eggs, salt, pepper and oregano; mix well. Spoon into shells. Pour small amount of spaghetti sauce in 13 × 9-inch baking dish. Place shells in single layer over sauce. Cover with remaining sauce. Sprinkle with additional Parmesan cheese. Bake at 350 degrees for 40 minutes. Yield: 8-10 servings.

Laura Wooldridge, Pres.
Beta Gamma No. 3310
Lynchburg, Virginia

Macaroni-Fruit Buffet

4 c. elbow macaroni
2 c. sour cream
2 c. creamed cottage cheese
¼ c. chopped pecans
1 tsp. salt
½ tsp. cinnamon
2 1-lb. 4½-oz. cans pineapple chunks
2 c. orange sections
Salad greens
2 1-lb. 14-oz. cans apricot halves, drained

Prepare macaroni according to package directions; drain. Combine macaroni, sour cream, cottage cheese, pecans, salt and cinnamon; mix well. Drain pineapple, reserving 3 tablespoons juice. Combine reserved juice, pineapple and orange sections; mix well. Add to macaroni mixture; toss lightly. Chill until flavors blend. Mount on salad greens; surround with apricots. Yield: 12 servings.

Photograph for this recipe on page 105.

Manicotti

1 pkg. manicotti
2 c. ricotta or cottage cheese
1 8-oz. package mozzarella cheese, shredded
½ c. grated Parmesan cheese
2 eggs, slightly beaten
1 tsp. salt
1 tsp. chopped parsley
⅛ tsp. pepper
3 c. spaghetti sauce

Prepare manicotti according to package directions; drain. Place in single layer on a paper towel to dry. Combine cheeses, eggs, salt, parsley and pepper; mix well. Fill manicotti with desired amount of cheese mixture. Spread thin layer of spaghetti sauce in large deep baking pan. Place manicotti on spaghetti sauce. Cover with remaining spaghetti sauce. Sprinkle with additional Parmesan cheese. Bake at 350 degrees for 35 minutes or until heated through.

Frances M. Bobbitt
Eta Nu No. 9929
Cullowhee, North Carolina

Noodle-Spinach Ring

1 8-oz. package wide noodles
2 10-oz. packages frozen chopped spinach, thawed and drained
1 onion, chopped
½ c. butter
3 eggs, slightly beaten
1 c. sour cream

Prepare noodles according to package directions; drain. Combine noodles and spinach; mix well. Saute onion in butter until browned. Add to noodle mixture; mix well. Fold in eggs. Add sour cream; blend well. Pour into greased 6-cup ring mold; place in pan of hot water. Bake at 350 degrees for 45 minutes. Serve on heated platter with steamed mushrooms in center. Yield: 8 servings.

Tina Duncan, Librarian
Epsilon Rho
North Wilkesboro, North Carolina

Mushrooms And Rice

2⅔ c. minute rice
6 tbsp. oil
2 sm. cans mushrooms, drained
2 green onions, chopped
2 cans beef consomme
2 tbsp. soy sauce
½ tsp. salt

Combine all ingredients; mix well. Pour into casserole; cover. Bake at 350 degrees for 30 to 45 minutes or until liquid is absorbed. Yield: 6 servings.

Jody Hartnett, Treas.
Xi Psi X2129
Emmett, Idaho

California Casserole

1 c. chopped onion
¼ c. margarine
4 c. cooked rice
2 c. sour cream
1 c. cream-style cottage cheese
½ tsp. salt
⅛ tsp. pepper
2 cans green chilies, diced
2 c. grated sharp Cheddar cheese

Saute onion in margarine for 5 minutes or until lightly browned. Remove from heat. Add remaining ingredients; mix well. Spoon into lightly-greased 2-quart baking dish. Bake at 375 degrees for 25 minutes or until hot and bubbly. Yield: 6 servings.

Barbara Boan, Pres.
Preceptor Alpha Theta XP726
Cortez, Colorado

Pamela's Rice And Mushrooms

2 c. rice
2 cans cream of mushroom soup
1 stick margarine, cubed
½ c. sliced mushrooms
3 tbsp. instant beef bouillon granules
1 tsp. pepper

Combine all ingredients with 2 cups boiling water in slow cooker; mix well. Cook on Low for 8 to 10 hours or on High for 2 to 4 hours, stirring occasionally.

Pamela Aliff Rose, Rec. Sec.
Epsilon Mu No. 10203
Elkview, West Virginia

Pasta Confetti Bake
(1940)

1½ c. scalded milk
1 c. soft bread crumbs
¼ c. chopped pimento
1 tbsp. minced onion
1 tbsp. minced green pepper (opt.)
¼ c. butter or margarine
1½ c. grated American cheese
3 eggs, beaten
½ tsp. salt
1 tsp. pepper
1 c. macaroni

Pour milk over bread crumbs. Saute pimento, onion and green pepper in margarine until tender. Add pimento mixture to bread crumb mixture; mix well. Add cheese, eggs, salt and pepper; mix well. Prepare macaroni according to package directions; drain. Add to bread crumb mixture; mix well. Pour into greased 9 × 12-inch shallow baking dish. Bake at 325 degrees for 50 minutes. Yield: 6-8 servings.

Gwen I. Higgins
Xi Mu Upsilon X3701
Bedford, Texas

Pilaf Extraordinaire

½ c. butter or margarine
2 c. long grain rice
1 tsp. salt
¼ tsp. saffron
Freshly ground pepper
3 10½-oz. cans consomme
2 med. onions, sliced
1 c. dark seedless raisins

Melt ¼ cup butter in heavy skillet. Add rice; cook over Low heat until rice is browned, stirring. Stir in seasonings and consomme; cover. Bake at 325 degrees for 1 hour and 30 minutes. Saute onions in remaining butter until tender. Stir raisins into rice mixture. Let stand for 5 minutes. Spoon onto serving platter. Top with onions. Yield: 6 servings.

Photograph for this recipe on page 107.

Sour Cream Rice

2 c. sour cream
2 tsp. pepper
1 tbsp. sugar
2½ tbsp. chopped onion
Tabasco sauce to taste
¼ c. sliced black olives
3 c. cooked rice
4 c. grated Cheddar cheese

Combine sour cream, pepper, sugar, onion, Tabasco sauce and olives; mix well. Alternate layers of rice, sour cream mixture and cheese in buttered 2-quart casserole, ending with cheese. Bake at 425 degrees for 30 minutes. Yield: 6 servings.

Donna Pool, Pres.
Alpha Kappa Kappa No. 8946
Mesquite, Texas

Springtime Rice
(1940)

1 c. rice
2 tbsp. olive oil
½ c. chopped bell pepper
½ c. chopped spring onion
½ to 1 c. sliced mushrooms (opt.)
2 tbsp. parsley flakes
2 to 2½ c. chicken broth

Saute rice in oil in 10-inch skillet over Medium-low heat until lightly browned. Add bell pepper, onion and mushrooms; stir-fry for 1 to 2 minutes. Pour into 1-quart casserole. Add chicken broth; cover. Bake at 350 degrees for 35 to 45 minutes or until liquid is absorbed. Toss well. Yield: 6 servings.

Susan Milholland, Ext. Off.
Epsilon Rho No. 8332
Wilkesboro, North Carolina

Donna's Wild Rice

1 box Uncle Ben's long grain and wild rice
1 c. chopped celery
1 c. chopped onion
¼ c. margarine
1 4-oz. can button mushrooms, drained
1 can cream of mushroom, celery or chicken soup

Prepare rice according to package directions. Saute celery and onion in margarine over Low heat until tender. Combine rice, celery mixture, mushrooms and soup; mix well. Pour into casserole. Bake at 350 degrees for 45 minutes or until lightly browned. Yield: 6 servings.

Jo Ann Carlson, Treas.
Nu Pi No. 8760
Troy, Missouri

Sandy's Wild Rice Casserole

6 oz. long grain wild rice
1 green pepper, chopped
1 onion, chopped
4 oz. mushrooms, sliced

½ c. margarine
8 slices American cheese, grated
1 c. half and half

Prepare rice according to package directions. Saute green pepper, onion and mushrooms in margarine. Alternate layers of rice, green pepper mixture and cheese in casserole, ending with cheese. Cover with half and half. Bake at 400 degrees for 30 minutes.

Sandy Gibson, Pres.
Epsilon Delta No. 3774
Lamoni, Iowa

Wild Rice Casserole
(1950)

2 med. onions, chopped
1 stalk celery, chopped
1 stick margarine
1 pkg. long grain rice
1 can mushroom soup
1 sm. can mushrooms, drained
½ lb. Velveeta cheese, cubed

Saute onions and celery in margarine in large skillet. Prepare rice according to package directions. Add soup and mushrooms to onion mixture; mix well. Add cheese; cook until cheese is melted. Add rice;

mix well. Pour into buttered 9 × 13 × 2-inch Pyrex casserole. Let stand for 1 hour. Bake at 325 degrees for 1 hour. Yield: 6-8 servings.

Marjorie L. Fogle, Pres.
Nu Kappa No. 8556
Aurora, Missouri

Quiche Lorraine

½ c. mayonnaise
½ c. milk
2 eggs
1 tbsp. cornstarch
1½ c. cubed cooked ham
1½ c. chopped Swiss cheese
⅓ c. sliced green onions
Dash of pepper
1 unbaked 9-in. pie shell

Combine mayonnaise, milk, eggs and cornstarch; beat until smooth. Add ham, cheese, onions and pepper; mix well. Pour into pie shell. Bake at 350 degrees for 35 to 40 minutes or until knife blade inserted near center comes out clean.

Dorothy N. Ball, City Coun. Adv.
Laureate Alpha PL319
Somerset, New Jersey

Chinese Fried Rice

1½ c. rice
¾ c. chopped onion
¾ c. chopped celery
3 tbsp. oil
3 tbsp. soya sauce
1 c. leftover chopped chicken, turkey or pork

Prepare rice according to package directions. Cool. Saute onion and celery in oil. Add cold rice and soya sauce; stir-fry. Add meat; stir until heated through. Yield: 12 servings.

Norma Robson, Pres.
Preceptor Tau XP1631
Courtenay, British Columbia, Canada

Coco-Rice

2 c. cooked long grain white rice
1 c. cooked wild rice
1 c. shredded coconut
Grated rind of 1 lemon
Grated rind of 1 orange
3 tbsp. butter
3 tbsp. Grand Marnier or Cointreau liqueur

Combine hot rice, coconut and grated rind in serving bowl. Add butter and liqueur; mix until butter is melted. Yield 8 servings.

Sharon Marbach, Pres.
Xi Epsilon X5429
West Germany

Donna's Rice Casserole

1 sm. onion, chopped
1 tbsp. butter
1 tsp. salt
1 can cream of mushroom soup
Milk
1 8-oz. jar Cheez Whiz
1 pkg. frozen broccoli bits, thawed
1⅓ c. minute rice

Saute onion in butter in 10-inch skillet. Add salt, soup, ½ soup can milk and Cheeze Whiz; blend well. Add broccoli and rice; mix well. Pour into 1½-quart casserole. Bake at 400 degrees for 30 minutes. Yield: 4-6 servings.

Donna Lawhorn, V.P
Alpha Nu No. 2614
Attleboro, Massachusetts

Green Rice Casserole
(1930)

2 eggs, beaten
1 c. evaporated milk
½ c. finely chopped parsley
1 clove of garlic, finely chopped
1 sm. onion, minced
2 c. cooked rice
½ c. medium sharp Cheddar cheese
½ tsp. salt
2 tbsp. cooking oil
1 can mushroom soup
½ c. milk

Combine eggs and evaporated milk, mixing well. Add parsley, garlic and onion; mix well. Stir in rice, cheese and salt. Pour oil into 8-inch square baking dish. Add rice mixture. Bake at 325 degrees for 35 minutes. Combine soup and milk in saucepan; mix well. Cook until heated through. Serve over rice. Yield: 9 servings.

Virginia Grace Chiene, Ext. Off.
Preceptor Iota XP244
Seattle, Washington

Maxie's Green Rice

2 c. rice
8 oz. Old English cheese, grated
1⅓ c. chopped parsley
3 eggs, slightly beaten
2⅓ c. evaporated milk
2 cloves of garlic, chopped
⅓ tsp. Accent
1 tsp. Lawry's Seasoned Salt
⅔ tsp. pepper
1⅓ tsp. salt
1 tbsp. lemon juice
1 tsp. grated lemon rind
1⅓ c. butter-flavored oil
Paprika to taste

Prepare rice according to package directions; rinse and drain. Combine rice, cheese and parsley; mix well. Combine eggs, evaporated milk, garlic, Accent, seasoned salt, pepper, salt, lemon juice and rind; mix well. Add oil gradually, beating with hand mixer. Fold into rice mixture. Pour into two 2½-quart casseroles. Sprinkle with paprika. Place in shallow pan of water. Bake at 350 degress for 1 hour. Yield: 15 servings.

Maxie DeLaney, Rec. Sec.
Alpha Phi XL1059
Paris, Missouri

Mary's Special Rice

½ c. chopped onion
½ c. butter or margarine
1½ c. rice
3 c. bouillon
Chopped parsley to taste
½ c. slivered almonds

Brown onion in butter. Add rice; cook until bubbly. Add remaining ingredients; mix well. Pour into 1½-quart casserole; cover. Bake at 350 degrees for 30 minutes. Bake, uncovered, for 10 minutes longer. Yield: 8 servings.

Mary E. Hahn, Pres.
Laureate Alpha Epsilon PL378
Riverside, California

Zita's Rice and Mushrooms

1 c. rice
1 can Campbell's onion soup
1 4-oz. can mushrooms, drained
½ stick butter or margarine

Rinse rice; drain. Place rice in 2-quart casserole. Add remaining ingredients and 1 soup can water; mix well. Bake at 350 degrees for 1 hour. Yield: 6 servings.

Zita Scheiding, Pres.
Alpha No. 6532
Beatrice, Nebraska

Old-Fashioned Rice
(1930)

1 lg. onion, chopped
½ lb. chicken livers
1 c. margarine
2 carrots, chopped
2 stalks celery, chopped
2 tbsp. chopped parsley
1 1-lb. package rice, cooked

Saute onion and chicken livers in margarine. Add carrots and celery. Simmer for 10 minutes or until carrots are tender. Add parsley; stir for 1 minute. Add to rice; mix well. Yield: 6-10 servings.

Marie DeFeo, Pres.
Xi Alpha Upsilon XP1667
Somerset, New Jersey

Rice Consomme

1 c. rice
1 can consomme
1 stick margarine
1 beef bouillon cube
Salt and pepper to taste

Combine all ingredients; mix well. Place in 1½-quart casserole. Bake at 350 degrees for 1 hour. Yield: 6 servings.

Sandra Stubbs, Pres.
Eta Omega No. 9517
Colorado Springs, Colorado

Spicy Wild Rice

1 lb. hot sausage
2 bunches green onions, chopped
2 med. cans mushrooms
1 pkg. wild rice

Brown sausage; drain. Add green onions and mushrooms; mix well. Prepare rice according to package directions. Combine rice and sausage mixture; mix well. Place in 4 x 6 x 2-inch baking pan. Bake at 350 degrees for 15 minutes or until heated through. Yield: 6-8 servings.

Faye Harper, Pres.
Xi Epsilon Zeta X3708
Sikeston, Missouri

Corn Bread Stuffing

6 c. chopped celery
3 c. chopped onion
Butter
12 c. corn bread crumbs
12 slices bread, cubed
7 c. turkey or chicken broth
3 eggs, slightly beaten
1 tsp. pepper
3 tsp. salt
1 tsp. thyme
4 tsp. poultry seasoning
1 tsp. sage

Saute celery and onion in butter until browned. Add remaining ingredients; mix well. Pour into 2 buttered baking pans. Bake at 350 degrees for 40 minutes or until lightly browned. Yield: 15 servings.

Kathryn Barr Park, Pres.
Epsilon Xi No. 4848
Lake Park, Florida

Breads

Nothing makes the mouth water faster than the delicious smell of home-baked bread fresh from the oven. And tho Beta Sigma Phis have always been known as skillful bakers, bread making methods have improved so much in the last fifty years that even the novice cook can bake bread "like Mother used to."

From early packaged biscuits to beer bread, Beta Sigma Phis have used bread making imaginatively, both for entertaining and for family meals.

In this chapter, you will find the quick and easy way to make corn bread, biscuits and muffins as well as the old-fashioned coffee cakes and kneaded favorites. The aromas will make it hard to keep family members out of the kitchen!

Angel Flake Biscuits

5 c. flour
2 tsp. baking powder
1 tsp. soda
3 tbsp. sugar
1 tsp. salt
1 c. shortening
1 pkg. yeast
2 c. buttermilk

Sift dry ingredients together; mix well. Cut in shortening. Dissolve yeast in ¼ cup warm water. Add yeast mixture and buttermilk to mixture to form dough. Shape dough into a ball. Place in greased plastic bag; seal tightly. Refrigerate for 12 hours. Roll out on floured surface; cut as desired. Bake at 350 degrees for 10 to 15 minutes. Dough keeps well refrigerated.

Maxine Wilson, Corr. Sec.
Preceptor Alpha Lambda XP834
Pleasant Hope, Missouri

Baking Powder Biscuits

2 c. sifted flour
3 tsp. baking powder
1 tsp. salt
¼ c. shortening
⅔ c. milk

Sift flour, baking powder and salt together. Cut in shortening with 2 knives or pastry blender. Add milk; blend well. Turn out on lightly floured surface; knead. Pat out to ½-inch thickness; cut with biscuit cutter. Place in greased baking pan. Bake at 450 degrees for 12 minutes. Yield: 12 servings.

Karen Mason
Phi Alpha Theta P1441
Independence, Missouri

Light-As-A-Feather Biscuits
(1958)

2 c. sifted flour
1 tbsp. sugar
4 tsp. baking powder
½ tsp. salt
½ c. margarine or butter
1 egg, beaten
⅔ c. milk

Sift dry ingredients together. Cut in margarine until mixture resembles coarse crumbs. Combine egg and milk; add to flour mixture. Stir until dough leaves side of bowl. Turn out on lightly floured board; knead 20 times. Roll dough to ¾-inch thick square. Cut as desired. Place on cookie sheet. Bake at 450 degrees for 10 to 14 minutes or until golden brown. Yield: 18 servings.

Judithan Williamson, City Coun. Pres.
Xi Gamma Zeta X3720
Pearl River, New York

Crispy Corn Sticks

½ c. finely chopped onion
2 tbsp. butter or margarine, melted
1 14-oz. package corn muffin mix
1 12-oz. can whole kernel yellow corn, drained
Corn syrup

Saute onion in butter. Prepare muffin mix according to package directions. Stir in onion and corn, mixing only until blended. Pour into well-oiled corn stick pans. Keep remaining batter refrigerated until baked. Bake at 400 degrees for 20 minutes. Remove from pan. Brush with corn syrup.

Photograph for this recipe on page 113.

Corn Bread Muffins
(1938)

1 egg, slightly beaten
1 tbsp. sugar
½ tsp. salt
¾ c. milk
1 c. yellow cornmeal
½ c. flour
3 tsp. baking powder
2 tbsp. melted shortening

Combine egg, sugar, salt and milk; blend well. Combine cornmeal, flour and baking powder; mix well. Stir into batter. Add shortening; beat well. Pour into greased and heated muffin pan. Bake at 425 degrees for 25 to 30 minutes. Yield: 8 muffins.

Hazel M. Cornelison, Pres.
Preceptor Beta Delta XP1192
Poplar Bluff, Missouri

Russian Corn Bread

3 c. self-rising cornmeal
3 eggs
1 c. chopped onion
3 hot peppers, chopped
½ c. shredded cheese
½ c. oil
2 c. buttermilk

1 8-oz. can cream-style corn
2 tbsp. sugar

Combine all ingredients; mix well. Pour into 12 × 9-inch baking pan. Bake at 375 degrees for 45 minutes. Yield: 15 servings.

Audra Miller
Xi Beta Theta X3312
Northfork, West Virginia

Spanish Corn Bread

1 c. buttermilk
1 c. yellow cornmeal
1 c. sifted flour
3 tsp. sugar
1 tsp. salt
1 tsp. baking powder
1 tsp. soda
1 egg, beaten
¼ c. melted shortening
1 8-oz. can whole kernel corn, drained
1 4-oz. can green chili peppers, drained and
   chopped
1 4-oz. can pimento, drained and chopped
½ c. grated Cheddar cheese

Combine buttermilk and cornmeal in small bowl; let stand for 30 minutes. Sift flour, sugar, salt, baking powder and soda together. Add egg, shortening and buttermilk mixture; stir well. Add corn, peppers, and pimento; stir well. Add cheese; mix well. Pour into greased 9 × 13-inch baking pan. Bake at 375 degrees for 30 minutes. Yield: 8-10 servings.

Jo Anne Hoffer, Pres.
Lambda Nu No. 3992
Sunnyvale, California

Southern Corn Bread
(1935)

2 eggs
¼ c. Wesson oil
1 c. cream-style corn
1 c. self-rising cornmeal
1 c. sour milk or buttermilk

Combine ingredients in order listed; mix well. Pour into 8-inch square baking pan. Bake at 400 degrees for 20 minutes. Yield: 6 servings.

Virginia M. Rider, V.P.
Preceptor Alpha Epsilon XP648
Burlington, Kentucky

Tar Heel Hush Puppies

1 lb. fine cornmeal
1 egg, slightly beaten
1 tbsp. salt
1 tbsp. sugar
Pinch of soda
1 c. buttermilk

Combine all ingredients with enough water to form batter of consistency to drop from a spoon. Cook in deep hot fat until golden brown. Yield: 12 servings.

Virginia Putzka, Corr. Sec.
Laureate Alpha PL124
Kansas City, Missouri

Beer Bread

3 c. sifted self-rising flour
3 tbsp. sugar
1 12-oz. can beer

Combine all ingredients; mix well. Batter will be lumpy. Pour into greased loaf pan. Bake at 400 degrees for 40 minutes. Yield: 10 servings.

Virginia Chenault, Sec.
Laureate Nu PL337
Littleton, Colorado

Beverly's Monkey Bread

4 cans refrigerator biscuits, quartered
1⅔ c. sugar
2 tbsp. cinnamon
1 stick margarine

Place biscuits, 1 cup sugar and 1 tablespoon cinnamon in plastic bag. Shake to coat biscuits. Place biscuits in well-greased tube pan. Combine ⅔ cup sugar, 1 tablespoon cinnamon and margarine in saucepan. Cook on Low heat until melted and well blended. Pour over biscuits. Bake at 350 degrees for 35 minutes. Remove from pan immediately.

Beverly T. Mayes, Corr. Sec.
Xi Psi No. 1217
Richmond, Virginia

Monkey Bread

1 c. milk
Butter
¼ c. sugar
1 tsp. salt
2 pkg. dry yeast
2 eggs
4 c. flour

Combine milk, ¼ cup butter, sugar and salt in saucepan; bring to a boil. Cool to lukewarm. Dissolve yeast in 2 tablespoons warm water in large bowl. Add milk mixture to yeast mixture; mix well. Add eggs and 2 cups flour; beat well. Add remaining flour; beat until smooth. Place dough in large greased bowl; let rise for 1 hour or until doubled in bulk. Turn out on floured board; knead for 5 minutes. Roll into ½-inch thick rectangle. Cut into 2-inch squares. Dip squares in ⅓ cup melted butter. Place squares in greased tube pan. Let rise for 50 minutes. Bake at 350 degrees for 30 minutes. Yield: 10 servings.

Mary Greer, Pres.
Alpha Tau Omicron No. 10996
Graham, Texas

Old-Fashioned Crackling Bread
(1930)

2 tsp. bacon drippings
1½ c. chopped cracklings
1½ c. cornmeal
3 tbsp. flour
1 tsp. salt
1 tsp. soda
2 c. buttermilk
1 egg, beaten

Pour bacon drippings into 10-inch iron skillet. Place in 450-degree oven until hot. Combine cracklings, cornmeal, flour, salt and soda; mix well. Combine buttermilk and egg; add to crackling mixture, stirring until just moistened. Pour into hot skillet. Bake at 450 degrees for 25 minutes.

Gayle Attkisson
Alpha Psi No. 2504
Columbia, Tennessee

Onion-Topped Bread

1½ c. biscuit mix
¾ tsp. salt
½ c. milk
1 3-oz. can French-fried onions
1 egg
1 c. sour cream

Combine biscuit mix, ¼ teaspoon salt and milk; mix well. Spread in greased 8-inch baking pan. Sprinkle with ½ of the onions. Combine egg, sour cream and ½ teaspoon salt; beat well. Spoon over onions. Top with remaining onions. Bake at 375 degrees for 25 minutes or until bread tests done.

Freda F. Pirtle, Pres.
Preceptor Gamma Mu X1975
West Frankfort, Illinois

Blueberry Muffins
(1955)

1½ c. sifted flour
½ c. sugar
2 tsp. baking powder
½ tsp. salt
1 egg, beaten
½ c. oil
½ c. milk
1 c. blueberries

Sift dry ingredients together. Combine egg, oil and milk; mix well. Add to dry ingredients, stirring until creamy. Fold in blueberries. Pour into muffin pan. Bake at 375 degrees for 20 to 25 minutes. Yield: 12 muffins.

Sarah Giambrone, Pres.
Eta Beta No. 5990
Brocton, New York

Sweet Potato Muffins

1 stick butter, softened
1¼ c. sugar
1¼ c. sweet potatoes, mashed
2 eggs
1½ c. flour
1 tsp. baking powder
1 tsp. cinnamon
¼ tsp. nutmeg
¼ tsp. salt
1¼ c. milk
¼ c. chopped pecans or walnuts
½ c. raisins, chopped

Cream butter, sugar and sweet potatoes until smooth. Add eggs; blend until smooth. Sift flour, baking powder, cinnamon, nutmeg and salt together. Add dry ingredients to sweet potato mixture alternately with milk. Fold in pecans and raisins. Pour into greased muffin cups. Sprinkle with additional sugar and cinnamon. Bake at 400 degrees for 25 minutes or until muffins test done.

Barbara Pfeiffer
Preceptor Nu No. 1498
Middletown, Maryland

Apple Coffee Cake

½ c. shortening
1 c. sugar
1 egg, slightly beaten
½ c. orange juice
1 tsp. vanilla extract
Flour
½ tsp. salt
1 tsp. soda
2 c. chopped apples
½ c. (firmly packed) brown sugar
1 tsp. cinnamon
½ c. chopped nuts

Cream shortening, sugar and egg until smooth. Add orange juice, vanilla, 1½ cups flour, salt and soda; mix well. Dredge applies in 2 tablespoons flour; add to batter, mixing well. Pour into 9-inch square pan. Combine brown sugar, cinnamon and nuts; mix well. Sprinkle over batter. Bake at 350 degrees for 35 to 40 minutes. Yield: 6-8 servings.

Ellarea Davison, Soc. Comm. Chm.
Preceptor Alpha Sigma XP1773
Corydon, Iowa

Chocolate Chip Coffee Cake

1 stick margarine, softened
1 c. sugar
2 eggs
1 tsp. soda
1 tsp. baking powder
¼ tsp. salt
2 c. flour
1 c. sour cream
1 tsp. vanilla extract
1 c. chocolate chips

Cream margarine and sugar until smooth. Add eggs; beat well. Sift soda, baking powder, salt and flour together. Add to creamed mixture alternately with sour cream, beating well after each addition. Stir in vanilla. Pour into greased bundt or angel food pan. Bake at 350 degrees for 45 minutes. Yield: 6 servings.

Terry Taylor, V.P.
Kappa Kappa No. 7545
Lansing, Michigan

Easy Coffee Cake

1 pkg. yellow cake mix
3 eggs, slightly beaten
1 1-lb. can applesauce
¼ c. plus 2 tbsp. sugar
2 tsp. cinnamon

Combine cake mix, eggs and applesauce in large mixer bowl; blend well. Beat with electric mixer according to cake mix package directions. Combine sugar and cinnamon; mix well. Sprinkle greased tube or bundt pan with 2 tablespoon sugar mixture. Pour ½ of the batter over sugar mixture. Sprinkle with remaining sugar mixture. Add remaining batter. Bake at 350 degrees for 35 to 45 minutes.

Peggy W. Cox, Rec. Sec.
Preceptor Nu No. 1760
Anniston, Alabama

Cinnamon Loaf
(1954)

½ c. margarine
1 c. sugar
2 eggs
2 c. flour
Salt
1 tsp. soda
½ tsp. baking powder
1 c. sour milk
1 tsp. vanilla extract
½ c. (firmly packed) brown sugar
1 tsp. cinnamon

Cream margarine and sugar until smooth. Add eggs, one at a time, beating well after each addition. Sift flour, ½ teaspoon salt, soda and baking powder together. Add to egg mixture alternately with sour milk, beating well after each addition. Add vanilla. Pour ½ of the batter into baking pan. Combine brown sugar, cinnamon and ⅛ teaspoon salt; mix well. Sprinkle ½ of the brown sugar mixture over batter. Top with remaining batter. Sprinkle with remaining brown sugar mixture. Bake at 350 degrees for 1 hour.

Karen Ellsworth
Beta Tau No. 3892
Essex, Ontario, Canada

Peanut Butter-Crumb Coffee Cake
(1930)

2 c. (firmly packed) brown sugar
2½ c. sifted flour
½ tsp. salt
⅓ c. butter, softened
½ c. peanut butter
1 tsp. soda
1 tsp. vanilla extract
1 c. sour milk
2 eggs, beaten

Combine brown sugar, flour and salt; mix well. Cut in butter and peanut butter until mixture resembles coarse crumbs. Reserve ⅔ cup of crumb mixture. Dissolve soda in 1 teaspoon water and vanilla. Add soda mixture, milk, and eggs to remaining crumb mixture; beat well. Pour into greased and floured 9 × 13-inch pan. Sprinkle with reserved crumb mixture. Bake at 375 degrees for 30 minutes or until cake tests done. Drizzle with favorite confectioners sugar glaze recipe, if desired. Yield: 12 servings.

Joyce Horvath, Corr. Sec.
Xi Iota Gamma X4347
Wellington, Ohio

Quick Coffee Cake

Butter
1½ c. sugar
1 egg
2½ c. flour
2 tsp. baking powder
1 c. milk
2 tsp. cinnamon
¼ tsp. nutmeg

Cream ½ cup butter and 1 cup sugar until smooth. Add egg; beat well. Combine 2 cups flour and baking powder; mix well. Add to creamed mixture alternately with milk, beating well after each addition. Pour into greased and floured 9 × 13-inch pan. Combine ½ cup flour, ½ cup sugar, 2 tablespoons melted butter, cinnamon and nutmeg; mix well. Sprinkle over batter. Bake at 350 degrees for 20 minutes. Yield: 12-15 servings.

Jacqueline Rae Dehmer, Past Pres.
Theta Eta No. 5649
Ferguson, Missouri

Aloha Banana Bread

2 c. flour
1 c. sugar
1 tsp. soda
½ tsp. salt
½ c. butter or margarine, softened
2 eggs, slightly beaten
¼ c. milk
2 med. bananas, mashed
1 tbsp. grated orange rind
1 tsp. vanilla extract
½ tsp. almond extract
1 c. flaked coconut
½ c. chopped nuts

Combine all ingredients except coconut and nuts in large mixer bowl. Beat at Low speed of electric mixer until dry ingredients are moistened. Beat at Medium speed for 3 minutes. Stir in coconut and nuts. Grease bottom only of 9 × 5-inch loaf pan. Pour batter into greased loaf pan. Bake at 350 degrees for 60 to 70 minutes or until bread tests done. Remove from pan immediately; cool.

Theresa Weller
Xi Eta Epsilon
Circleville, Ohio

Avocado Bread

1 egg
½ c. mashed avocado

½ c. buttermilk
⅓ c. vegetable oil
2 c. flour
¾ c. sugar
½ tsp. soda
½ tsp. baking powder
¼ tsp. salt
¾ c. chopped pecans

Combine egg, avocado, buttermilk and oil in medium bowl; blend well. Stir in flour, sugar, soda, baking power, salt and pecans; mix only until blended. Pour into greased 9 × 5-inch loaf pan. Bake at 350 degrees for 1 hour or until bread tests done. Cool for 10 minutes. Remove from pan; slice. Serve warm with butter.

DeAnn Bumgardner
Delta Gamma No. 3906
Wichita, Kansas

Date-Nut Bread

1 8-oz. package pitted dates, chopped
2 c. sugar
½ c. shortening
2 tsp. soda
2 tsp. salt
4 c. flour
1 c. chopped nuts
3 tsp. vanilla extract

Pour 2 cups boiling water over dates. Cream sugar and shortening until smooth. Sift soda, salt and flour together. Add to creamed mixture alternately with date mixture, beating well after each addition. Stir in nuts and vanilla. Remove labels from ten 10½-ounce soup cans. Pour batter into cans, filling ½ full. Bake at 350 degrees for 50 to 60 minutes. Let stand for 5 minutes. Invert cans; remove bread. Batter may be poured into 2 loaf pans and baked at 350 degrees for 60 to 70 minutes.

Marla Egbert, Ext. Off.
Beta Xi No. 7896
American Falls, Idaho

Governor Tea Bread
(1940)

½ c. shortening
⅔ c. sugar
2 eggs
1 c. ground apples
2 c. flour
1 tsp. baking powder
1 tsp. soda
½ tsp. salt
½ c. grated American cheese
¼ c. chopped walnuts

Cream shortening and sugar until smooth. Beat eggs; add apples, mixing well. Sift flour, baking powder, soda and salt together; add alternately with egg mixture to creamed mixture. Add cheese and walnuts; mix well. Pour into greased loaf pan. Bake at 350 degrees for 1 hour or until bread tests done.

Helene Cable, Pres.
Preceptor Gamma XP505
Charlotte, North Carolina

Grape-Nut Bread
(1950)

½ c. Grape Nuts
1 c. sour milk
½ c. sugar
1 egg
½ tsp. salt
½ tsp. soda
1 tsp. baking powder
2 c. flour
1 tbsp. shortening, softened

Combine Grape Nuts and sour milk; let stand for 5 minutes. Add remaining ingredients; mix well. Pour into greased 9 × 5-inch loaf pan. Bake at 350 degrees for 30 minutes or until bread tests done.

Phyllis J. Sanzone, V.P.
Gamma Iota No. 2163
Rome, New York

Harvest Bread
(1930)

1½ c. finely chopped dried apples
½ c. butter, softened
⅔ c. sugar
2 eggs
2 c. sifted flour
1 tsp. soda
½ tsp. salt
¾ c. shredded natural Cheddar cheese
½ c. chopped black walnuts

Place apples in water to cover in saucepan; cover. Cook for 20 to 25 minutes; drain. Cream butter and sugar until light and fluffy. Add eggs; beat well. Sift flour, soda and salt together. Add dry ingredients to creamed mixture. Stir in apples, cheese and walnuts. Pour into greased 9 × 5 × 3-inch loaf pan. Bake at 350 degrees for 50 to 55 minutes. Cool for 10 minutes in pan. Remove from pan; cool on rack.

Patricia A. Williams
Preceptor Alpha Iota XP817
Gladstone, Missouri

Bonanza Bread

1 c. sifted flour
1 c. whole wheat flour
½ tsp. salt
½ tsp. soda
2 tsp. baking powder
⅔ c. nonfat dry milk powder
⅓ c. wheat germ
½ c. honey
¼ c. chopped nuts
½ c. raisins
3 eggs
½ c. vegetable oil
½ c. molasses
¾ c. orange juice
2 bananas, mashed
⅓ c. chopped dried apricots

Combine first 10 ingredients in large mixing bowl; blend well. Beat eggs until frothy; add oil, molasses, orange juice and bananas, beating well after each addition. Add apricots; blend well. Add egg mixture to dry ingredients, stirring until just moistened. Pour into 2 greased 4 × 8 × 2-inch loaf pans. Bake at 325 degrees for 1 hour or until center is firm. Cool slightly. Remove from pans. Cool. Wrap securely. Let stand overnight. Yield: 2 loaves.

Gail Boros, Pres.
Epsilon Phi No 10924
Monroeville, Alabama

Poppy Seed Bread
(1930)

4 eggs, beaten
2 c. sugar
1⅓ c. corn oil
3 c. flour
1 can condensed milk
1 tsp. vanilla extract
¼ tsp. lemon juice
1½ tsp. soda
1 tsp. salt
5 tbsp. poppy seed

Combine all ingredients in order listed in large mixer bowl, blending well after each addition at Low speed of electric mixer. Beat for 2 minutes with electric mixer. Pour into 2 well-greased and floured loaf pans. Bake at 325 degrees for 1 hour and 15 minutes or until top is dry and edges pull away from sides of pan.

Patricia Cramer, Corr. Sec.
Xi Phi X3359
Hot Springs, South Dakota

Hobo Bread

1½ c. raisins
2 tsp. soda
1 c. sugar
3 tbsp. oil
1 egg, slightly beaten
2 c. flour
½ tsp. salt
¾ tsp. aniseed
½ c. chopped nuts

Combine raisins and soda in large mixing bowl. Add 1 cup boiling water. Cool. Add remaining ingredients in order listed; mix well. Pour into 2 greased loaf pans. Bake at 350 degrees for 45 to 50 minutes. Serve with cheese.

Norma J. Hoyt
International Honorary Mem.
Anchorage, Alaska

Irish Bread

2 c. buttermilk
1 tsp. soda
1 tsp. salt
1¼ c. sugar
4 tbsp. melted shortening
4 c. sifted flour
1 c. mixed candied fruit
Milk

Combine buttermilk, soda, salt, sugar, shortening and 2 cups flour; mix well. Add fruit and remaining flour, mixing well. Pour into greased loaf or angel food pans. Bake at 350 degrees for 1 hour and 10 minutes. Brush top with small amount of milk. Bake for 10 minutes longer. Yield: 12-15 servings.

Genevieve F. Perry, Pres.
Xi Epsilon Pi X4143
Meadville, Pennsylvania

Sharon's Date-Nut Bread
(1930)

1 c. chopped dates
1 tsp. soda
1 tsp. butter
1 egg
1 tsp. salt
1 tsp. vanilla extract
1 c. sugar
2 c. flour
½ c. chopped nuts

Sprinkle dates with soda; cover with 1 cup boiling water. Set aside. Combine butter, egg, salt, vanilla and sugar; mix well. Add date mixture to egg mixture alternately with flour, mixing well after each addition. Stir in pecans. Pour into well-greased 9 × 5 × 3-inch loaf pan. Bake at 325 degrees for 1 hour or until bread tests done.

Sharon Maltzberger, Pres.
Xi Eta Beta X1932
Santa Maria, California

Strawberry Bread

2 pkg. frozen strawberries, thawed
4 eggs
1¼ c. vegetable oil
3 c. flour
1 tsp. soda
1 tsp. salt
3 tsp. cinnamon
2 c. sugar
1 to 1¼ c. chopped pecans

Combine strawberries, eggs and vegetable oil; mix well. Sift all but ½ cup flour, soda, salt, cinnamon and sugar together. Add dry ingredients to strawberry mixture; stir until well blended. Combine pecans and reserved ½ cup flour; mix well. Add to batter; mix well. Pour into 2 well-greased and floured 9 × 5-inch loaf pans. Bake at 350 degrees for 1 hour or until bread tests done. Yield: 30 servings.

Myrtle L. Burks, V.P.
Xi Alpha Lambda X1066
Peru, Indiana

Lemon Bread

½ c. shortening
1¼ c. sugar
Grated rind of 1 lemon
2 eggs, slightly beaten
1⅔ c. flour
1 tsp. baking powder
½ tsp. salt
½ c. milk
Juice of 1 lemon

Combine shortening, 1 cup sugar, lemon rind and eggs; cream until smooth. Add dry ingredients to creamed mixture alternately with milk. Pour into medium loaf pan or two 3 × 6-inch loaf pans. Bake at 350 degrees for 55 minutes. Cool for 10 minutes. Combine lemon juice and ¼ cup sugar; mix well. Pour over loaf.

Judy N. McKee
Xi Epsilon X558
Beatrice, Nebraska

Zucchini Bread

1 c. cooking oil
2 c. sugar
3 eggs
2 c. flour
¼ tsp. baking powder
2 tsp. soda
1 tsp. salt
3 tsp. cinnamon
2 c. grated zucchini
1 c. chopped walnuts
2 tsp. vanilla extract

Combine oil and sugar in large mixing bowl; blend well. Add eggs; beat well. Sift dry ingredients together. Add dry ingredients to egg mixture alternately with zucchini, beating well after each addition. Stir in walnuts and vanilla. Pour into 2 greased bread pans. Bake at 350 degrees for 1 hour. Yield: 24 servings.

Teresa Cusemano, Rec. Sec.
Beta Mu No. 1808
Jamestown, New York

Delicious Pancakes
(1955)

2 c. flour
5 tsp. baking powder
1 tsp. salt
2 tbsp. sugar
2 c. milk
2 egg yolks
7 tbsp. oil
2 egg whites, stiffly beaten

Sift dry ingredients together. Add milk and egg yolks; stir just to blend. Stir in oil. Fold in egg whites. Bake on hot griddle on both sides until lightly browned. Yield: 5 servings.

Pat Ketner, Pres.
Preceptor Gamma Pi XP850
Brawley, California

Sweet Applets

1 c. sugar
⅓ c. shortening, softened
1 egg, slightly beaten
⅓ c. milk
1½ c. shredded apples
1½ c. flour
2 tsp. baking powder
½ tsp. salt
½ tsp. nutmeg

¼ c. melted butter
1 tsp. cinnamon

Cream ½ cup sugar and shortening until smooth. Add egg, milk and apples; mix well. Combine flour, baking powder, salt and nutmeg; mix well. Add to apple mixture; mix well. Pour into greased muffin cups, filling ⅔ full. Bake at 400 degrees for 20 to 25 minutes. Remove from pan; cool. Dip in butter. Combine cinnamon and ½ cup sugar; mix well. Roll muffins in cinnamon mixture. Yield: 12 servings.

Hannah Jane Moore, Rec. Sec.
Alpha Delta Preceptor XP647
Greenfield, Ohio

Waffles

1 c. sifted flour
½ tsp. soda
1½ tsp. baking powder
½ tsp. salt
5 tbsp. butter
2 egg yolks, beaten
1 c. buttermilk
2 egg whites, stiffly beaten

Sift dry ingredients together in mixing bowl. Cut in butter until mixture resembles coarse meal. Combine egg yolks and buttermilk; mix well. Add to flour mixture, mixing only until moistened. Fold in egg whites. Bake in preheated waffle iron until steaming stops.

Photograph for this recipe on page 119.

Anadama Bread

½ c. yellow cornmeal
1 pkg. dry yeast
½ c. molasses
2 tsp. salt
1 tbsp. butter or margarine
4½ c. flour

Place cornmeal in large mixing bowl. Add 2 cups boiling water, stirring until smooth. Let stand for 30 minutes. Sprinkle yeast over ½ cup warm water. Let stand for 5 minutes or until yeast is dissolved; do not stir. Add molasses, salt, butter and yeast mixture to cornmeal mixture; mix well. Stir in flour; beat well. Pour into 2 well-greased loaf pans; cover. Let rise in warm place, free from draft, until doubled in bulk. Bake at 350 degrees for 45 to 50 minutes or until bread tests done. Remove from pans; cool on rack

Gladys Armstrong, Soc. Chm.
Xi Epsilon Eta X2149
Worthington, Ohio

Dilly Casserole Bread

1 pkg. dry yeast
1 c. creamed cottage cheese, heated to
    lukewarm
2 tbsp. sugar
1 tbsp. minced onion
1 tbsp. butter
2 tsp. dillseed
1 tsp. salt
¼ tsp. soda
1 egg
2¼ to 2½ c. sifted flour

Soften yeast in ¼ cup warm water. Combine yeast mixture and remaining ingredients except flour in large mixing bowl. Add flour gradually, beating well after each addition, to form stiff dough. Cover; let rise in warm place for 50 to 60 minutes or until doubled in bulk. Punch dough down. Place in well-greased 1½ or 2-quart casserole. Let rise for 30 to 40 minutes or until light. Bake at 350 degrees for 40 to 50 minutes or until golden brown. Brush with additional butter. Sprinkle with additional salt.

Patricia Gallagher, Pres.
Psi Mu No. 5667
Chula Vista, California

Herbed-Cheese Bread

1 pkg. dry yeast
¼ c. butter
1 c. seasoned mashed potatoes
1 tbsp. sugar
2 tsp. salt
¾ c. milk, scalded
2 eggs, beaten
½ tsp. oregano
½ tsp. basil
4 to 4½ c. sifted flour
2 c. shredded Cheddar Cheese

Dissolve yeast in ¼ cup warm water. Combine butter, potatoes, sugar, salt and scalded milk, mixing well; cool. Add yeast mixture, eggs, oregano, basil and 1 cup flour; mix well. Add cheese and remaining flour to make stiff dough. Turn out on lightly floured board; knead until smooth and elastic. Place dough in greased bowl, turning once to grease surface; cover. Let rise in warm place until doubled in bulk. Turn out on floured board. Divide dough into 6 equal portions. Roll each portion into 15-inch long strand. Braid 3 strands together. Place on greased baking sheet or in greased 8 × 4 × 2-inch loaf pan. Repeat, using remaining dough. Brush top with melted butter, if desired. Let rise until doubled in bulk. Bake at 350 degrees for 45 minutes or until bread tests done. Cool on rack.

Photograph for this recipe on page 110.

Meal Bread

1 c. oats
1 c. whole wheat cereal
1 c. yellow cornmeal
2 tbsp. dry yeast
2 tsp. salt
2 c. whole wheat flour
6 to 8 c. flour
½ c. honey

Combine first 3 ingredients; cover with 4 cups boiling water. Cool. Dissolve yeast and salt in 1 cup hot water. Add to cornmeal mixture; mix well. Stir in honey. Add whole wheat flour, ½ cup at a time, mixing well after each addition. Add flour, one cup at a time, mixing well after each addition. Dough will be stiff and sticky. Turn out on well-floured board; knead for 5 minutes. Dough will be sticky. Place in greased bowl; cover with damp cloth. Let rise in warm place for 1 hour or until doubled in bulk. Shape into 4 loaves. Place in greased bread pans. Cover with waxed paper. Let rise for 1 hour or until doubled in bulk. Bake at 350 degrees for 1 hour and 5 minutes or until done.

Helen M. Kroeger, Tres.
Xi Beta Phi X5205
Cody, Nebraska

Shredded Wheat Loaves

(1954)

2 lg. shredded wheat biscuits, crumbled
3 tbsp. shortening
1 tsp. salt
⅔ c. molasses
1 pkg. yeast
5½ to 6 c. flour

Place shredded wheat in large mixing bowl. Add 2 cups boiling water. Add shortening, salt and molasses; mix well. Cool to lukewarm. Dissolve yeast in ½ cup warm water. Add to shredded wheat mixture; mix well. Stir in flour gradually. Turn out onto floured board. Cover; let rest for 10 minutes. Knead until smooth. Place in greased bowl, turning to grease top; cover. Let rise in warm place for 1 hour and 15 minutes or until doubled in bulk. Punch dough down. Divide dough into 2 parts. Place in 2 greased 8 × 4 × 2-inch loaf pans. Cover; let rise in warm place for 1 hour or until doubled in bulk. Bake at 350 degrees for 40 to 45 minutes or until done.

Pauline E. Hall, Corr. Sec.
Preceptor Mu XP1477
Glen Burnie, Maryland

Cinnamon Crescents

4½ to 4¾ c. flour
1 pkg. dry yeast
¾ c. milk
Sugar
Butter or margarine
½ tsp. salt
3 eggs
1 c. raisins
½ c. chopped walnuts
1 tsp. cinnamon

Combine 2½ cups flour and yeast in large mixer bowl. Combine milk, ⅓ cup sugar, 6 tablespoons butter and salt in saucepan; heat until butter is melted, stirring constantly. Add to flour mixture. Add eggs; beat at Low speed of electric mixer for 30 seconds, scraping sides of bowl constantly. Beat at High speed for 3 minutes. Stir in enough remaining flour to form soft dough. Turn out on lightly floured surface; knead for 8 to 10 minutes or until dough is smooth and elastic. Shape into ball. Place in lightly greased bowl, turning once to grease surface; cover. Let rise in warm place for 1 hour or until doubled in bulk. Punch dough down. Turn out on lightly floured surface. Divide dough in half; cover. Let rest for 10 minutes. Roll each half into 12 × 10-inch rectangle. Combine raisins, ½ cup sugar, walnuts, 2 table-spoons melted butter and cinnamon; mix well. Sprinkle ½ of the raisin mixture over each rectangle. Roll as for jelly roll, starting with long edge; seal. Place, seam side down, on greased baking sheet, curving to form crescent and pinching ends to seal; cover. Let rise in warm place for 30 minutes or until doubled in bulk. Bake at 375 degrees for 10 minutes. Cover with aluminum foil. Bake for 15 minutes longer. Frost with favorite confectioners' sugar icing, if desired. Yield: 24 servings.

Barbara Everett
Xi Eta Omicron X4003
Tampa, Florida

Whole Wheat Bread

2 c. milk
3 tbsp. oil
1 tbsp. salt
½ c. honey
2 tbsp. dry yeast
5½ c. whole wheat flour
Melted butter

Place milk in saucepan; heat to simmer. Add oil and salt. Add honey, in a fine stream. Pour into large mixer bowl. Cool to lukewarm. Dissolve yeast in ½ cup lukewarm water for 4 minutes. Add yeast to honey mixture. Add 3 cups flour. Mix on Low with electric mixer for 8 minutes. Add 2 cups flour; mix well. Turn dough onto floured board; knead until smooth and elastic. Knead in remaining flour as needed. Place in greased bowl; cover. Let rise in warm place, free from draft, for 1 hour or until doubled in bulk. Punch down; cover. Let rise until doubled in bulk. Punch down; shape into 2 loaves. Place in greased loaf pans; cover. Let rise until almost doubled in bulk. Bake at 375 degrees for 30 to 40 minutes. Remove from pans; cool on wire rack. Brush with melted butter.

Carol M. Shaw, Pres.
Xi Iota X422
Garden City, Kansas

Honey-Wheat Surprise Loaves

4¼ c. flour
2 c. whole wheat flour
1 tbsp. salt
1 pkg. Fleischmann's Dry Yeast
¼ c. honey
Margarine
1 c. golden raisins
¼ c. sugar
¼ tsp. ground cinnamon

Combine flours; mix well. Combine 2½ cups flour mixture, salt and yeast in large mixer bowl; mix well. Combine honey, 3 tablespoons margarine and 2 cups water in saucepan; heat just until warmed. Add to dry ingredients; mix at Medium speed of electric mixer for 2 minutes, scraping bowl occasionally. Add 1 cup flour mixture, mixing until thickened. Beat at High speed of electric mixer for 2 minutes, scraping bowl occasionally. Stir in raisins and remaining flour mixture to make soft dough. Turn out on lightly floured board. Cover dough with bowl; let rest for 10 minutes. Knead for 8 to 10 minutes or until smooth and elastic. Place in greased bowl, turning once to grease surface; cover. Let rise in warm place, free from draft, for 1 hour or until doubled in bulk. Combine sugar and cinnamon; mix well. Punch dough down. Turn out on lightly floured board. Divide dough in half. Roll ½ of the dough into 12 × 8-inch rectangle. Brush with melted margarine. Sprinkle with ½ of the sugar mixture. Roll as for jelly roll; seal edges. Seal ends of loaf; fold underneath. Place, seam side down, in greased 8 × 4 × 2-inch loaf pan. Repeat procedure with remaining dough. Cover; let rise in warm place, free from draft, for 1 hour and 30 minutes or until doubled in bulk. Bake at 400 degrees for 30 to 35 minutes or until bread tests done. Remove from pans; cool on wire racks.

Photograph for this recipe on page 123.

Butterhorns

(1935)

½ c. butter, melted
½ c. lard, melted
½ c. sugar
2 eggs, slightly beaten
1 c. milk, scalded
1 pkg. yeast
1 tsp. salt
4 c. flour

Combine butter, lard, sugar and eggs; mix well. Dissolve yeast in warm scalded milk. Add to mixture; mix well. Add 2 cups flour; mix well. Add remaining flour; mix well. Let stand overnight. Divide dough into 3 parts; roll each part on lightly floured surface to 9-inch circle, ½-inch thick. Cut each circle into wedge-shaped pieces. Roll each wedge, starting with wide end and rolling to point. Arrange in greased baking pans. Bake at 425 degrees for 15 to 20 minutes.

Alyce D. Vanek
International Honorary Mem.
Laguna Hills, California

Refrigerator Potato Rolls

4½ to 5 c. flour
2 pkg. dry yeast
1 c. milk, scalded
½ c. shortening
½ c. sugar
1 tsp. salt
2 c. mashed potatoes
2 eggs

Combine 2 cups flour and yeast in large mixer bowl; mix well. Combine hot milk, shortening, sugar and salt; mix well. Add potatoes; mix well. Cool. Add potato mixture to flour mixture; mix well. Add eggs; beat at Low speed of electric mixer for 30 seconds, scraping sides of bowl constantly. Beat at High speed of electric mixer for 3 minutes. Stir in enough remaining flour to make stiff dough. Place dough in greased bowl, turning once to grease surface; cover. Refrigerate for several hours. Divide dough in half. Shape each half into 16 rolls. Place rolls in two 9 × 9 × 2-inch baking pans; cover. Let rise for 1 hour or until doubled in bulk. Bake at 375 degrees for 25 to 30 minutes.

Royetta Otto, Pres.
Xi Iota Epsilon X4443
Defiance, Ohio

Desserts

Who doesn't have a fond memory of watching her mother bake, helping frost a cake, cutting out cookies, rolling out a pie crust, and licking the bowl?

Beta Sigma Phis have made good memories of their own with desserts, for no rush party, tea or initiation would be the same without a delicious array of goodies. And at home, nothing makes a child clean the plate faster than thoughts of a freshly baked dessert.

Here are the desserts mothers fixed—as well as recipes from the most modern kitchen. Create your own memory-maker with these tantalizing cakes, cookies, candies, pies and puddings. Truly, this collection takes the cake!

Chocolate Candy Eggs
(1930)

12 oz. coconut
½ lb. butter, softened
1 jar marshmallow creme
2 lb. confectioners' sugar
1 sm. jar peanut butter
1 12-oz. package semisweet chocoalte
⅓ stick paraffin

Combine first 5 ingredients; mix by hand until smooth. Shape into eggs. Chill on foil or waxed paper overnight. Melt chocolate and paraffin in top of double boiler. Dip eggs. Chill until firm. Yield: 36 servings.

Mary G. O'Brien, Treas.
Gamma Lambda No. 3436
Sanford, Florida

Crockett Balls

1 c. peanut butter
1 c. confectioners' sugar
1 c. chopped walnuts
1 c. chopped glazed cherries
2 tbsp. butter
1 box semisweet chocolate
1 tbsp. paraffin

Combine first 5 ingredients in mixing bowl; mix well. Roll into balls. Melt chocolate and paraffin in top of double boiler. Dip balls in chocolate mixture, using toothpicks. Place on waxed paper. Yield: 30 servings.

Dona Miller
Xi Theta
Nelson, British Columbia, Canada

Date-Nut Candy
(1930)

1 c. chopped dates
3 c. sugar
1 c. milk
¼ tsp. salt
1 c. chopped pecans or walnuts
2 tsp. vanilla extract

Combine dates, sugar, milk and salt in large saucepan; mix well. Bring to a boil over Medium heat, stirring constantly. Cook to soft-ball stage. Remove from heat. Stir in pecans and vanilla; beat until thickened. Spoon onto damp cloth. Roll as for jelly roll. Chill until firm. Cut into slices. Yield: 2 pounds.

Carolyn Reece, Soc. Chm.
Upsilon Psi No. 5385
Lake Elsinore, California

Peanut Butter Fudge

1½ sticks butter
1 c. peanut butter
1 1-lb. package confectioners' sugar
½ c. chocolate chips

Melt butter in saucepan; remove from heat. Add peanut butter; beat well. Add confectioners' sugar; beat well. Add chocolate chips; mix only until marbleized. Pour into buttered 8-inch square pan. Refrigerate overnight. Cut into squares.

Phyllis Hall
Beta Sigma Phi
Cincinnati, Ohio

Quick Fudge
(1958)

1⅔ c. sugar
2 tbsp. margarine
½ tsp. salt
⅔ c. evaporated milk
1½ c. chocolate chips
1½ c. miniature marshmallows
1 tsp. vanilla extract
½ c. chopped nuts (opt.)

Combine sugar, margarine, salt and evaporated milk in large saucepan. Bring to a boil over Medium heat, stirring occasionally. Boil for 5 minutes, stirring constantly. Remove from heat. Stir in chocolate chips, marshmallows, vanilla and nuts. Pour into greased 8-inch square baking pan. Chill until firm. Cut into squares. Yield: 64 servings.

Joanne Roth, Pres.
Xi Gamma Psi X3975
Pekin, Illinois

Cheesecake
(1950)

¼ c. margarine, melted
1 pkg. graham crackers, crushed
1 3-oz. package lemon or strawberry gelatin
1 8-oz. package cream cheese, softened
½ pt. whipping cream, whipped
½ c. sugar
2 tsp. vanilla extract

Combine margarine and graham cracker crumbs; mix well. Press into 9-inch square pan to form crust. Set aside. Dissolve gelatin in 1 cup boiling water. Chill until partially congealed. Combine cream cheese and whipped cream; mix well. Add sugar and vanilla; mix well. Combine cream cheese mixture and chilled mixture, mixing well. Pour evenly over crust. Chill for 1 to 2 hours or until set. Yield: 8 servings.

Delores Jean Lowis, Rec. Sec.
Xi Gamma Gamma X2829
Plainwell, Michigan

Cheesecake Cupcakes

3 8-oz. packages cream cheese, softened
1¼ c. sugar
6 eggs, beaten
3 tsp. vanilla flavoring
1 c. sour cream

Combine cream cheese, 1 cup sugar and eggs; cream until smooth. Stir in 2 teaspoons vanilla. Pour into paper-lined muffin cups, filling ⅔ full. Bake at 325 degrees for 40 minutes or until cupcakes test done. Cool. Combine sour cream, ¼ cup sugar and 1 teaspoon vanilla; mix well. Spoon sour cream mixture onto cupcakes. Bake at 325 degrees for 5 minutes. Cool. Keep refrigerated in airtight container.

Eleanor Brooks, Pres.
Xi Beta Xi No. 4589
Burlington, North Carolina

Cheesecake Squares

⅔ c. (firmly packed) brown sugar
2 c. sifted flour
⅔ c. butter, melted
1 8-oz. package cream cheese, softened
¼ c. sugar
1 egg
1 c. sour cream
½ tsp. vanilla extract

Combine brown sugar and flour in large bowl; stir in butter, blending until light and crumbly. Press in 9 × 13-inch baking pan. Bake at 350 degrees for 15 minutes. Combine remaining ingredients in mixer bowl; heat until smooth. Pour over baked layer. Bake at 350 degrees for 30 minutes. Cool. Cut into squares. Freezes well. Yield: 40 squares.

Paula Harkins
Upsilon Upsilon No. 5734
Abilene, Texas

Cherry Cheesecake

1 pkg. Dream Whip
1 8-oz. package cream cheese, softened
½ c. confectioners' sugar
1 graham cracker crust
1 16-oz. can cherry pie filling

Prepare Dream Whip according to package direc-

tions. Add cream cheese; beat well. Add confectioners' sugar; mix well. Spoon into graham cracker crust. Top with pie filling; chill until firm.

Martha M. Level
Alpha No. 294
Lewiston, New York

Gateway-To-The-Delta

1⅓ c. flour
1 c. chopped pecans
1 stick margarine, softened
3 3-oz. packages cream cheese, softened
1¼ c. confectioners' sugar
1 21-oz. can blueberry pie filling
Dream Whip or whipped cream

Combine first 3 ingredients; mix well. Press into 9 × 13-inch glass baking dish. Bake at 400 degrees for 15 minutes or until lightly browned. Cool. Combine cream cheese and confectioners' sugar in mixer bowl; beat with electric mixer until smooth. Spread over cooled crust. Cover with pie filling. Top with Dream Whip. Chill thoroughly. Yield: 15 servings.

Elrose Migl, Pres.
Xi Upsilon Epsilon X5214
Halletsville, Texas

Icebox Dessert

1 c. flour
1 stick margarine, melted
1 c. chopped nuts
1 8-oz. package cream cheese, softened
1 c. confectioners' sugar
1 lg. carton Cool Whip
2 pkg. instant butter-pecan pudding mix
3 c. milk

Combine flour, margarine and nuts; mix well. Press into 9 × 11-inch baking pan or 2 pie pans to form crust. Bake at 350 degrees for 20 minutes; cool. Combine cream cheese, confectioners' sugar and 1 cup Cool Whip; beat until smooth. Pour into cooled crust. Combine pudding mix and milk; mix until smooth. Spread over cream cheese mixture. Top with remaining Cool Whip. Chill until set. Yield: 16 servings.

Margaret Hook, Pres.
Gamma Tau No. 3816
Syracuse, Kansas

Heavenly Cheesecake

5 8-oz. packages cream cheese, softened
1 pt. sour cream
6 eggs, beaten
2 c. sugar
1 tbsp. vanilla extract
2 tbsp. cornstarch

Combine all ingredients; mix well. Pour into greased and floured 9-inch springform pan. Bake at 325 degrees for 20 minutes. Turn oven off; open door. Let cheesecake stand in oven for 1 hour. Chill until set. Yield: 16 servings.

Rose E. Kondur
Xi Gamma Omega
Mercer Island, Washington

Individual Cheesecakes

18 vanilla wafers
2 8-oz. packages cream cheese, softened
¾ c. sugar
2 eggs
1 tsp. vanilla extract
1 tbsp. lemon juice
Pie filling

Place 1 vanilla wafer in each paper-lined muffin cup. Combine remaining ingredients in mixer bowl; mix with electric mixer for 5 minutes. Pour into muffin cups. Bake at 375 degrees for 20 minutes or until lightly browned. Cool. Top with pie filling. Chill until serving time. Yield: 18 servings.

Jeanette Parsons, Pres.
Xi Beta Lambda X1011
Malvern, Ohio

Lemon Cheesecake

1 3½-oz. can flaked coconut
¼ c. chopped pecans
2 tbsp. butter, melted
2 c. cottage cheese
2 3¾-oz. packages lemon instant pudding mix
1¾ c. milk
2 tbsp. grated lemon rind
½ c. sour cream

Combine coconut, pecans and butter; mix well. Press into bottom and sides of 9-inch pie plate to form crust. Bake at 325 degrees for 15 to 20 minutes or until coconut is lightly browned. Cool. Place cottage cheese in mixer bowl; beat until smooth. Prepare pudding mix according to package directions using 1¾ cups milk. Stir in cottage cheese and lemon rind.

Pour into cooled crust. Top with sour cream. Sprinkle with additional pecans. Chill until set.

Photograph for this recipe on page 129.

Peanut Butter Cheesecake

⅓ c. butter or margarine, melted
1 c. graham cracker crumbs
¾ c. finely chopped dry-roasted peanuts
12 oz. cream cheese, softened
⅔ c. creamy peanut butter
1 14-oz. can sweetened condensed milk
⅓ c. lemon juice
1 tsp. vanilla extract
4½ oz. nondairy whipping cream

Combine butter, graham cracker crumbs and peanuts, reserving 2 tablespoons peanuts for garnish; mix well. Press into pie plate. Chill. Combine cream cheese and peanut butter; beat until fluffy. Add sweetened condensed milk; beat until smooth. Stir in lemon juice and vanilla. Fold in whipped cream. Pour into cooled crust. Top with reserved peanuts. Chill until firm.

Tamara L. Reed, V.P.
Omega
Spokane, Washington

Praline Cheesecake

1 c. graham cracker crumbs
3 tbsp. margarine
3 tbsp. sugar
3 8-oz. packages cream cheese, softened
1¼ c. (firmly packed) brown sugar
2 tbsp. flour
3 eggs
1½ tsp. vanilla extract
½ c. chopped pecans
Maple syrup

Combine crumbs, margarine and sugar; mix well. Press into 9-inch springform pan. Bake at 350 degrees for 10 minutes. Combine cream cheese, brown sugar and flour; blend well. Add eggs, one at a time, beating well after each addition. Stir in vanilla and pecans. Pour over crust. Bake at 350 degrees for 50 to 55 minutes. Loosen cake from rim of pan. Cool before removing from pan. Chill until set. Brush with maple syrup. Garnish with pecan halves.

Marjorie Kleier, Pres.
Preceptor Phi XP632
Lawrence, Kansas

Simply Yummy Cheesecake Bars

2 c. flour
1 c. chopped nuts (opt.)
⅔ c. (firmly packed) brown sugar
⅔ c. margarine, softened
½ c. jelly
2 8-oz. packages cream cheese, softened
½ c. sugar
¼ c. milk
2 eggs, slightly beaten
¼ c. lemon juice
1 tsp. vanilla extract

Combine first 4 ingredients; mix until crumbly. Reserve 1¼ cups crumb mixture. Press remaining crumb mixture into 13 × 9-inch pan. Bake at 350 degrees for 15 minutes. Spread jelly over crumb mixture. Combine cream cheese, sugar, milk, eggs, lemon juice and vanilla in mixer bowl; beat at Medium speed of electric mixer for 2 minutes. Pour over jelly. Sprinkle with reserved crumbs. Bake at 350 degrees for 35 to 40 minutes or until browned. Cool. Cut into bars. Yield: 36-48 servings.

Kathy Wicklund, City Coun. V.P.
Xi Epsilon X741
South Daytona, Florida

Mara's Chocolate Delight

1 c. flour, sifted
1 stick butter
1 c. chopped nuts
1 lg. carton Cool Whip
1 c. confectioners' sugar, sifted
1 8-oz. package cream cheese, softened
1½ c. evaporated milk
1 3-oz. package vanilla pudding mix
1 3-oz. package chocolate pudding mix

Combine flour and butter; blend until smooth. Press into shallow 3-quart casserole. Bake at 325 degrees for 20 to 25 minutes. Cool. Sprinkle nuts over crust; set aside. Combine 1 cup Cool Whip and confectioners' sugar; mix well. Add cream cheese; blend until smooth. Spread onto cooled crust. Combine pudding mixes, milk and 1¼ cups water in saucepan; blend until smooth. Cook on Low heat until thickened. Cool. Spread over creamed cheese mixture. Top with remaining Cool Whip. Decorate with chocolate curls. Chill for at least 3 hours. Cut into squares. Yield: 15-20 servings.

Margie Gourley
Preceptor Alpha Psi XP1126
Miami, Florida

Butter-Pecan Dessert

1 stick margarine
1 c. graham cracker crumbs
1 c. cracker crumbs
2 pkg. instant vanilla pudding mix
1 c. milk
1 qt. butter-pecan ice cream, softened
1 lg. carton Cool Whip
2 lg. Heath bars, crushed

Melt margarine; add crumbs, mixing well. Press into baking dish. Combine pudding mix and milk; beat well. Fold in ice cream. Spread over crumbs. Top with Cool Whip. Sprinkle with crushed candy. Chill until set. Yield: 12-15 servings.

Joy Fisher, Pres.
Laureate Kappa PL375
Wilmington, Ohio

Butterscotch Trifle

1 pkg. butterscotch pudding mix
1½ c. milk
⅔ c. shredded coconut
1¼ c. fine graham cracker crumbs
¼ c. (firmly packed) brown sugar
⅓ c. melted butter
½ c. whipping cream, whipped

Prepare pudding according to package directions, using 1½ cups milk. Stir in coconut. Cool. Combine 1 cup crumbs, brown sugar and butter; mix well. Press into 10 × 6 × 2-inch pan. Chill. Spread cooled pudding over crust. Chill until set. Cut into rectangles. Fold remaining ¼ cup crumbs into whipped cream. Serve over Trifle.

Sara F. Lowery
Preceptor Beta Kappa XP1378
Bushnell, Florida

Chocolate Delight Pie

1 c. flour
½ c. chopped nuts
1 stick butter, softened
1 c. Cool Whip
1 8-oz. package cream cheese, softened
1 c. confectioners' sugar
1 4½-oz. package instant chocolate pudding

Combine first 3 ingredients in bowl; mix until crumbly. Spread in 8 × 12-inch glass dish. Bake at 350 degrees for 15 minutes. Cool. Combine Cool Whip, cream cheese and confectioners' sugar in bowl. Spread over crust. Make pudding according to directions on package. Spread over filling. Cover with additional Cool Whip. Chill thoroughly.

Mary Ammerman, Serv. Chm.
Preceptor Delta Beta XP1393
Stafford, Texas

Chocolate Swirl Delight

1 pkg. chocolate wafers
1 3-oz. package vanilla pudding and pie filling mix
½ pt. whipping cream
1 tsp. vanilla extract
1 to 1½ c. confectioners' sugar
1 sq. semisweet chocolate, melted

Line 9-inch square pan with ½ of the chocolate wafers. Prepare pudding according to package directions. Pour over wafers. Chill. Combine whipping cream and vanilla; beat until stiff peaks form. Spread whipped cream over pudding. Top with remaining chocolate wafers. Combine confectioners' sugar and enough hot water until of spreading consistency. Spread glaze over wafers, reserving small amount. Combine reserved glaze and chocolate; mix well. Drizzle over wafers in swirl design. Refrigerate overnight. Yield: 12-16 servings.

Gloria VanDam, V.P.
Epsilon Kappa No. 6670
Guelph, Ontario, Canada

Dream Whip Squares

1 c. butter
1 c. flour
2 tbsp. confectioners' sugar
⅔ c. sugar
2 eggs
1 tsp. vanilla extract
2 sq. semisweet chocolate, melted
1 env. Dream Whip

Combine ½ cup butter, flour and confectioners' sugar; cream until smooth. Spread in 8-inch square pan. Bake at 350 degrees for 10 to 12 minutes or until lightly browned. Cool. Combine ½ cup butter, sugar, eggs, vanilla and chocolate; beat at Medium speed of electric mixer for 10 minutes. Spread over cooled crust. Prepare Dream Whip according to package directions. Spread over chocolate mixture, forming an uneven surface. Cover. Chill overnight or until firm. Decorate with finely grated chocolate, chocolate chips or chocolate shot. Yield: 12-16 servings.

Shirley Furlong, Rec. Sec.
Omicron No. 7182
Amhurst, Nova Scotia

Cranberry-Raspberry Star

1 3-oz. package raspberry gelatin
1 3-oz. package lemon gelatin
1 10-oz. package frozen raspberries
1 16-oz. can jellied cranberry-raspberry sauce
1 7-oz. bottle lime-lemon carbonated beverage

Dissolve gelatins in 1½ cups boiling water. Add raspberries, stirring to break large pieces. Mash cranberry-raspberry sauce with fork; add to gelatin mixture. Chill for 5 minutes or until partially congealed. Pour in lime-lemon beverage gradually, stirring. Pour into 6-cup mold. Chill for 6 hours or until firm. Unmold on crisp greens. Yield: 8-10 servings.

Annette Volkers
Alpha Upsilon
Nevada, Iowa

Four-Layer Dessert

1½ c. flour
1½ sticks margarine, softened
½ c. chopped nuts
8 oz. cream cheese
2 sm. cartons Cool Whip
1½ c. confectioners's sugar
1 lg. package instant pudding mix
3⅓ c. milk

Combine flour, margarine and nuts; mix until crumbly. Press into 9×13-inch pan. Bake at 375 degrees for 20 minutes. Cool. Combine cream cheese, half the Cool Whip and confectioners' sugar; beat well. Spread over cooled crust. Combine pudding mix and milk; beat until thickened. Spread over cream cheese mixture. Chill until firm. Top with remaining Cool Whip. Garnish with nuts. Yield: 12 servings.

Sue Case, Pres.
Pi Lambda No. 7878
Olney, Illinois

Ginger's Strawberry Surprise

2 c. flour
1 c. butter, softened
1 c. chopped nuts
1 8-oz. package cream cheese, softened
1 c. confectioners' sugar
1 9-oz. carton Cool Whip
1 can strawberry pie filling

Combine flour, butter and nuts; mix well. Press into 9×13-inch baking dish to form crust. Bake at 350 degrees for 20 minutes; cool. Combine cream cheese and confectioners' sugar; beat until smooth. Fold in

Cool Whip. Pour into cooled crust. Top with pie filling. Chill until set. Yield: 8-12 servings.

Ginger Tyler, Pres.
Delta Tau No. 6656
Thomaston, Georgia

Lemon Pudding Surprise

½ c. chopped pecans
1 c. flour
1 stick margarine, softened
1 8-oz. package cream cheese, softened
1 c. confectioners' sugar
1 sm. carton Cool Whip
2 sm. packages lemon pudding mix

Combine pecans, flour and margarine; mix well. Spread in glass baking dish. Bake at 425 degrees for 15 minutes. Cool. Combine cream cheese, confectioners' sugar and 1 cup Cool Whip; mix well. Spread over cooled pecan mixture. Prepare pudding mix according to package directions. Combine pudding and remaining Cool Whip; mix well. Spread over cream cheese mixture. Chill. Store in refrigerator covered with plastic wrap. Yield: 12 servings.

Lois Coulson, Pres.
Delta Eta No. 2401
Muncie, Indiana

Party Dessert

1 stick butter or margarine
1 c. flour
½ c. chopped pecans
¼ c. (firmly packed) light brown sugar
½ lb. marshmallows
½ c. milk
3 tbsp. Sherry
1 c. whipping cream, whipped

Melt butter in baking dish. Add flour, pecans and brown sugar; mix well. Bake at 300 degrees until mixture resembles coarse crumbs, stirring occasionally. Reserve ½ of crumb mixture. Spread remaining crumb mixture evenly in baking dish. Combine marshmallows, milk and Sherry in saucepan; heat just until marshmallows are melted. Fold in whipped cream. Spread over crumb mixture. Top with reserved crumb mixture. Refrigerate overnight.

Peggy S. Oliver, V.P.
Preceptor Xi
Raleigh, North Carolina

Flapper Pudding
(1930)

1 c. vanilla wafer crumbs
¾ c. butter or margarine, softened
2 c. sifted confectioners' sugar
2 eggs yolks, room temperature
2 eggs whites, room temperature
1 9-oz. can crushed pineapple, drained
½ c. chopped walnuts
½ c. shredded coconut (opt.)

Spread ½ cup crumbs in 10 × 6 × 1-inch baking dish. Cream butter in mixer bowl; add confectioners' sugar gradually, beating until light and fluffy. Add egg yolks, one at a time, beating well after each addition. Beat for 1 minute. Beat egg whites until stiff peaks form. Fold egg whites into egg yolk mixture. Fold in pineapple and walnuts. Spread over crumbs. Top with remaining ½ cup crumbs. Sprinkle with coconut. Chill until firm. Cut into squares. Garnish with cherries. Yield: 10 servings.

Emily F. Miller
Alpha Laureate PL108
West Chester, Pennsylvania

Paradise Pudding
(1950)

2 tbsp. butter, softened
¾ c. confectioners' sugar
2 egg yolks
⅔ c. graham cracker crumbs
1 c. heavy cream, whipped
1 c. drained crushed pineapple
¼ c. chopped walnuts

Cream butter and confectioners' sugar until smooth. Add eggs yolks, one at a time, beating well after each addition. Spread ⅓ cup crumbs in 9 × 5 × 3-inch dish. Cover with egg yolk mixture. Top with remaining crumbs. Combine whipped cream, pineapple and walnuts; mix well. Spread over crumbs. Chill for 4 hours. Yield: 6 servings.

Gail S. Fox, Pres.
Xi Nu X1150
Los Alamos, New Mexico

Pineapple Fluff
(1950)

Butter or margarine
1¼ c. vanilla wafer crumbs
¼ c. chopped walnuts
2½ c. crushed pineapple and syrup
1 3-oz. package lemon gelatin
4 eggs, separated

¼ tsp. salt
½ c. sugar

Melt ¼ cup butter. Add crumbs and walnuts; mix well. Reserve ¼ cup crumb mixture. Press remaining crumb mixture into 10 × 6 × 1-inch baking dish. Chill. Combine pineapple, gelatin and slightly beaten egg yolks in saucepan; cook, stirring until mixture thickens. Stir in 2 tablespoons butter. Chill until partially congealed. Beat egg whites with salt until soft peaks form. Add sugar gradually, beating until stiff peaks form. Fold into pineapple mixture. Pour over crust. Sprinkle with reserved crumbs. Chill until firm. Cut into 6 squares.

Delores Silverman, Sec.
Laureate Eta PL321
Terre Haute, Indiana

Prune Fancy

3 egg whites
½ c. sugar
1 c. apple-cranberry sauce
½ c. plumped prunes, pitted and chopped
Juice of ½ lemon
2 tsp. Angostura aromatic bitters

Beat egg whites until stiff peaks form. Add sugar gradually, beating until stiff and glossy. Fold in remaining ingredients. Spoon into serving glasses. Chill until serving time. Yield: 6 servings.

Photograph for this recipe on page 133.

Sisters' Raspberries and Cream

3 10-oz. packages frozen raspberries
1 c. sifted light brown sugar
1 tsp. ginger
1½ pt. whipping cream, whipped

Thaw raspberries; drain well. Fold brown sugar and ginger into whipped cream. Fold raspberries into whipped cream mixture. Chill for 1 hour. Stir gently before serving. Yield: 10 servings.

Sheri Perkins
Beta Rho No. 3461
Paris, Tennessee

Snowflake Pudding

1 c. sugar
1 env. unflavored gelatin
½ tsp. salt
1¼ c. milk
1 tsp. vanilla extract
1 3½-oz. can flaked coconut

2 c. heavy cream, whipped
1 10-oz. package frozen raspberries, thawed
    and crushed
1½ tsp. cornstarch
½ c. red currant jelly

Combine sugar, gelatin and salt in saucepan; mix well. Add milk; mix well. Cook over Medium heat, stirring, until sugar and gelatin are dissolved. Chill until partially congealed. Add vanilla. Fold in coconut and whipped cream. Spoon into 1½-quart mold. Chill for 4 hours or until firm. Combine raspberries and cornstarch in saucepan; mix well. Add jelly; bring to a boil. Cook until mixture is clear and slightly thickened. Strain. Chill. Unmold pudding. Serve with raspberry sauce. Yield: 8 servings.

Vicki Lee Cooper, City Coun. Rep.
Xi Tau X1171
Roseburg, Oregon

Carrot-Brownie Bars

Butter
1½ c. (firmly packed) brown sugar
2 c. flour
2 tsp. baking powder

½ tsp. salt
2 eggs
2 c. finely grated carrots
½ c. chopped walnuts
2 oz. cream cheese, softened
1 tsp. vanilla extract
1½ c. confectioners' sugar

Melt ½ cup butter in large saucepan. Add brown sugar; stir until blended. Remove from heat; cool. Sift flour, baking powder and salt onto waxed paper. Add eggs to cooled butter mixture, one at a time, beating well after each addition. Stir in flour mixture; blend well. Add carrots and walnuts; mix well. Pour into 2 greased 8×8-inch baking pans. Bake at 350 degrees for 30 minutes. Cool for 10 minutes on wire rack. Remove from pans; cool. Combine cream cheese and ⅓ cup butter in small mixer bowl; beat until smooth. Add vanilla and confectioners' sugar; beat until smooth. Spread over top. Cut into squares.

Kathleen L. Radcliffe, Rec. Sec.
Preceptor Kappa XP416
Lancaster, Pennsylvania

Angel Cookies

1 c. sugar
½ c. butter, melted
1 8-oz. package chopped dates
2 c. Rice Krispies
1 c. coconut
Confectioners' sugar

Combine sugar, butter and dates in saucepan; cook over Low heat, stirring until blended. Stir in Rice Krispies and coconut. Shape into walnut-sized balls. Roll in confectioners' sugar. Store in airtight container.

Aileen Hurley, Sec.
Tau Delta No. 10545
Decatur, Illinois

Brambles
(1930)

1 egg, slightly beaten
⅔ c. sugar
½ c. raisins
¼ c. fine cracker crumbs
¼ c. melted butter or margarine
¼ c. lemon juice
1½ c. flour
½ tsp. salt
½ c. shortening

Combine egg, sugar, raisins, crumbs, butter and lemon juice; mix well. Set aside. Combine flour and salt; mix well. Cut in shortening until of pea consistency. Sprinkle with 4 to 5 tablespoons cold water, one tablespoon at a time, tossing well after each addition. Shape dough into ball. Turn out on floured surface. Roll to ⅛-inch thickness. Cut into 3-inch rounds with floured biscuit cutter. Place rounds in 1¾-inch muffin pans. Top with 1 tablespoon raisin mixture. Bake at 400 degrees for 15 to 18 minutes. Cool slightly. Remove from pans. Yield: 24 servings.

Leecia Hillyard, Historian
Gamma Theta No. 7036
Falls City, Nebraska

Golden Carrot-Lemon Squares

1 c. melted butter, cooled
1½ c. sugar
4 eggs
1 c. mashed cooked carrots, cooled
2 c. flour
1 tsp. baking powder
1½ tsp. vanilla extract
¼ tsp. lemon extract
2½ c. confectioners' sugar

Place butter in large mixer bowl; add sugar gradually, beating well. Add eggs, one at a time, beating well after each addition. Add carrots, flour and baking powder; beat for 1 minute. Stir in vanilla and ¾ teaspoon lemon extract. Spread in greased 15 × 10 × 1-inch pan. Bake at 350 degrees for 25 minutes. Cool on rack. Combine confectioners' sugar, ¼ cup water and 1½ teaspoon lemon extract; beat until smooth. Spread over cooled mixture. Cut into squares. Yield: 10-15 servings.

Lorraine L. Kirkpatrick
Xi Eta Kappa X1963
Barstow, California

Cinnamon-Coffee Bars
(1950)

¼ c. shortening, softened
1 c. (firmly packed) brown sugar
1 egg
½ c. hot coffee
1½ c. sifted flour
1 tsp. baking powder
¼ tsp. soda
¼ tsp. salt
½ tsp. cinnamon
½ c. seedless raisins
¼ c. chopped nuts

Cream shortening, brown sugar and egg until smooth. Stir in coffee. Sift flour, baking powder, soda, salt and cinnamon together. Add to coffee mixture; mix well. Stir in raisins and nuts. Pour into greased and floured 13 × 9-inch pan. Bake at 350 degrees for 15 to 20 minutes. Frost with favorite quick cream icing. Cut into squares.

Marilyn Romsdahl, V.P.
Preceptor Iota XP244
Seattle, Washington

Caramel-Layer Chocolate Squares

1 14-oz. package light caramels
⅓ c. evaporated milk
1 pkg. German chocolate cake mix
½ c. butter, softened
1 c. chopped nuts
1 6-oz. package semisweet chocolate pieces

Combine caramels and evaporated milk in heavy saucepan; cook over Low heat until caramels are melted, stirring constantly. Keep warm. Combine cake mix, butter, nuts and 1 tablespoon water; stir with fork until crumbly but holds together. Press ½ of the dough into greased and floured 13 × 9-inch pan. Bake at 350 degrees for 6 minutes. Sprinkle chocolate pieces over baked crust. Cover with caramel mixture. Top with remaining dough. Bake at 350 degrees for 15 to 20 minutes. Cool. Cut into squares.

Christina Pitsch, Pres.
Beta Upsilon No. 4883
Appleton, Wisconsin

Chocolate Drop Cookies
(1940)

½ c. shortening, softened
1 c. (firmly packed) brown sugar
2 sq. chocolate, melted
1 egg, beaten
1 tsp. vanilla extract
½ c. milk
2 c. flour, sifted
½ tsp. soda

Cream shortening and brown sugar. Add chocolate; mix well. Combine egg, vanilla and milk; mix well. Sift flour and soda together. Add flour mixture to creamed mixture alternately with milk mixture, beating well after each addition. Drop by spoonfuls onto greased cookie sheet. Bake at 375 degrees for 10 to 12 minutes.

Dorothy Sinex, Pres.
Preceptor Delta XP199
Lafayette, Indiana

Cocoa-Bread Crumb Cookies
(1934)

¼ c. butter
½ c. sugar
¼ c. Hershey's cocoa
2 eggs
1 tsp. vanilla extract
1 c. fine bread crumbs
Jam or jelly

Cream butter, sugar and cocoa. Add eggs and vanilla; mix well. Stir in bread crumbs. Batter will be consistency of cake batter. Spread into well-greased 8 × 8 × 2-inch cake pan. Bake at 300 degrees for 20 minutes. Cut into desired shape. Spread half the cookies with jam; top with remaining cookies. Frost with favorite chocolate icing recipe. Yield: 24 servings.

Jane D. Speight, Pres.
Preceptor Rho No. 1182
Suffolk, Virginia

Chocolate Shortcake

2 c. sugar
2 c. flour
1 c. margarine
7 tbsp. cocoa
½ c. shortening
½ c. buttermilk
2 eggs
1 tsp. soda
2 tsp. vanilla extract
6 tbsp. milk
1 1-lb. package confectioners' sugar
1 c. chopped nuts

Combine sugar and flour in mixing bowl; mix well. Combine ½ cup margarine, 3½ tablespoons cocoa, 1 cup water and shortening in saucepan; bring to a boil. Add to sugar mixture; beat well. Add buttermilk, eggs, soda and 1 teaspoon vanilla; mix well. Pour into 11 × 16-inch baking pan. Bake at 400 degrees for 20 to 25 minutes. Heat ½ cup margarine, 3½ tablespoons cocoa and milk in saucepan, beating until margarine is melted and smooth. Stir in confectioners' sugar, nuts and 1 teaspoon vanilla. Spread over hot cake. Cut into squares.

Maxine I. Barr, Rec. Sec.
Xi Sigma X4882
Homer, Alaska

Fork Cookies
(1950)

1 c. brown sugar
1 c. sugar
1 c. butter or lard
3 eggs, slightly beaten
2 tsp. soda
2 tsp. cream of tartar
¼ tsp. salt
3½ c. flour
1 tsp. vanilla extract

Combine sugars, butter and eggs; cream until smooth. Add dry ingredients; mix well. Add vanilla. Shape into walnut-sized balls. Place on cookie sheet. Flatten with floured tines of fork. Bake at 350 degrees until lightly browned.

Donna Lovekamp, City Coun. Pres.
Eta Theta No. 10069
Stuarts Draft, Virginia

Filbert Confection Creams

1 c. chopped filberts
Butter
¼ c. sugar
2 tbsp. cocoa
2 tsp. vanilla extract
¼ tsp. salt
2 eggs
1¾ c. vanilla wafer crumbs
½ c. flaked coconut
½ tsp. peppermint extract
2 c. sifted confectioners' sugar
4 1-oz. squares semisweet chocolate

Spread filberts in shallow baking pan. Bake at 350 degrees for 5 to 10 minutes or until lightly browned, stirring occasionally. Combine ½ cup butter, sugar, cocoa, vanilla, salt and 1 egg in saucepan; cook over Low heat until glossy and thickened. Combine crumbs, filberts and coconut; mix well. Add to cocoa mixture, mixing well. Press into 9-inch square pan. Cream ⅓ cup butter. Add 1 egg and peppermint extract, beating well. Add confectioners' sugar; beat until smooth and creamy. Spread over chocolate base. Chill until icing is firm. Melt chocolate over hot water. Spread over icing. Cut into oblong bars. Chill until serving time.

Photograph for this recipe on page 137.

Frosted Chocolate Drop Cookies
(1958)

½ c. shortening, softened
1 c. (firmly packed) brown sugar
1 egg, beaten
2 tsp. vanilla extract
2 1-oz. squares unsweetened chocolate, melted
1⅔ c. cake flour
½ tsp. salt
½ tsp. soda
½ c. milk
½ c. chopped black walnuts
6 tbsp. cocoa
6 tbsp. hot coffee
6 tbsp. butter
3 c. confectioners' sugar

Cream shortening and brown sugar. Add egg, 1 teaspoon vanilla and chocolate; mix well. Sift dry ingredients together. Add sifted ingredients to chocolate mixture alternately with milk, mixing well after each addition. Stir in walnuts. Drop from teaspoon 2 inches apart onto greased cookie sheet. Bake at 350 degrees for 10 to 12 minutes. Combine cocoa and coffee; mix well. Add butter and 1 teaspoon vanilla; beat until smooth. Add sugar

gradually, beating until of spreading consistency. Frost warm cookies. Yield: 2½ dozen.

Ruth E. Kile
Preceptor Alpha Delta X1912
Prescott, Arizona

Holiday Orange Chip Cookies
(1930)

1 c. butter
½ c. sugar
½ c. (firmly packed) brown sugar
1 egg
2 tbsp. orange juice
1 tbsp. grated orange rind
2¾ c. flour
¼ tsp. soda
¼ tsp. salt
1 1-oz. square semisweet chocolate, grated

Cream butter and sugars. Add egg, juice and grated rind; mix well. Sift flour, soda and salt together. Add to creamed mixture; mix well. Stir in chocolate. Shape into walnut-sized balls. Wrap in waxed paper. Refrigerate for several hours or overnight. Cut into slices. Place on cookie sheet. Bake at 375 degrees for 10 to 12 minutes. Yield: 3-4 dozen.

Linda Dean, V.P.
Alpha Epsilon No. 6905
Rock Springs, Wyoming

Kiss Cookies

1 c. butter or margarine, softened
½ c. sugar
1 tsp. vanilla extract
1¾ c. flour
1 c. finely chopped walnuts
1 9-oz. package milk-chocolate kisses
Confectioners' sugar

Combine butter, sugar and vanilla in large mixer bowl; cream until smooth. Add flour and walnuts; beat at Low speed of electric mixer until well blended. Cover; chill. Place scant tablespoon of dough around each kiss, covering completely. Shape into ball. Place on cookie sheet. Bake at 375 degrees for 10 to 12 minutes or until bottom edges are browned. Cool slightly. Place on wire racks; cool. Dust with confectioners' sugar. Yield: 54 servings.

Rose L. DeRoven
Theta Mu No. 10963
New Iberia, Louisiana

Old-Fashioned Brownies
(1952)

3 c. sugar
⅔ c. cocoa
2 sticks butter, melted
6 eggs, beaten
1½ c. flour
½ tsp. salt
3 tsp. vanilla extract
1 c. chopped nuts

Combine sugar, cocoa and butter in large mixing bowl; mix well. Add eggs, stirring well. Sift flour and salt together; add to cocoa mixture, mixing well. Stir in vanilla and nuts. Pour into aluminum foil-lined 9 × 13-inch pan. Bake at 300 degrees for 50 minutes. Cut into squares.

Audrey D. Porter, Pres.
Xi Pi Xi No. 4460
Terrell, Texas

Cry-Babies
(1940)

1 c. lard
2 c. molasses
4 tbsp. sugar
2 tsp. cinnamon
1 c. milk
4 c. flour
2 tsp. soda

Cream lard, molasses, sugar and cinnamon until smooth. Add remaining ingredients, mixing well. Drop by tablespoonsful onto greased shallow pan. Bake at 350 degrees for 25 minutes.

Ann Jones
Xi Alpha Alpha No. 2262
Mantua, New Jersey

Stork Nests

2 c. coconut
¾ c. chopped nuts
3 tbsp. (heaping) cocoa
2 egg whites
1 c. sugar
¼ c. chopped raisins
1 egg

Combine all ingredints in saucepan; bring to a boil. Cook for 5 minutes. Drop from teaspoon onto cookie sheet. Bake at 300 degrees for 15 minutes.

Mary Osborne
Xi Beta Delta No. 1727
Webb City, Missouri

Peanut Goody Bars

1 12-oz. package chocolate chips
1 12-oz. package butterscotch chips
1 c. chunky-style peanut butter
1 lb. salted peanuts
1 10-oz. package unflavored miniature
   marshmallows

Combine chocolate chips, butterscotch chips and peanut butter in top of double boiler; heat over boiling water until melted, stirring constantly. Add peanuts; stir to coat well. Remove from heat. Add marshmallows, stirring only until marshmallows are partially melted. Pour into 12 × 9 × 2-inch pan. Cool. Cut into squares.

Paula Schroeder, Corr. Sec.
Xi Nu Nu X3907
Littlefield, Texas

German Squares

4 eggs
1 16-oz. package brown sugar
2½ c. flour
1 tsp. cinnamon
Dash of salt
½ tsp. cloves
1 c. chopped nuts
1 c. confectioners' sugar

Combine eggs and brown sugar; beat until smooth. Sift dry ingredients together; add to egg mixture, mixing well. Add nuts; mix well. Spread on greased 11 × 16-inch cookie sheet. Bake at 400 degrees for 15 to 25 minutes. Combine confectioners' sugar and ¼ cup cold water; mix well. Pour over hot cake. Cool. Cut in squares.

Florence Longworth, W. and M. Chm.
Xi Beta Upsilon X2058
Key West, Florida

Ginger Cookies
(1940)

1 c. sugar
2 tsp. cinnamon
1 tsp. ginger
½ tsp. salt
½ tsp. cloves
1 tsp. nutmeg
¾ c. strained bacon drippings
1 c. molasses
2 tsp. soda
2 tbsp. vinegar
3½ c. flour

Combine first 6 ingredients; mix well. Add bacon drippings; mix well. Stir in molasses. Dissolve soda in vinegar; add to batter. Stir in flour to form thick dough. Roll out on floured board. Cut as desired. Bake at 375 degrees for 15 minutes. Yield: 4-5 dozen.

Frances Schneider
Xi Delta Kappa X1947
Champaign, Illinois

Gone-With-The-Wind Cookies
(1940)

3 egg whites
1 c. sugar
1 c. coconut
1 c. finely chopped nuts
3½ c. corn flakes

Beat egg whites until soft peaks form. Add sugar gradually, beating well. Fold in coconut, nuts and corn flakes. Drop by teaspoonfuls onto greased cookie sheet. Bake at 375 degrees for 12 to 15 minutes.

Mary Louise Simpson, Corr. Sec.
Preceptor Delta XP371
Alexandria, Virginia

Holiday Fruit Drops
(1940)

½ c. lard
½ c. butter
2 c. (firmly packed) brown sugar
2 eggs
½ c. sour milk or buttermilk
3½ c. flour
1 tsp. soda
1 tsp. salt
1½ c. chopped nuts
½ c. candied green cherries
½ c. candied red cherries
1 c. chopped dates
Pecan halves

Cream lard, butter, sugar and eggs. Stir in sour milk. Sift flour, soda and salt together. Add to sour milk mixture; mixing well. Stir in nuts, cherries and dates. Chill for 1 hour. Drop by spoonfuls onto cookie sheet. Top with pecan half. Bake at 400 degrees for 8 to 10 minutes. Yield: 6 dozen.

Barbara A. Fischer, Corr. Sec.
Iota Lambda No. 6775
Crystal Spring, Pennsylvania

Holiday Squares

1½ c. sugar
1 c. butter
4 eggs
2 c. flour
1 tsp. lemon extract
1 20-oz. can pie filling
Confectioners' sugar

Combine sugar and butter in mixer bowl; cream until light and fluffy. Add eggs, one at a time, beating well after each addition. Add flour and lemon extract; mix at Low speed of electric mixer. Pour into greased 15 × 10 × 1-inch jelly roll pan. Score for 20 squares. Place 1 heaping tablespoon of pie filling on each square. Bake at 350 degrees for 45 minutes. Sift confectioners' sugar over warm cake. Cool. Cut into squares.

Ingrid E. Smith, Corr. Sec.
Xi Beta Epsilon X650
North Pekin, Illinois

Kisses

4 egg whites
1 c. sugar
1 tbsp. lemon juice

Beat egg whites until stiff peaks form. Add ⅔ cup sugar and lemon juice; mix well. Fold in remaining sugar. Drop by spoonfuls onto greased or foil-covered baking sheet. Bake at 250 degrees for 1 hour. Turn off heat. Let stand in oven until cooled. Store in airtight container. Yield: 8 servings.

Jane I. Juszli, Pres.
Preceptor Beta XP250
Claremont, New Hampshire

Honey Drops

3¼ c. sifted flour
½ tsp. salt
3 tsp. baking powder
½ tsp. nutmeg
1 c. butter, softened
1⅓ c. (firmly packed) light brown sugar
½ c. honey
1 egg, slightly beaten
1 c. seedless raisins
1 c. coarsely chopped nuts
1 tsp. vanilla extract

Sift flour, salt, baking powder and nutmeg together; set aside. Cream butter and brown sugar. Add honey and egg; beat well. Stir in sifted ingredients. Add raisins, nuts and vanilla; mix well. Chill. Drop by level tablespoonfuls onto greased baking sheet. Bake at 350 degrees for 10 to 12 minutes. Yield: 6 dozen.

Photograph for this recipe on page 139.

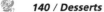

Icebox Cookies
(1930)

½ lb. butter, softened
½ c. (firmly packed) brown sugar
½ c. sugar
2 eggs, slightly beaten
1 tsp. cinnamon
1 tsp. vanilla extract
3 c. flour
½ tsp. soda
1 c. chopped walnuts

Cream butter. Add sugars, eggs, cinnamon, vanilla, flour and soda, mixing well after each addition. Stir in walnuts. Chill for 3 hours. Cut into slices. Place on cookies sheet. Bake at 400 degrees for 8 to 10 minutes. Yield: 5 dozen.

Eleanor V. Harris, Tel. Chm.
Epsilon Nu No. 8262
Centerville, Virginia

Iced Peanut Squares

½ c. corn syrup
½ c. (firmly packed) brown sugar
1 c. peanut butter
3 c. corn flakes or Rice Krispies
1 tsp. vanilla extract

Combine corn syrup and brown sugar in large saucepan over Medium heat; stir until blended. Remove from heat. Add peanut butter; mix well. Stir in vanilla. Add corn flakes; mix well. Press into 8 × 8-inch pan. Chill. Frost with favorite white icing recipe. Cut into squares. Keep refrigerated. Yield: 16 servings.

Elizabeth Tappen, Pres.
Tau No. 10088
Belleville, Ontario, Canada

Lemon Squares
(1955)

1 c. butter, softened
½ c. confectioners' sugar
Flour
4 eggs, slightly beaten
Juice and grated rind of 2 lemons
2 c. sugar

Combine butter, confectioners' sugar and 2 cups sifted flour; mix well. Press into 9 × 13-inch baking pan to form crust. Bake at 350 degrees for 20 minutes. Combine eggs, lemon juice and rind, sugar and 4 tablespoons flour; mix well. Pour into crust. Sprinkle with additional confectioners' sugar. Bake

at 350 degrees for 20 to 25 minutes. Cool. Cut into squares. Yield: 24 servings.

Delores A. Brown, Treas.
Laureate Zeta PL489
Martinsburg, West Virginia

Noels
(1955)

2 tbsp. butter
2 eggs
1 c. (firmly packed) brown sugar
5 tbsp. flour
⅛ tsp. soda
1 tsp. vanilla extract
1 c. chopped nuts
Confectioners' sugar

Melt butter in 9-inch square pan. Remove from heat. Beat eggs slightly. Combine dry ingredients; stir into eggs. Stir in vanilla and nuts. Pour over melted butter; do not stir. Bake at 350 degrees for 20 minutes. Invert on rack. Dust with confectioners' sugar. Cut into bars.

Sandra Bell, Pres.
Xi Beta Sigma X1120
Shelby, Ohio

Oatmeal-Spice Cookies
(1940)

1 c. raisins
1 c. shortening
1 c. sugar
3 eggs, beaten
2 c. flour
½ tsp. salt
½ tsp. soda
2 tsp. cinnamon
½ tsp. allspice
½ tsp. cloves
2 c. quick-cooking oatmeal
½ c. chopped nuts
1 12-oz. package chocolate chips

Cover raisins with boiling water; let stand for 30 minutes. Drain, reserving 6 tablespoons liquid. Cream shortening and sugar. Add eggs; beat well. Sift flour, salt, soda, cinnamon, allspice and cloves together. Add oatmeal; mix well. Add flour mixture to creamed mixture alternately with reserved liquid, mixing well after each addition. Add raisins, nuts and chocolate chips; mix well. Drop by spoonfuls onto greased cookie sheet. Bake at 400 degrees for 10 to 12 minutes. Yield: 4-6 dozen.

Susan E. Andrus
Xi Omega X499
Oakland, California

Lace Cookies

½ c. butter or margarine, melted
½ c. sugar
⅓ c. sifted flour
¼ tsp. salt
1 c. quick-cooking oats
2 tbsp. milk

Combine all ingredients in order listed; mix well. Drop by scant teaspoonfuls, 3 inches apart, onto greased and floured cookie sheets. Spread thinly with spatula. Bake at 375 degrees for 5 to 7 minutes or until edges are browned. Remove from oven. Let stand for 1 minute. Remove from cookie sheets with wide spatula. Cool.

Photograph for this recipe on page 141.

Raisin Mumbles
(1940)

2½ c. raisins
½ c. sugar
2 tbsp. cornstarch
3 tbsp. lemon juice
¾ c. margarine, softened
1 c. (firmly packed) brown sugar
1¾ c. sifted flour
½ tsp. salt
¼ tsp. soda
1½ c. quick-cooking oats

Combine raisins, sugar, cornstarch, lemon juice and ¾ cup water in saucepan; cook until thickened, stirring constantly. Cream margarine and brown sugar until smooth. Add flour, salt and soda; mix well. Add oats, mixing well. Press ½ of the oat mixture into greased 9 × 13 × 2-inch pan. Spread with raisin mixture. Top with remaining oat mixture. Bake at 400 degrees for 20 to 30 minutes. Cool. Cut into squares. Yield: 15-20 servings.

Pamela Burg, Corr. Sec.
Eta Gamma No. 4808
Holland, Michigan

Saucy Oat Cakes
(1954)

1¾ c. quick-cooking oats
1½ c. flour
1 tsp. salt
1 tsp. baking powder
1 tsp. cinnamon
½ tsp. nutmeg
½ tsp. soda
½ c. butter or margarine, softened
1 c. (firmly packed) brown sugar
½ c. sugar
1 egg, slightly beaten
¾ c. applesauce
1 c. chocolate bits
1 c. raisins
1 c. chopped nuts

Combine first 7 ingredients; mix well. Combine butter and sugars in large mixing bowl; cream until smooth. Add dry ingredients to creamed mixture alternately with applesauce; mix well. Stir in remaining ingredients. Drop by level tablespoonfuls onto greased cookie sheet. Bake at 375 degrees for 15 minutes.

Susan Laffredo, City Coun. V.P.
Theta Beta No. 5423
Norristown, Pennsylvania

Peanut Butter Cookies
(1950)

½ c. shortening, softened
½ c. (firmly packed) brown sugar
½ c. sugar
1 egg
½ c. crunchy peanut butter
1 c. flour
½ tsp. soda
¼ tsp. salt
1 tsp. vanilla extract

Combine shortening, sugars, egg, peanut butter and 1 tablespoon water; mix well. Sift flour, soda and salt together. Add sifted ingredients to peanut butter mixture; mix well. Stir in vanilla. Drop by teaspoonfuls onto greased cookie sheet. Bake at 250 degrees for 15 to 20 minutes. Yield: 3 dozen.

Carnell Waymack, Pres.
Preceptor Lambda XP1236
Pine Bluff, Arkansas

Perfect Raisin Drop Cookies
(1930)

2 c. raisins
1 tsp. soda
2 c. sugar
1 c. shortening
1 tsp. vanilla extract
3 eggs, beaten
4 c. flour
1 tsp. baking powder
½ tsp. salt
1 tsp. cinnamon
¼ tsp. nutmeg
1 c. chopped walnuts

Boil raisins in 1 cup water for 5 minutes. Cool. Add soda; let stand for 5 minutes. Drain, reserving liquid. Cream sugar and shortening until light and fluffy. Add vanilla, eggs and reserved liquid; mix well. Sift flour, baking powder, salt, cinnamon and nutmeg together. Add to creamed mixture; mix well. Stir in walnuts and raisins. Drop from teaspoon onto greased baking sheet. Bake at 375 degrees for 13 minutes. Store in airtight container. Yield: 9 dozen.

Elizabeth A. Shea, Pres.
Xi Theta Eta No. 4284
Palm Bay, Florida

Pineapple-Coconut Delight

7/5/82
Good

1 c. coconut
1 14-oz. can crushed pineapple
½ c. shortening, softened
¾ c. sugar
2 eggs, slightly beaten
2 c. flour
1 tsp. baking powder
½ tsp. soda
½ tsp. salt

Combine coconut and ¾ cup pineapple; mix well. Set aside. Cream shortening, sugar and eggs. Sift flour, baking powder, soda and salt together. Add to creamed mixture; mix well. Stir in remaining pineapple. Pour into 15 × 10 × 1-inch jelly roll pan. Sprinkle with coconut mixture. Bake at 375 degrees for 25 minutes.

Patricia A. Pavel, V.P.
Lambda Omega No. 10674
Carmichaels, Pennsylvania

Prague Tea Squares
(1940)

¾ c. butter, softened
1 c. sugar

1 egg, slightly beaten
1 tsp. vanilla extract
2 c. flour
¼ tsp. nutmeg
1 c. finely chopped almonds
Raspberry or strawberry jam
Confectioners' sugar

Combine butter, sugar, egg and vanilla in mixer bowl; beat until creamy. Add flour, nutmeg and almonds; blend well. Spread half the batter in 9 × 9-inch baking pan. Cover with jam. Cover with remaining batter; press down with fork. Bake at 350 degrees for 35 minutes. Sprinkle with sifted confectioners' sugar. Cut into squares. Yield: 36 servings.

Georgina L. Montrose
Honorary Member
Windsor, Ontario, Canada

Pumpkin Bars

4 eggs
1⅔ c. sugar
1 c. oil
1 16-oz. can pumpkin, drained
2 c. flour
1 tsp. salt
2 tsp. baking powder
2 tsp. cinnamon
1 tsp. soda
1 3-oz. package cream cheese, softened
½ c. butter, softened
1 tsp. vanilla extract
2 c. confectioners' sugar

Combine eggs, sugar, oil and pumpkin; beat until light. Combine next five ingredients; mix well. Stir into pumpkin mixture. Pour into 15 × 10 × 1-inch baking pan. Bake at 350 degrees for 25 to 30 minutes. Cool. Combine cream cheese, butter, vanilla and confectioners' sugar; beat until smooth. Spread over cooled mixture. Cut into bars.

Barbara Borton, V.P.
Gamma Mu No. 4213
Kennewick, Washington

Raspberry Macaroons
(1935)

3 egg whites
⅛ tsp. salt
3½ tbsp. raspberry gelatin
¾ c. sugar
1 c. chocolate chips

Beat egg whites with salt until foamy. Combine gelatin and sugar; add to egg whites gradually,

beating until stiff peaks form. Fold in chocolate chips. Drop by teaspoonfuls onto unrecycled brown paper. Bake at 250 degrees for 25 minutes. Turn oven off. Let stand for 30 minutes in oven. Yield: 30 servings.

Marie Woodyard
Laureate Alpha PL124
Kansas City, Missouri

Grandma's Sugar Cookies
(1930)

1 c. margarine, softened
1 c. sugar
2 eggs, slightly beaten
½ tsp. nutmeg
½ tsp. soda
½ tsp. salt
1 tsp. cream of tartar
2½ to 3 c. flour

Cream margarine until fluffy. Add sugar; beat until smooth. Add eggs, nutmeg, soda, salt and cream of tartar; beat well. Add flour gradually, beating until smooth. Roll on floured surface; cut as desired. Place on baking sheet. Bake at 350 degrees for 5 to 8 minutes or until browned. Yield: 3-4 dozen.

Nora Gross, Pres.
Gamma No. 4467
St. John's, Newfoundland, Canada

Old-Fashioned Sugar Cookies
(1930)

3 c. flour
1½ tsp. baking powder
½ tsp. salt
1 c. sugar
1 c. butter, softened
1 egg, slightly beaten
3 tbsp. cream or half and half
1 tsp. vanilla extract

Sift dry ingredients together. Cut in butter. Add remaining ingredients; blend well. Chill. Roll out on floured board or between waxed paper. Cut as desired. Place on cookie sheet. Bake at 400 degrees for 5 to 8 minutes. Yield: 5 dozen.

Gail P. Matthews, Soc. Chm.
Eta No. 1172
Montgomery, Alabama

Watergate Cookies

1 pkg. white cake mix
1 3-oz. package instant pistachio pudding mix
½ c. oil
3 tbsp. 7-Up
2 eggs
½ c. chopped nuts
½ c. coconut

Combine all ingredients; mix well. Drop by tea-spoonfuls 2 inches apart on greased baking sheet. Bake at 350 degrees for 10 to 12 minutes.

Sue Schmidt, Pres.
Xi Epsilon Alpha X4626
Baldwin City, Kansas

Scottish Shortbread
(1940)

1 c. confectioners' sugar
3 c. flour
1 c. cornstarch
1 lb. butter, softened

Sift dry ingredients together. Blend in butter. Knead until mixture holds together. Roll with rolling pin until ¼ inch thick. Cut to desired shape. Place on ungreased baking sheet. Bake at 350 degrees for 13 minutes.

Judy Wright, Pres.
Preceptor Beta Pi XP1916
Peterborough, Ontario, Canada

Coffee Ice Cream Pie

1¾ oz. slivered almonds
½ c. butter or margarine, melted
1 c. sugar
1 c. coconut
2½ c. crushed Rice Chex
½ gal. ice cream, softened

Brown almonds in butter in large saucepan. Add sugar, coconut and Rice Chex. Mix well, stirring, until sugar dissolves. Cool. Press half of mixture in 9 × 13-inch pan. Spread ice cream over mixture. Sprinkle remaining Rice Chex mixture over ice cream. Press in. Freeze. Serve with a small amount of chocolate sauce. Yield: 10 to 12 servings.

Marjorie A. Bailey
Preceptor Delta XP1385
Kittery Point, Maine

Cranberry Ice

2 c. cranberries
2 c. sugar
Juice of 2 oranges
Juice of 1 lemon

Cook cranberries in 2 cups water until skins pop. Strain. Add sugar, stirring until sugar is dissolved. Add juices; mix well. Pour into 2 refrigerator trays. Freeze. Spoon into sherbet glasses. Yield: 12-16 servings.

Darlene Nolan, Treas.
Alpha Rho XP1721
Perry, Iowa

Frozen Lemon Pie
(1948)

1½ to 2 c. vanilla wafers crumbs
3 eggs, separated
½ c. plus 1 tbsp. sugar
Grated rind and juice of 1 lemon
1 c. whipping cream, chilled

Press crumbs into buttered 8 × 8-inch pan. Combine egg yolks and ½ cup sugar in top of double boiler. Heat over boiling water, beating with rotary beater, for 3 minutes or until thick. Add rind and lemon juice. Cool. Beat egg whites and 1 tablespoon sugar in large bowl until stiff. Beat whipping cream in large bowl until stiff. Fold in egg whites and lemon mixture. Spread over crust. Sprinkle with additional vanilla wafer crumbs. Freeze until firm. Yield: 9 servings.

Mary Susan Lyons, Corr. Sec.
Xi Alpha Sigma X983
Shippensburg, Pennsylvania

Frozen Pumpkin Pie

1 qt. vanilla ice cream, softened
1 9-in. baked pie shell, chilled
1 c. canned pumpkin
¾ c. sugar
¾ tsp. pumpkin pie spice
½ tsp. salt
1 c. whipping cream, whipped
½ c. chopped walnuts

Spoon ice cream evenly into pie shell. Freeze until firm. Combine pumpkin, sugar, spice and salt; mix well. Fold in whipped cream. Spread over ice cream. Top with walnuts. Freeze until firm. Yield: 6 servings.

Mildred R. Burns, Pres.
Laureate Epsilon PL247
Alamosa, California

Frozen Strawberry Fluff

1 stick margarine, softened
1 c. flour
½ c. chopped nuts
1 10-oz. package frozen strawberries, thawed
1 tbsp. lemon juice
1 c. sugar
2 egg whites
1 pkg. Dream Whip

Combine margarine, flour and nuts; mix well. Spread on cookie sheet. Bake at 350 degrees for 15 minutes, stirring every 5 minutes. Spoon into 9 × 13-inch glass casserole or two 8-inch square casseroles. Combine strawberries, lemon juice, sugar and egg whites in large mixer bowl; beat on High speed of electric mixer for 20 minutes. Prepare Dream Whip according to package directions; fold into strawberry mixture. Spread over crumb mixture. Cover with foil. Freeze until firm. Cut into squares.

Rosemary Hohman, V.P.
Xi Epsilon Psi X2749
Brookport, Illinois

Fudge Sundae Pie

1 c. evaporated milk
1 c. chocolate chips
1 c. miniature marshmallows
¼ tsp. salt
Vanilla wafers
1 qt. vanilla ice cream

Combine first 4 ingredients in heavy saucepan. Cook over Medium heat, stirring, until chocolate and marshmallows melt and mixture thickens. Remove from heat. Cool. Line bottom and sides of 9-inch pie pan or 9 × 13-inch pan with vanilla wafers. Spoon half of ice cream over wafers. Cover with half of chocolate mixture. Repeat layers. Garnish with pecan halves. Freeze for 3 to 5 hours.

Dorothy Brewer, Pres.
Preceptor Zeta Alpha XP1898
Waco, Texas

Grasshopper Pie

1½ c. chocolate wafer crumbs
6 tbsp. butter or margarine, melted
6½ c. miniature marshmallows
¼ c. milk
¼ c. green Creme de Menthe
2 tbsp. white Creme de Cacao
2 c. whipping cream, whipped

Combine crumbs and butter in bowl; mix well. Spread evenly in 9-inch pie pan. Chill for 1 hour.

Combine marshmallows and milk in large saucepan. Cook over Low heat, stirring constantly, until marshmallows melt. Remove from heat. Cool, stirring every 5 minutes. Combine Creme de Menthe and Creme de Cacao. Stir into marshmallow mixture. Fold in whipping cream. Pour into crust. Freeze several hours or overnight. Garnish with chocolate curls.

Pennie Smith, Pres.
Delta Psi No. 10676
Palisade, Nebraska

Peanut Butter Pie

1 4-oz. package cream cheese
1 c. confectioners' sugar
½ c. peanut butter
½ c. milk
1 9-oz. carton frozen nondairy whipped cream, softened
1 9-in. graham cracker crust

Beat cream cheese until fluffy. Stir in confectioners' sugar and peanut butter. Add milk; mix well. Fold in whipped cream. Pour into graham cracker crust. Freeze. Yield: 8 servings.

Nancy Messing, Pres.
Preceptor Alpha Iota X917
Clearwater, Florida

Pistachio Ice Cream Pie

32 Ritz crackers, crushed
½ stick butter, melted
1 qt. vanilla ice cream
1½ c. milk
2 3-oz. packages instant pistachio pudding mix
6 oz. Cool Whip
1 lg. Heath bar, crushed

Combine cracker crumbs and butter; mix well. Press into 8 × 8-inch baking pan. Bake at 300 degrees for 10 minutes. Cool. Combine ice cream, milk and pudding mix; blend until smooth. Pour over cooled crust. Freeze until firm. Spread Cool Whip over ice cream mixture. Top with crushed Heath bar. Freeze until firm. Let stand at room temperature for 30 minutes before serving.

Suzen Fyffe, Pres.
Xi Rho Epsilon X4659
Arlington, Texas

Refreshing Frozen Dessert

1 20-oz. can crushed pineapple, drained
½ c. maraschino cherries
½ c. chopped nuts
1 c. whipping cream, whipped
1 c. sour cream
1 tbsp. lemon juice
¾ c. sugar
⅛ tsp. salt
3 lg. bananas, chopped

Combine pineapple, cherries and nuts; mix well. Combine whipped cream, sour cream, lemon juice, sugar and salt; mix well. Add to pineapple mixture; mix well. Add bananas. Freeze for 6 to 8 hours. Serve in paper or plastic cups. Yield: 16 servings.

Lois A. Carlson
Laureate Gamma PL167
Spencer, Iowa

Lotus Ice Cream

2 lemons
Juice of 4 lemons
3 c. sugar
6 c. light cream
3 c. milk

Cut ends from lemons; discard. Cut into very thin slices. Remove seeds; cut lemon slices in half. Combine lemon juice and sugar; mix well. Add lemon slices; cover. Refrigerate overnight. Combine cream and milk in ice cream freezer container; refrigerate for 10 to 15 minutes. Add lemon mixture to chilled mixture; mix well. Freeze according to freezer directions.

Bettye H. Donley, Pres.
Xi Theta Zeta X4262
Tyndall AFB, Florida

Orange-Apricot Ice Cream
(1945)

12 lg. marshmallows
1 c. orange juice
1 c. apricot syrup
⅛ tsp. salt
¾ c. mashed apricots
1½ c. whipping cream
¼ c. sugar

Combine marshmallows, orange juice, apricot syrup and salt in saucepan. Cook over Low heat until marshmallows are melted, stirring. Add apricots; cool. Pour into refrigerator trays. Freeze until slightly thickened. Whip cream until thick. Add sugar; beat until soft peaks form. Fold into apricot mixture. Pour into refrigerator trays. Freeze until firm. Yield: 4-6 servings.

Frances S. Passey, Pres.
Preceptor Mu X1693
Taber, Alberta, Canada

Apple Crisp
(1948)

8 to 10 apples, peeled, cored and diced
1 c. raisins
1 c. sugar
½ tsp. cinnamon
⅛ tsp. nutmeg
¼ tsp. allspice
1 c. flour
1 stick butter, softened
¼ c. (firmly packed) brown sugar
1 c. chopped nuts (opt.)

Place apples and raisins in buttered 9 × 13-inch pan. Combine sugar and spices; mix well. Sprinkle over apples. Combine flour, butter and brown sugar; blend until smooth. Spread over apples. Top with nuts. Bake at 350 degrees for 35 to 40 minutes. Serve with cream, whipped cream or ice cream. Yield: 15 servings.

Sherry K. Moore, Corr. Sec.
Xi Gamma Psi X3441
Bloomfield Hills, Michigan

Apple Dump

2 eggs, beaten
1 c. oil
2 c. sugar
2 c. flour
2 tsp. soda
1 tsp. salt
1 c. raisins
1 c. nuts
1 tsp. vanilla extract
1 can apple pie filling

Combine first 9 ingredients in large mixer bowl; mix well. Add pie filling. Pour into greased and floured 9 × 13-inch pan. Bake at 350 degrees for 40 to 45 minutes.

Patricia G. Arthaud
Xi Alpha Omega X1650
Hazleton, Iowa

Apple Dumplings
(1936)

3 c. sifted flour
1½ tsp. salt
1 c. shortening
4 c. chopped apples
2 tsp. cinnamon
3 c. sugar
1 stick margarine

Combine flour and salt. Cut in half the shortening with pastry blender until mixture resembles coarse meal. Cut in remaining shortening until of pea consistency. Sprinkle with 6 tablespoons water, one tablespoon at a time, mixing with fork after each addition. Shape dough into ball. Divide dough into 3 parts. Roll to ⅛-inch thickness. Cut into 10-inch squares. Fill each square with 1 cup apples. Sprinkle with ½ teaspoon cinnamon. Bring opposite points of pastry over apples; overlap. Moisten; seal. Combine sugar, margarine and 3 cups water in large baking pan; bring to a boil. Boil for 3 minutes. Drop dumplings into hot syrup. Bake at 425 degrees for 40 minutes or until crust is browned. Serve with hot syrup. Yield: 4 servings.

Maude Carrier, Pres.
Xi Alpha Omicron No. 2385
Enid, Oklahoma

Kay's Apple Crisp
(1950)

6 lg. tart apples, peeled and sliced
Juice of 1 lemon
½ c. sugar
½ tsp. cinnamon
¾ c. flour
½ c. sugar
¼ tsp. salt
6 tbsp. margarine, softened

Place apples in 8 × 8 × 2-inch baking dish. Add lemon juice. Combine sugar and cinnamon; mix well. Sprinkle over apples. Combine flour, sugar, salt and margarine; mix well. Spread over apples. Bake at 350 degrees for 35 to 45 minutes. Yield: 4-6 servings.

Kay McClintock, V.P.
Kappa Tau No. 9849
Louisburg, Kansas

Blueberry Delight

1 c. flour
1 stick margarine, softened
½ c. chopped pecans
1 c. confectioners' sugar

1 8-oz. package cream cheese
1 9-oz. carton Cool Whip
2 20-oz. cans blueberry pie filling

Combine flour, margarine and pecans; mix until crumbly. Press into 9 × 13-inch pan to form crust. Bake at 350 degrees for 15 minutes. Cool. Combine confectioners' sugar and cream cheese; beat until smooth. Fold in 1 cup Cool Whip. Spread over crust. Spread with pie filling. Top with remaining Cool Whip. Chill until set. Yield: 15 servings.

Sherri Ousley, V.P.
Xi Gamma Sigma X2664
Elwood, Indiana

Cherry Pudding
(1930)

1 egg
1 c. milk
½ tsp. salt
1 tbsp. melted butter
1½ c. flour
1 tsp. baking powder
2 c. unsweetened cherries
½ c. sugar

Combine first 6 ingredients in order listed; mix well. Pour into greased baking pan. Press cherries into batter. Sprinkle with sugar. Bake at 350 degrees for 30 minutes. Serve hot with milk or cream.

Veronica Ehrhart, Pres.
Xi Zeta Iota X4684
Dallastown, Pennsylvania

Cherry Torte

1¼ c. flour
2 tbsp. sugar
¼ lb. butter or margarine, softened
2 pkg. vanilla pudding mix
1 can cherry pie filling
Cool Whip or whipped cream

Combine flour and sugar; mix well. Cut in butter. Press into 8 × 12-inch pan. Bake at 350 degrees for 25 minutes. Prepare pudding according to package directions; cool slightly. Spread over baked crust. Chill until firm. Cover with cherry pie filling. Top with Cool Whip. Yield. 8 servings.

Cindy Acker, Pres.
Epsilon Eta No. 7505
Smyrna, Georgia

Golden Peach Cobbler
(1958)

2½ c. sugar
3 tbsp. margarine, softened
3 tsp. baking powder
½ tsp. salt
1½ c. flour
¾ c. milk
1 tsp. vanilla extract
2 c. sliced peaches

Cream 1½ cups sugar and margarine until smooth. Sift dry ingredients together. Add to creamed mixture alternately with milk, mixing well after each addition. Stir in vanilla. Pour into large iron skillet. Sprinkle peaches with 1 cup sugar. Spoon peaches onto batter. Cover with 1½ cups hot water. Bake at 375 degrees for 45 minutes or until browned. Yield: 6-8 servings.

Sandra K. Vaught, Pres.
Epsilon Pi No. 9763
Jacksonville, Arkansas

Peach Cobbler
(1930)

6 peach halves
1 c. sugar
¼ c. butter
1 c. milk
2 eggs, beaten
1 c. sifted flour
½ tsp. salt
½ tsp. cinnamon
2 tsp. baking powder

Place peaches in buttered casserole. Sprinkle with ½ of the sugar. Cream remaining sugar and butter until smooth. Add eggs; beat well. Add remaining ingredients; beat until smooth. Pour over peaches. Bake at 375 degrees for 30 minutes. Serve with cream. Yield: 6 servings.

Margaret W. Stocks, Rec. Sec.
Epsilon Nu No. 6303
Moses Lake, Washington

Peach Dumplings

1 recipe pie pastry
6 peaches, peeled and pitted
Sugar or brown sugar
1 c. confectioners' sugar
½ c. butter
3 tbsp. cream
5 tbsp. honey

Prepare pie pastry. Roll out; cut into squares. Sprinkle peaches with sugar. Place peaches in pastry squares; seal. Place in shallow cake pan. Bake at 400 degrees for 40 minutes. Heat remaining ingredients in top of double boiler. Serve over dumplings. Yield: 6 servings.

Julia Ingomells
Delta Xi No. 2853
Stanley, Iowa

Pineapple-Pear Crisp

½ c. butter or margarine, melted
½ c. (firmly packed) light brown sugar
1⅔ c. toasted whole wheat bread crumbs
4½ tsp. cornstarch
1 tbsp. sugar
1½ c. pineapple juice
1 1-lb. 13-oz. can pears, drained and sliced
Whipped Cream

Combine butter and brown sugar; mix well. Stir in bread crumbs; set aside. Combine cornstarch and sugar in saucepan; mix well. Stir in pineapple juice. Bring to a boil; boil for 1 minute, stirring constantly. Remove from heat. Stir in pears gradually. Press all but ⅓ cup bread crumb mixture into 1½-quart rectangular baking dish to form crust. Pour pear mixture over crust. Sprinkle with remaining crumb mixture. Bake at 425 degrees for 5 minutes or until top is browned. Chill until serving time. Serve with whipped cream. Yield: 6-8 servings.

Photograph for this recipe on page 149.

Pineapple Rice
(1935)

1 c. rice
1 tsp. salt
1 20-oz. can crushed pineapple, drained
4 tbsp. sugar
1 tsp. vanilla extract
1 pt. heavy cream, whipped

Place rice in 2 quarts salted boiling water; cook for 10 to 15 minutes. Drain; cool. Add pineapple; mix well. Add sugar and vanilla; mix well. Fold whipped cream into rice mixture. Yield: 8-10 servings.

Linda M. Brumski, Pres.
Xi Alpha Alpha X538
Carlisle, Pennsylvania

Maple-Nut Torte

3 egg whites
Sugar
1 tsp. vanilla extract
14 soda crackers, crushed
½ tsp. baking powder
1 c. chopped walnuts
1 c. heavy cream
1 tsp. maple flavoring

Beat egg whites until foamy. Add 1 cup sugar gradually; beat until stiff peaks form. Stir in vanilla. Fold in cracker crumbs, baking powder and walnuts. Pour into buttered 8-inch square baking dish. Bake at 350 degrees for 30 minutes; cool. Whip cream until thickened. Add 4 to 5 teaspoons sugar and maple flavoring; beat until stiff peaks form. Spread over cooled torte. Refrigerate for 4 hours. Yield: 9 servings.

Tommye F. Adams, Pres.
Xi Theta Rho X2276
Needles, California

Pavlova
(1930)

4 egg whites
⅛ tsp. cream of tartar
1 c. sugar
½ tsp. vanilla extract
2 tsp. vinegar
2 tsp. cornstarch
1 c. whipped cream
Sliced peaches, strawberries or kiwi fruit

Combine egg whites and cream of tartar; beat until stiff peaks form. Add half the sugar; beat well. Fold in remaining sugar. Fold in next 3 ingredients and 1 tablespoon water one at a time in order listed. Mound in 9-inch circle on aluminum foil-lined cookie sheet. Bake at 300 degrees for 2 hours. Invert; cool. Fill depression with whipped cream. Top with fruit. Yield: 8 servings.

Margaret E. Poole, Serv. Chm.
Preceptor Alpha XP169
Kaneohe, Hawaii

Rhubarb Dessert
(1950)

3 c. bread cubes
4 c. diced rhubarb
1½ c. sugar
¼ c. melted butter
½ tsp. cinnamon
½ tsp. nutmeg

Combine all ingredients; mix well. Pour into greased 9-inch square baking dish; cover. Bake at 375 degrees for 30 minutes. Bake, uncovered, for 10 minutes longer. Yield: 9 servings.

Gwen Beck, Rec. Sec.
Xi Chi X783
Jefferson City, Missouri

Applesauce Custard Pie
(1950)

1½ c. applesauce
¾ c. sugar
⅛ tsp. nutmeg
½ c. milk
2 eggs, beaten
½ tsp. vanilla
1 baked 8-in. pie shell

Combine first 6 ingredients. Pour into pie shell. Bake at 350 degrees for 30 to 40 minutes or until firm.

Paula Sebesta
Preceptor Eta No. 1189
Salt Lake City, Utah

Glazed Apricot-Cheese Pie

1 17-oz. can apricot halves
1 baked 9-in. pie shell
1 8-oz. package cream cheese, softened
2 c. cold milk
1 lg. package vanilla instant pudding and pie filling mix
3 maraschino cherry halves
2 tbsp. corn syrup

Drain apricots, reserving ⅓ cup juice. Set aside 6 apricot halves for garnish. Arrange remaining apricot halves in pie shell. Beat cream cheese until smooth. Add 1 cup milk gradually, blending until smooth. Add 1 cup milk, reserved juice and pie filling mix; beat at Low speed of electric mixer for 1 minute or until smooth. Pour over apricots. Chill for 5 minutes. Cut reserved apricots into thirds. Arrange on pie to resemble 3 flowers. Place cherry half in center of each flower. Brush fruit with corn syrup. Chill for 3 hours.

Photograph for this recipe on page 151.

Banana Paradise Pie

4 c. sliced bananas
¼ c. pineapple juice
2 tbsp. lemon juice
1½ tsp. grated lemon rind
¼ c. sugar
Cinnamon
1 unbaked 8-in. pie pastry
1 tsp. cornstarch
⅓ c. chopped macadamia nuts
¾ c. flour
¾ c. (firmly packed) brown sugar
6 tbsp. butter

Combine bananas, pineapple juice and lemon juice; let stand for 20 minutes. Drain, reserving juices. Sprinkle bananas with lemon rind, sugar and ½ teaspoon cinnamon. Place in pastry-lined pie plate. Place reserved juices in saucepan; cook until heated through. Add cornstarch, stirring until thickened. Pour over bananas. Combine macadamia nuts, flour, brown sugar, ¾ teaspoon cinnamon and butter; cut with two knives or pastry blender until crumbly. Sprinkle over bananas. Bake at 400 degrees for 20 minutes or until crust is browned. Yield: 6-8 servings.

Melanie Drennon, Corr. Sec.
Omicron Chi No. 9442
Arnold, Missouri

Buttermilk Pie
(1943)

2 c. sugar
4 tbsp. flour
4 eggs, beaten
1 c. buttermilk
2 tsp. vanilla extract
4 tbsp. melted butter
1 unbaked 9-in. pie crust.

Combine sugar and flour in mixer bowl; mix well. Add eggs; mix well. Add buttermilk gradually, stirring constantly. Add vanilla and butter; mix well. Pour into pie crust. Bake at 425 degrees for 10 minutes. Reduce heat to 350 degrees. Bake for 50 to 60 minutes.

Carolyn S. Henderson, Corr. Sec.
Preceptor Nu XP387
Salina, Kansas

Bicentennial Cherry Pie

3 1-lb. cans tart red cherries, packed in water
1½ c. sugar
⅓ c. cornstarch
⅛ tsp. salt

1 tbsp. grated orange peel
½ tsp. cinnamon
½ tsp. red food coloring
¼ c. butter or margarine
2 unbaked 9-in. pie shells

Drain cherries, reserving 1½ cups liquid. Combine sugar, cornstarch and salt in medium saucepan. Stir in cherry liquid. Bring to a boil, stirring until mixture thickens. Boil for 1 minute, stirring constantly. Stir in orange peel, cinnamon, food coloring, butter and cherries. Cover. Chill for 30 minutes. Pour into pie shells. Bake at 425 degrees for 35 to 40 minutes. Cool. Chill. Garnish with Cool Whip.

Shirley L. Grassle, Pres.
Xi Gamma Omicron X1480
Park Forest, Illinois

Easy Pink Salad Pie

1 21-oz. can cherry pie filling
1 8-oz. carton Cool Whip
1 15¼-oz. can crushed pineapple, drained
1 11-oz. can mandarin oranges, drained
2 c. miniature marshmallows

1 c. chopped pecans
2 baked 9-in. pie shells, cooled

Combine first 4 ingredients in large bowl; mix well. Add marshmallows and pecans; mix. Pour into pie shells. Chill for 2 hours. Yield: 2 pies.

Natalie Ann Dorsett, Pres.
Beta Lambda No. 4378
Lovington, New Mexico

Grape Pie
(1950)

1 egg, slightly beaten
1⅓ c. sugar
2 c. seeded Concord grapes
1 recipe 2-crust pie pastry
Butter

Combine egg, sugar and grapes; mix well. Ease bottom crust into pie plate. Add grape mixture. Dot with butter. Add top crust. Bake at 450 degrees for 10 minutes. Reduce heat to 350 degrees. Bake at 350 degrees for 35 minutes longer or until grapes are tender. Yield: 6 servings.

Georgia M. Cuneo
Preceptor Alpha XP311
Winston Salem, North Carolina

Chocolate Cream Pie
(1934)

2 c. milk, scalded
3 sq. baking chocolate, melted
2 tbsp. flour
3 tbsp. cornstarch
1½ c. sugar
½ tsp. salt
½ cup milk
4 eggs, separated
2 tbsp. butter
1½ tsp. vanilla extract
1 baked 9-in. pie shell
½ tsp. cream of tartar

Combine first 2 ingredients in top of double boiler. Heat over simmering water, stirring until smooth. Sift flour, cornstarch, 1 cup sugar and salt together twice. Combine with remaining ½ cup milk. Add to chocolate mixture, stirring constantly, until thickened. Cook for 10 minutes. Remove from heat. Gradually stir small amount of chocolate mixture into beaten egg yolks. Return to double boiler. Cook 2 minutes, stirring occasionally. Remove from heat. Add butter and vanilla. Pour into pie shell. Beat egg whites with cream of tartar in large bowl until frothy. Add ½ cup sugar, 1 tablespoon at a time; beat until stiff peaks form. Pile meringue over filling; seal edges. Bake in 425-degree oven for 5 minutes. Cool. Chill thoroughly.

Judy Henson, Pres.
Alpha Sigma Nu No. 10719
Van Horn, Texas

Chocolate Marvel Pie
(1948)

1 pkg. graham cracker crumbs
½ c. margarine
1 6-oz. package chocolate chips
3 tbsp. milk
2 tbsp. sugar
4 eggs, separated
1 tsp. vanilla extract

Combine graham cracker crumbs and margarine as for pie crust. Combine chocolate chips, milk and sugar in double boiler; melt and blend. Cool. Add egg yolks, one at a time, beating well after each addition. Add vanilla. Fold stiffly beaten egg whites into chocolate mixture. Pour into pie shell. Chill. Garnish with whipped cream.

Corinne L. Mullins
Xi Delta Lambda X5412
Canon City, Colorado

Indiana Pie

¾ c. sugar
½ c. flour
2 eggs, beaten
¼ lb. margarine, melted and cooled
⅓ c. light corn syrup
½ c. pecan pieces
1 6-oz. package chocolate chips
½ tsp. vanilla extract
1 unbaked 9-in. pie shell

Mix sugar and flour together by hand. Add eggs, margarine, corn syrup, pecans, chocolate chips and vanilla. Pour into pie shell. Bake at 325 degrees for 1 hour. Serve warm.

Pat Koeppen, Pres.
Preceptor Alpha Tau XP1756
Bloomington, Indiana

Mrs. Jacobs' Kentucky Derby Pie
(1955)

½ c. melted butter
2 eggs, slightly beaten
1 c. sugar
½ c. flour, sifted
1 c. chopped pecans
1 c. semisweet chocolate chips
1 unbaked pie shell

Combine butter, eggs, sugar, flour, pecans and chocolate chips; mix well. Pour into pie shell. Bake at 375 degrees for 45 minutes. Yield: 8 servings.

Roberta Jacobs Butera
Xi Nu Alpha X3802
San Antonio, Texas

Mother's Coconut Cream Pie
(1941)

2 tbsp. flour
1 c. sugar
½ tsp. salt
2 egg yolks, beaten
1½ c. milk
1 tsp. vanilla
1 c. coconut
1 baked 9-in. pie shell

Combine flour, ¾ cup sugar and salt in top of double boiler. Add egg yolks and milk. Cook over boiling water until thickened. Cool. Add vanilla and coconut. Pour into pie shell. Beat egg whites until stiff. Add ¼ cup sugar; beat until stiff peaks form. Spread over filling; seal edges. Sprinkle with additional coconut. Bake at 350 degrees until browned.

Betty K. Farris
Alpha Omega No. 6191
N. Augusta, South Carolina

Funny-Cake Pie
(1930)

3 c. sugar
½ c. cocoa
½ c. shortening
2 eggs
1 c. milk
2 tsp. baking powder
2 c. flour
1 tsp. vanilla extract
2 unbaked 9-in. pie shells

Combine 1 cup sugar, cocoa and ¾ cup hot water in saucepan. Bring to a boil. Cool. Combine 2 cups sugar, shortening, eggs and milk in mixer bowl; mix well. Sift baking powder and flour together. Add to creamed mixture. Add vanilla; mix well. Pour half of cocoa mixture into each pie shell. Add half of creamed mixture to each pie shell. Do not stir. Bake at 350 degrees for 40 minutes. Yield: 2 pies.

Rhonda M. Clapper, Corr. Sec.
Kappa Omicron No. 8089
Shawnee-on-Delaware, Pennsylvania

Impossible Pie

5 eggs
½ c. sugar
2 c. milk
½ c. flour
1 c. shredded coconut
2 tbsp. melted butter
2 tsp. vanilla, orange, banana or pineapple
    extract

Combine all ingredients in order listed in blender container; mix until smooth. Pour into lightly-greased 9-inch pie pan. Bake at 350 degrees for 40 to 45 minutes or until knife blade inserted into center comes cut clean. Yield: 6 servings.

Jeanette Miles, Treas.
Preceptor Sigma XP465
Monte Vista, Colorado

Irish Coffee Pie

1 3½-oz. package vanilla whipped dessert mix
2 tsp. instant coffee granules
½ c. cold milk
2 tbsp. Irish whiskey
½ c. whipping cream, whipped
1 baked 8-in. pastry shell, cooled

Combine dessert mix and coffee granules in large mixer bowl; mix well. Add milk; beat at High speed of electric mixer for 1 minute. Blend in whiskey and ⅓ cup water; beat at High speed for 2 minutes or until fluffy. Fold in whipped cream. Pour into pastry shell. Chill for 3 to 4 hours or until set. Garnish with whipped cream and chocolate shavings.

Chris McWaters, Rec. Sec.
Theta Rho No. 8156
New Hampton, Iowa

Lemon Chess Pie
(1958)

½ c. margarine, softened
1½ c. sugar
3 eggs, beaten
1 tsp. lemon flavoring
1 tbsp. vinegar
1 unbaked 9-in. pie shell

Cream margarine and sugar. Add eggs; beat well. Add lemon flavoring and vinegar. Pour into pie shell. Bake at 300 degrees for 10 minutes. Increase oven temperature to 350 degrees. Bake for 35 minutes longer.

Loretta G. Thompson, Pres.
Va. Eta Sigma No. 10767
Catlett, Virginia

Lemon Curd Tarts

1 c. butter
4 tbsp. confectioners' sugar
1½ c. flour
4 eggs, beaten
2 c. sugar
Grated rind and juice of 2 lemons

Combine ½ cup butter and confectioners' sugar in mixer bowl. Beat until creamy. Add flour; mix. Press into small greased tart pans. Bake at 350 degrees for 10 minutes. Cool. Combine eggs, sugar, ½ cup butter, grated rind and juice of 2 lemons in top of double boiler. Cook, stirring often, until thickened. Pour into tart shells. Yield: 18 servings.

Muriel Ball, V.P.
Exemplar Preceptor XP796
Charlottetown, P.E.I. Canada

Lemon Luscious

1 can Eagle Brand milk
1 6-oz. can frozen lemonade, thawed
1 lg. carton Cool Whip
1 graham cracker crust

Combine milk and lemonade; mix well. Fold in Cool Whip. Pour into crust. Chill for several hours.

DeRette LaRue, V.P.
Xi Delta X376
Tucson, Arizona

Green Tomato Pie

8 med. green tomatoes, quartered, ground and drained
1 c. raisins
2 tbsp. butter
2 tbsp. vinegar
1¼ c. sugar
4 tbsp. cornstarch
1 tsp. cinnamon
¼ tsp. ground cloves
1 recipe 2-crust pie pastry

Measure 2½ cups tomato pulp. Combine with raisins, butter and vinegar in saucepan. Blend sugar, cornstarch, cinnamon and cloves together in small bowl. Add to tomato mixture; mix well. Cook over Moderate heat, stirring constantly, until thickened. Divide pastry in half; roll each half to fit 9-inch pie plate. Fit half the pastry into plate; add tomato mixture. Fit remaining pastry over top. Seal edges; cut steam vents. Sprinkle crust with additional sugar and cinnamon. Bake in preheated 425-degree oven for 25 minutes. Reduce heat to 350 degrees. Bake for 20 to 25 minutes longer. Filling may be made ahead and frozen.

Mary Tempero, Soc. Chm.
Xi Gamma Beta X2538
Scott City, Kansas

Macadamia Nut Pie
(1932)

4 eggs, beaten
1 c. light corn syrup
⅔ c. sugar
¼ c. butter, melted
2 tbsp. flour
1 tsp. vanilla extract
Dash of salt
1 unbaked 9-in. pastry shell
½ c. chopped macadamia nuts

Combine eggs, corn syrup, sugar, butter, flour, vanilla and salt in large mixing bowl. Beat with rotary beater until smooth. Pour into pastry shell. Sprinkle with nuts. Bake at 350 degrees for 50 minutes or until knife blade inserted into center comes out clean. Cool.

Juretta L. Lewis, Pres.
Xi Gamma X5377
Pahala, Hawaii

Million Dollar Pie

1 8-oz. can Eagle Brand milk
1 lg. can crushed pineapple
¼ c. lemon juice
1 lg. carton Cool Whip
½ c. chopped pecans
2 c. miniature marshmallows
1 c. coconut
2 graham cracker crusts

Combine first 6 ingredients; mix well. Spoon into crusts. Chill until set.

Reda Diane Malone, Treas.
Preceptor Alpha Epsilon XP648
Hebron, Kentucky

Old-Fashioned Sugar-Cream Pie

3 tbsp. butter, melted
1 c. sugar
3 tbsp. cornstarch
1 egg
1 13-oz. can evaporated milk
Milk
Pinch of salt
1 unbaked 10-in. pie shell
Nutmeg to taste

Combine butter, sugar, cornstarch and egg; mix well. Combine evaporated milk and enough milk to measure 2 cups. Add salt; mix well. Add to butter mixture, mixing well. Pour into pie shell. Sprinkle with nutmeg. Bake at 450 degrees for 13 minutes or until bubbly. Reduce oven temperature to 350 degrees. Bake for 5 minutes longer. Let stand until set. Yield: 8-10 servings.

Lynda L. Miesse, V.P.
Beta Omega XP1766
Lancaster, Ohio

Peach-Cheese Pie

1 8-oz. package cream cheese, softened
2 eggs
¾ c. sugar
2 tbsp. milk
1 tbsp. vanilla extract

1 unbaked 9-in. pie shell
1 29-oz. can sliced peaches
1 tbsp. cornstarch
1 tsp. lemon juice
¼ tsp. almond extract

Combine cream cheese, eggs, ½ cup sugar, milk and vanilla in mixer bowl; blend well. Pour into pie shell. Bake at 375 degrees for 30 minutes. Cool. Drain peaches, reserving 1 cup juice. Combine cornstarch and ¼ cup sugar. Stir in peach juice, lemon juice and almond extract. Cook, stirring, until thick. Arrange peaches, petal fashion, on filling. Garnish with maraschino cherry. Spoon glaze over fruit. Chill for 1 hour.

Laverne Smith, Treas.
Xi Beta Alphi X1534
New Albany, Indiana

Peach Melba Pie

¾ c. corn flake crumbs
½ c. finely chopped toasted blanched almonds
2 tbsp. light brown sugar
¼ c. butter or margarine, melted
1 qt. vanilla ice cream, slightly softened
½ c. currant jelly
1 c. seedless red raspberry preserves

1 1-lb. can cling peach slices, drained and chilled
Toasted whole blanched almonds

Combine crumbs, chopped almonds, brown sugar and butter; mix well. Press into bottom and sides of 9-inch pie plate to form crust. Bake at 375 degrees for 8 minutes. Cool on wire rack. Spoon ice cream into cooled crust; cover with aluminum foil or plastic wrap. Freeze until firm. Place jelly in saucepan; melt over Low heat. Stir in preserves. Arrange peach slices on ice cream. Sprinkle with almonds. Pour jelly mixture into serving dish; serve with pie. Yield: 6-8 servings.

Photograph for this recipe on page 155.

Peanut Butter Pie

2 1¾-oz. packages instant vanilla pudding mix
2 c. cold milk
⅓ c. crunchy peanut butter
1 graham cracker crust
Cool Whip or whipped cream

Combine pudding mix, milk and peanut butter in mixer bowl; beat with electric mixer until thickened. Pour into graham cracker crust. Top with Cool Whip. Chill until set. Yield: 6-8 servings.

Marie Kuper, Pres.
Preceptor Alpha Beta XP600
St. Joseph, Missouri

Pecan Pie
(1940)

2 eggs, slightly beaten
½ c. sugar
1 c. light corn syrup
¼ stick butter or margarine, softened
1 tsp. vanilla extract
1 c. pecans
1 recipe 9-in. pie pastry

Combine first 6 ingredients in order listed; mix well. Pour into unbaked pie shell. Bake at 350 degrees for 30 to 45 minutes. Yield: 6-8 servings.

Penny Phillips, City Coun. Pres.
Gamma Gamma No. 10025
Opelika, Alabama

Mom's Karo Pecan Pie
(1930)

3 eggs, beaten
1 c. sugar
2 tbsp. butter, softened
1 c. dark Karo syrup
1 c. pecans
Pinch of salt
1 tsp. vanilla extract
1 unbaked 9-in. pie shell

Combine first 7 ingredients in mixer bowl; blend well. Pour into pie shell. Bake at 325 degrees for 1 hour or until firm.

Katherine S. Hebert, Rec. Sec.
Xi Alpha Eta X3047
Houma, Louisiana

Crustless Pumpkin Pie

2 lg. eggs
2 c. canned pumpkin
1 c. nonfat dry milk powder
⅔ c. (scant) brown sugar
¼ tsp. salt
1 tsp. cinnamon
½ tsp. ginger
¼ tsp. nutmeg
½ tsp. vanilla extract
¼ c. whole wheat flour

Combine all ingredients in large mixing bowl; mix well. Add 1 cup water gradually, mixing well. Pour into greased 9-inch square pan. Bake at 350 degrees for 45 to 50 minutes or until knife blade inserted near center comes out clean. Yield: 8 servings.

Erma Dethlefsen, Treas.
Xi Alpha Alpha X1398
Chappell, Nebraska

Strawberry Pie

1 c. sugar
3 tbsp. cornstarch
1 c. 7-Up
½ pkg. strawberry Jell-O
1½ pt. strawberries
1 baked 9-in. pie shell

Combine sugar and cornstarch in saucepan; mix well. Add 7-Up; cook until thickened. Add Jell-O; mix well. Cool. Add strawberries; mix well. Pour into pie shell. Chill for 3 to 4 hours. Serve with Cool Whip or whipped cream. Yield: 6 servings.

Ruth Cravens, Pres.
Preceptor Omega
Anthony, New Mexico

Boiled Custard
(1942)

1 qt. milk
5 eggs
1 c. sugar
1 tsp. vanilla extract

Pour milk in top of double boiler; heat milk. Do not let milk boil. Beat eggs until light. Add sugar; mix well. Stir a small amount of hot milk into egg mixture; stir egg mixture into hot milk. Cook until mixture coats a spoon, stirring constantly. Add vanilla. Chill until serving time. Custard will thicken as it chills. Yield: 8 servings.

Barbara Richards, Treas.
Epsilon Rho No. 8379
Staunton, Virginia

Ella's Banana Pudding
(1930)

½ c. sugar
3 to 4 tbsp. flour
1½ c. milk
1 tsp. vanilla extract
2 to 3 bananas, sliced
Vanilla wafers
Whipped cream

Combine sugar, flour and milk in saucepan; cook until thickened. Stir in vanilla. Alternate layers of bananas, vanilla wafers and milk mixture in serving dish. Top with whipped cream. Yield: 6-8 servings.

Pat McEuin, Prog. Chm.
Preceptor Gamma Pi XP1286
Denton, Texas

Emperor's Mish-Mash
(1932)

6 eggs, separated
2 tbsp. sugar
1½ c. flour
1 c. milk
Pinch of salt
¾ c. seedless raisins
4 tbsp. butter
Confectioners' sugar

Beat egg yolks until frothy. Add sugar, flour, milk and salt; mix well. Beat egg whites until stiff peaks form. Fold egg whites into egg yolk mixture. Fold in raisins. Melt butter in large skillet. Pour batter over melted butter. Cook over Low heat until bottom is lightly browned. Cut into large pieces. Cook until browned. Invert on serving platter. Dust with confectioners' sugar. Serve with favorite rum sauce or fresh fruit. Yield: 6 servings.

Hermine Spiewak, Pres.
Xi Nu X1774
Bedford, Massachusetts

Capirotada
(1934)

3 tbsp. finely chopped scallions
3 tbsp. shortening
1½ lb. brown sugar
1 3-in. stick cinnamon
⅓ c. whole almonds
¼ c. raisins
1 loaf French bread, sliced and toasted
½ lemon, thinly sliced
¼ lb. Jack cheese, cut into strips

Saute scallions in shortening; set aside. Combine brown sugar, cinnamon and 1½ quarts water in large saucepan; bring to a boil. Boil for 15 minutes or until sugar is dissolved. Remove from heat; let stand. Soak almonds in hot water to cover for 30 minutes or until skins can be easily removed. Soak raisins in water to cover until raisins are puffy. Strain brown sugar mixture into large saucepan. Add raisins, almonds and scallions; mix well. Alternate layers of bread, lemon slices, cheese and raisin mixture in Dutch oven until all ingredients are used. Cover. Bring to a boil over Low heat; boil for 5 minutes. Serve hot. Yield: 20-25 servings.

Julia G. Schroder, Rec. Sec.
Xi Alpha Beta X2198
Smith, Nevada

Caramel Pudding

2 c. (firmly packed) brown sugar
1 c. sugar
⅓ c. flour
⅛ tsp. salt
2 eggs
2½ c. milk
1 sm. can crushed pineapple
1 c. chopped nuts
2 tsp. vanilla extract
1 tbsp. butter

Combine first 4 ingredients; blend well. Add eggs and milk; mix well. Pour into top of double boiler. Cook until creamy, stirring frequently. Add pineapple, nuts, vanilla and butter; stir until well blended. Chill until set. Serve with whipped cream. Yield: 8-10 servings.

Colleen Miller, Past Corr. Sec.
Xi Delta Nu X4841
Lamont, Oklahoma

Devil's Float
(1945)

1¼ c. sugar
½ c. (firmly packed) brown sugar
Cocoa
1 tsp. vanilla extract
½ tsp. salt
2 tbsp. shortening
1 egg
½ c. finely chopped nuts
1 c. sifted flour
1½ tsp. baking powder
½ c. milk

Combine ½ cup sugar, brown sugar, 5 tablespoons cocoa and 1 cup hot water in small saucepan; bring to a boil, stirring constantly. Cool. Combine vanilla, salt and shortening; cream until smooth. Add ¾ cup sugar gradually, mixing well after each addition. Add egg and nuts; beat well. Sift flour, baking powder and 1½ teaspoons cocoa together; add to creamed mixture alternately with milk, mixing well after each addition. Pour into greased 8-inch square pan. Pour cooled sauce over batter. Bake at 350 degrees for 30 minutes. Invert on serving plate. Serve with whipped cream. Yield: 4-6 servings.

Oreta R. Stuart, Pres.
Xi Alpha Nu X3829
Orofino, Idaho

Black Bottom Cups
(1933)

1 8-oz. package cream cheese, softened
1 egg
1⅓ c. sugar
Salt
1 c. chocolate chips
1½ c. flour
¼ c. cocoa
1 tsp. soda
⅓ c. oil
1 tbsp. vinegar
1 tsp. vanilla extract

Combine cream cheese, egg, ⅓ cup sugar, ⅛ teaspoon salt and chocolate chips; cream until smooth. Set aside. Sift flour, 1 cup sugar, cocoa, soda and ½ teaspoon salt together. Add oil, vinegar, vanilla and 1 cup water; mix well. Pour into muffin cups, filling ⅓ full. Top each with 1 teaspoon creamed mixture. Bake at 350 degrees for 25 to 30 minutes. Yield: 18-24 servings.

Helen Allan
Xi Beta Beta X2117
Kenmore, New York

Grannies' Chocolate Pudding
(1930)

1 c. sugar
2 tbsp. cocoa
2 eggs, separated
Vanilla wafers
Whipped cream

Combine sugar, cocoa and ¾ cup water in saucepan; boil for 10 minutes. Beat egg yolks until light; add to cocoa mixture, beating well. Beat egg whites until stiff peaks form; fold into cocoa mixture. Line serving dish with vanilla wafers. Alternate layers of cocoa mixture and whipped cream until all ingredients are used. Yield: 6 servings.

Geneva Murphy, Pres.
Preceptor Alpha Sigma XP760
San Angelo, Texas

Lemon Cake Pudding
(1949)

¼ c. flour
1 c. sugar
2 tbsp. butter
4 egg yolks, beaten
½ c. lemon juice
Rind of 2 lemons

4 egg whites, stiffly beaten
2 c. milk

Cream flour, sugar and butter. Add egg yolks, lemon juice and rind; mix well. Fold in egg whites. Add milk, stirring. Spoon into buttered 9 × 9-inch pan; place pan in tray of water. Bake at 350 degrees for 40 to 50 minutes or until lightly browned. Yield: 6 servings.

Beth Holland, Pres.
Alpha Nu No. 10099
Leouc, Alberta, Canada

Peach Custard Cake
(1945)

1½ c. flour
½ tsp. salt
½ c. margarine, softened
1 1-lb. 14-oz. can sliced peaches
½ c. sugar
1 tsp. cinnamon
1 egg, slightly beaten
1 c. evaporated milk

Combine flour, salt and margarine in 1½-quart mixing bowl; mix with pastry blender or 2 knives until mixture resembles coarse meal. Press on bottom and sides of greased 8-inch square baking pan to form crust. Drain peaches, reserving ½ cup juice. Arrange peaches over crust. Combine sugar and cinnamon; mix well. Sprinkle over peaches. Bake at 375 degrees for 20 minutes. Combine reserved juice, egg and evaporated milk; mix well. Pour over peaches. Bake for 30 minutes longer or until edges are firm. Let stand until center is firm. Yield: 9 servings.

Peggy L. Testrake, V.P.
Alpha No. 290
Erie, Pennsylvania

Apple Cake

1½ c. salad oil
2 c. sugar
2 eggs
1 tsp. vanilla extract
3 c. sliced apples
1 c. raisins
2 c. chopped nuts
1 tsp. soda
3 c. flour
½ tsp. salt
1 tsp. cinnamon

Combine oil, sugar and eggs in large mixing bowl; beat well. Stir in remaining ingredients. Pour into

9 × 13-inch pan. Bake at 350 degrees for 50 minutes. Serve with whipped cream. Yield: 15-20 servings.

Lucylle Doerr, Rec. Sec.
Preceptor Iota XP1278
Hettinger, North Dakota

Best Wishes Cake

2 California avocados, peeled and mashed
½ c. sugar
2 tsp. lemon juice
3 tbsp. Creme de Menthe
1 c. sour cream
1 loaf angel food cake

Combine avocados, sugar, lemon juice and Creme de Menthe in medium bowl; mix well. Stir in sour cream. Split cake into 3 horizontal layers. Spoon avocado cream between each layer; spread on top. Decorate with chocolate sprinkles. Chill until serving time. Yield: 8 servings.

Photograph for this recipe on page 159.

Banana-Nut Cake
(1950)

½ c. butter or margarine
½ c. sugar
¾ c. (firmly packed) brown sugar
1 egg
3 med. bananas, mashed
4 tbsp. milk
1 tsp. soda
1½ c. flour
¼ tsp. salt
1 tsp. vanilla extract
½ c. chopped nuts

Cream butter and sugars. Add egg, bananas and milk; mix well. Add dry ingredients; mix well. Stir in vanilla and nuts. Pour into greased and floured 11 × 6 × 2-inch baking dish. Bake at 350 degrees for 30 minutes or until browned. Frost with favorite butter icing recipe.

Ruthelma L. Doerr
Psi Epsilon No. 8981
Garland, Texas

Banana Split Cake

2 sticks butter or margarine, softened
2 c. graham cracker crumbs
2 eggs, slightly beaten
2 c. confectioners' sugar
2½ c. drained crushed pineapple
3 bananas, sliced
1 carton Cool Whip

Combine 1 stick butter and graham cracker crumbs; mix well. Press firmly into bottom of loaf pan. Combine remaining butter, eggs and confectioners' sugar; beat until fluffy. Spread over graham cracker crumbs. Add layer of pineapple and banana slices. Cover with Cool Whip. Decorate with nuts and maraschino cherries. Refrigerate for 8 hours.

Nancy L. Nelson, Pres.
Xi Alpha Kappa X590
Port Clinton, Ohio

Festive Banana Cake

3 c. flour
2 c. sugar
1 tsp. soda
1 tsp. salt
1 tsp. cinnamon
3 eggs, slightly beaten
1½ c. oil
1 tsp. almond extract
1 c. chopped or slivered almonds
2 c. chopped bananas
1 c. crushed pineapple in natural juices

Combine dry ingredients; mix well. Combine eggs, oil and almond extract; mix well. Add to dry ingredients, stirring to blend well. Stir in almonds, bananas and pineapple. Spoon into greased 10-inch tube pan. Bake at 325 degrees for 1 hour and 20 to 25 minutes. Allow to cool completely.

Kathy Gammon, Pres.
Gamma No. 1078
Winnipeg, Manitoba, Canada

Golden Apricot Chiffon Cake
(1950)

1 30-oz. can apricot halves
2¼ c. cake flour
Sugar
1 tbsp. baking powder
1 tsp. salt
½ c. salad oil
5 egg yolks
2 tsp. grated lemon rind
1 c. egg whites
½ tsp. cream of tartar
1 c. whipping cream
1½ tsp. lemon flavoring
½ c. toasted sliced almonds

Drain apricots, reserving ⅔ cup juice. Puree apricots; measuring 1 cup for cake. Chill remaining puree for garnish. Sift flour, 1½ cups sugar, baking powder and salt into large mixer bowl, making a well in center. Add salad oil, egg yolks, reserved apricot juice, 1 cup apricot puree and lemon rind; beat until smooth. Beat egg whites with cream of tartar until smooth stiff peaks form. Fold egg yolk mixture into egg whites. Pour into ungreased 10-inch tube pan. Bake at 325 degrees for 55 minutes. Increase temperature to 350 degrees; bake for 10 minutes longer or until cake tests done. Insert pan over neck of bottle; cool. Loosen cake; remove from pan. Cool on wire rack with narrow part of cake on bottom. Brush crumbs from cake. Whip cream with 2 tablespoons sugar and lemon flavoring until soft peaks form. Spread over cake. Sprinkle sides of cake with almonds. Drizzle chilled puree over top of cake. Yield: 10-12 servings.

Helen V. Still, Corr. Sec.
Mu Alpha No. 7918
Smithville, Missouri

Mockingbird Cake

3 c. sifted flour
1 tsp. soda
1 tsp. salt
1 tsp. cinnamon
2 c. sugar
1¼ c. Wesson oil
1 20-oz. can crushed pineapple, drained
1½ tsp. vanilla extract
3 eggs
2 c. mashed bananas
1 7-oz. can coconut
1 c. chopped pecans

Sift dry ingredients together. Add remaining ingredients in order listed; mix well with wooden spoon. Pour into greased and floured bundt pan. Bake at 350 degrees for 20 minutes. Yield: 20-24 servings.

Ruth Trus
Xi Upsilon Rho X5289
Overton, Texas

Blackberry Jam Cake
(1937)

3 c. sifted flour
2 tsp. baking powder
1 tsp. soda
Salt
1 tsp. cinnamon

1 tsp. cloves
⅔ c. shortening
1½ c. sugar
3 eggs, well beaten
1 c. blackberry jam
1 c. sour milk or buttermilk
¼ c. butter
2 c. confectioners' sugar
1 tsp. vanilla extract
3 tbsp. cream

Sift flour, baking powder, soda, ¼ teaspoon salt, and spices together. Cream shortening until smooth; add sugar gradually, beating until fluffy. Add eggs and jam; beat well. Add sifted ingredients gradually to jam mixture alternately with sour milk, beating well after each addition. Pour into 3 greased and floured layer pans. Bake at 350 degrees for 25 to 30 minutes or until cake tests done. Cream butter until smooth. Stir in 1 cup confectioners' sugar. Add vanilla and ⅛ teaspoon salt; mix well. Add remaining confectioners' sugar alternately with cream, beating well after each addition. Add additional cream if necessary for spreading consistency. Spread frosting between layers.

Faye Williams
International Coordinator
Xi Delta Pi X3376
Kennett, Missouri

Applesauce-Carrot Cake
(1959)

2¾ c. flour
3 tsp. soda
1 tsp. salt
3 tsp. cinnamon
1 tsp. nutmeg
4 eggs, beaten
¾ c. oil
2 c. sugar
1½ tsp. vanilla extract
1 15-oz. jar applesauce
3 c. shredded carrots
1 c. golden raisins
1 c. chopped walnuts
4 oz. cream cheese, softened
2 tbsp. butter or margarine, softened
¾ c. confectioners' sugar

Mix flour, soda, salt, cinnamon and nutmeg in large mixing bowl; set aside. Combine eggs, oil, sugar and 1 teaspoon vanilla in large bowl; mix well. Add applesauce and carrots; mix well. Add applesauce mixture to flour mixture, stirring just to moisten. Fold in raisins and ½ of the walnuts. Pour into greased and floured 9 × 13-inch pan. Sprinkle with remaining walnuts. Bake at 350 degrees for 45 minutes. Cool. Combine cream cheese, butter and ½

teaspoon vanilla in small mixer bowl; beat on Medium speed of electric mixer until smooth. Add confectioners' sugar gradually, beating until fluffy. Spread on cooled cake. Yield: 15-20 servings.

Joan C. Williams, Corr. Sec.
Preceptor Xi XP1501
Mount Laurel, New Jersey

Donna's Carrot Cake

2 c. flour
2 c. sugar
1½ tsp. soda
1 tsp. cinnamon
1¼ c. Wesson oil
4 eggs
3 c. finely grated carrots
½ stick margarine or butter, softened
4 oz. cream cheese
½ box confectioners' sugar
1 c. coconut
½ tsp. vanilla extract
1½ tbsp. cream
½ c. finely chopped nuts

Sift first 4 ingredients together. Combine oil and eggs in mixer bowl; beat until fluffy. Add carrots and dry ingredients; beat until smooth. Pour into 9 × 13-inch pan. Bake at 325 degrees for 35 minutes or until cake tests done. Combine remaining ingredients in large mixer bowl; blend well. Spread on cake.

Donna J. Stephens, Soc. Chm.
Delta Beta Beta No. 6924
Bayside, California

Kentucky Mountain Carrot Cake
(1940)

2 c. sugar
2 c. flour
1½ tsp. soda
1 tsp. salt
1½ tsp. nutmeg
½ c. vegetable oil
4 eggs, separated
1½ c. grated carrots
1¾ c. nuts

Sift dry ingredients. Combine with oil, egg yolks, carrots and nuts in large mixer bowl; mix well. Fold in stiffly beaten egg whites. Pour into greased tube pan. Bake at 325 degrees for 1 hour and 30 minutes or until cake tests done.

Betty Jo Shirley, Pres.
Xi Omega No. 3690
Bowling Green, Kentucky

Cherry-Nut Cake
(1950)

1 lb. butter or margarine
2 c. sugar
6 eggs, separated
¾ lb. candied cherries
¼ lb. candied pineapple, chopped
3 c. flour, sifted
3 c. chopped pecans
2 tbsp. lemon juice

Cream butter. Add sugar gradually; beat until light and smooth. Add beaten egg yolks; beat well. Combine cherries, pineapple and pecans; add flour, tossing to coat well. Add creamed mixture and lemon juice; mix well. Beat egg whites until stiff peaks form. Fold into batter. Pour into well-greased bundt pan. Bake at 300 degrees for 1 hour and 45 minutes. Cool for 15 minutes. Remove from pan. Yield: 20 servings.

Barbara Albright, Pres.
Xi Tau X1104
Lawton, Oklahoma

Black Sour Cream-Raisin Cake

2 c. flour
½ c. cocoa
1 tsp. cinnamon
1 tsp. cloves
½ tsp. salt
1 tsp. soda
1½ c. sugar
2 c. raisins
1 c. chopped nuts
1 c. sour cream
2 eggs, well beaten
¼ c. vegetable oil
1 tsp. vanilla extract

Sift dry ingredients together. Add raisins and nuts; mix well. Add sour cream, eggs, vegetable oil and vanilla; stir until blended. Pour into greased 8-inch tube pan. Bake at 325 degrees for 1 hour. Serve with whipped cream or ice cream.

Marilyn Vollmar, Ext. Off.
Preceptor Beta Kappa XP1366
Tontogany, Ohio

Chocolate-Applesauce Cake

2 c. flour
1 c. sugar
2 tbsp. cocoa
1 tbsp. cornstarch
1 tsp. salt
2 tsp. soda
¼ tsp. each cinnamon, cloves, allspice and
   nutmeg
1 c. chopped nuts
1 c. raisins
1½ c. applesauce
½ c. oil

Combine first 7 ingredients, stirring to mix well. Add nuts and raisins, stirring to mix well. Add applesauce and oil, stirring to mix well. Pour into greased and floured tube pan. Bake at 350 degrees for 1 hour. Frost as desired.

Marjorie McNealy, Pub. Chm.
Preceptor Alpha Nu XP644
El Paso, Texas

Chocolate Chip Cake

1 c. chopped dates
¾ c. shortening
1¼ c. sugar
2 eggs
2 c. sifted flour
1 tsp. soda
½ tsp. salt
3 tbsp. cocoa
2 6-oz. packages semisweet chocolate chips
2 c. chopped nuts

Cover dates with 1¼ cups boiling water; cool. Cream shortening and 1 cup sugar. Add eggs; beat well. Sift flour, soda, salt and cocoa together. Add sifted ingredients to creamed mixture alternately with date mixture, beginning and ending with sifted ingredients; mix well after each addition. Add half the chocolate chips; mix well. Pour into greased 13 × 9-inch baking pan. Combine ¼ cup sugar, nuts and remaining chocolate chips; mix well. Sprinkle over batter. Bake at 350 degrees for 35 minutes or until cake tests done.

Diane M. Vollbrecht, Ext. Off.
Xi Eta Delta X5393
Lake City, Pennsylvania

Chocolate Chip-Applesauce Cake

2 c. unsifted flour
1½ c. sugar
1½ tsp. soda
1 tbsp. cocoa
1½ tsp. cinnamon
1½ tsp. nutmeg
1½ tsp. allspice
1½ tsp. cloves
1 tsp. salt
½ c. shortening

2 c. applesauce
2 eggs
1 c. chocolate chips
1 c. chopped nuts
½ c. raisins
2 tbsp. brown sugar

Combine first 9 ingredients in large mixer bowl; mix well. Add shortening, applesauce, eggs, ½ cup chocolate chips, ½ cup nuts and raisins. Beat until smooth. Pour into greased 9 × 13-inch pan. Combine remaining ½ cup chocolate chips, ½ cup nuts and brown sugar. Sprinkle over batter. Bake in preheated 350-degree oven for 30 to 35 minutes or until cake tests done.

Jo Anne Klingenberg, Pres.
Gamma Omega No. 1433
Quincy, Illinois

Chocolate-Oatmeal Cake

1 c. quick-cooking oats
½ c. margarine
2 eggs, beaten
1½ c. sugar
1 tsp. vanilla extract
Cocoa
1 c. flour
1 tsp. soda
½ tsp. salt
4 tbsp. milk
1 stick butter, softened
1 1-lb. box confectioners' sugar
1 c. chopped nuts

Place oats in saucepan; add 1½ cups boiling water. Set aside. Combine margarine, eggs and sugar; cream until smooth. Add vanilla. Sift ½ cup cocoa, flour, soda and salt together. Add to creamed mixture. Stir in cooled oats. Pour into greased and floured sheet cake pan. Bake at 350 degrees for 20 to 25 minutes or until cake tests done. Pour milk in saucepan; heat thoroughly. Add butter and 4 tablespoons cocoa; stir until melted. Add confectioners' sugar; beat well. Add nuts; mix well. Pour over cake.

Nancy Jett, Pres.
Xi Beta Upsilon No. 2213
Sedalia, Missouri

Chocolate-Zucchini Cake

Butter
2 c. sugar
3 eggs, slightly beaten
2½ c. flour
½ tsp. soda

2½ tsp. baking powder
1 tsp. cinnamon
½ tsp. salt
½ c. cocoa
3 tsp. vanilla extract
2 c. shredded zucchini
½ c. milk
1 c. chopped nuts
3 oz. cream cheese, softened
⅓ to ½ box confectioners' sugar

Combine ¾ cup butter and sugar; cream until smooth. Beat in eggs. Sift flour, soda, baking powder, cinnamon, salt and cocoa together. Add to creamed mixture; mix well. Add two teaspoons vanilla, zucchini, milk and nuts; stir until well blended. Pour into greased and floured 9 × 13-inch pan. Bake at 350 degrees for 40 to 50 minutes. Combine cream cheese, 3 tablespoons butter, 1 teaspoon vanilla and confectioners' sugar; mix well. Spread on cooled cake.

Donna Schwartz, Rec. Sec.
Lambda Xi No. 10240
Neodesha, Kansas

Coca-Cola Cake

2 c. flour
2 c. sugar
Margarine
6 tbsp. cocoa
Coca-Cola
½ c. buttermilk
2 eggs, beaten
1 tsp. soda
1 tsp. vanilla extract
1½ c. miniature marshmallows
1 pkg. confectioners' sugar
1 c. chopped pecans or walnuts

Combine flour and sugar in large mixing bowl; mix well. Place 2 sticks margarine, 3 tablespoons cocoa and 1 cup Coca-Cola in saucepan; bring to boiling point. Pour over flour mixture; mix well. Add buttermilk, eggs, soda, vanilla and marshmallows; mix well. Pour into greased 9 × 13-inch cake pan. Bake at 350 degrees for 35 to 40 minutes. Combine ½ cup margarine, 3 tablespoons cocoa and 6 tablespoons Coca-Cola in saucepan; bring to boiling point. Place confectioners' sugar in large bowl. Add Coca-Cola mixture; beat well. Stir in pecans. Spread over hot cake. Yield: 20 servings.

Carol Ann Smith, Treas.
Gamma Psi No. 2150
Pimento, Indiana

Demon Cake
(1934)

4 sq. baking chocolate
1 c. butter
2¼ c. sugar
1½ c. buttermilk or sour cream
3 c. cake flour
1 tsp. soda
½ tsp. baking powder
½ tsp. salt
5 eggs, separated
1 tsp. vanilla extract

Melt chocolate over boiling water. Add butter and sugar; cream until smooth. Sift dry ingredients together; add to creamed mixture alternately with buttermilk, beginning and ending with sifted ingredients. Add well-beaten egg yolks. Fold in stiffly beaten egg whites and vanilla. Pour into 3 greased and floured 9-inch layer pans. Bake at 350 degrees for 30 to 35 minutes or until cake tests done. Frost with favorite white icing.

Elaine Myers, Ext. Off.
Xi Beta Iota No. 3705
Chamblee, Georgia

Devil's Food Cake
(1935)

½ c. shortening
2½ c. sugar
2¼ c. flour
2 tsp. soda
½ tsp. salt
3 tbsp. cocoa
3 eggs, beaten
½ c. sour milk
2 tsp. vanilla flavoring

Combine shortening and sugar; cream until smooth. Add dry ingredients; mix well. Add remaining ingredients and 1 cup boiling water; mix well. Pour into 2 greased and floured 8-inch round cake pans. Bake at 350 degrees for 50 to 60 minutes. Frost as desired. Yield: 12 servings.

Babs Brooks, Pres.
Zeta Iota No. 10721
Hamburg, Arkansas

Mississippi Mud Cake

3 sticks margarine, softened
2 c. sugar
1½ c. flour
4 eggs
2 tsp. vanilla extract

Cocoa
1½ c. coconut
1½ c. chopped nuts
1 7-oz. jar marshmallow creme
1 1-lb. box confectioners' sugar

Combine 2 sticks margarine, sugar, flour and eggs; beat for 1 minute. Add 1 teaspoon vanilla, 3 tablespoons cocoa, coconut and nuts; mix well. Pour into greased 9 × 13 × 2-inch cake pan. Bake at 300 degrees for 45 minutes. Spread hot cake with marshmallow creme. Cool. Combine 1 stick margarine, confectioners' sugar, ⅓ cup cocoa, 1 teaspoon vanilla and ¼ cup water; blend well. Spread on cooled cake. Yield: 18 servings.

Ann M. Hetrick, City Coun. Pres.
Preceptor Xi XP495
York, Pennsylvania

Mum-Mum Cake
(1940)

1 c. sugar
1 c. seeded muscat raisins
½ c. shortening
2 sq. unsweetened chocolate
1 tsp. cinnamon
1 tsp. cloves
¼ tsp. salt
1 tsp. soda
2 c. flour

Combine first 6 ingredients with 1½ cups water in medium saucepan. Bring to a boil; boil for 4 minutes. Cool. Dissolve soda in 1 tablespoon water. Add soda mixture, salt and flour to cooled mixture; mix well. Pour into loaf pan. Bake at 300 degrees for 1 hour or until cake tests done.

Denise Daniels, Pres.
Zeta Kappa No. 5126
Albany, New York

Snowy Day Chocolate Cake

1 c. sugar
2 c. shortening
1 egg
1½ tsp. soda
1 c. sour milk
½ c. cocoa
1½ c. sifted flour
½ tsp. salt
1 tsp. vanilla extract
Confectioners' sugar

Combine sugar and shortening in mixer bowl; cream until light and fluffy. Add egg; beat well. Dissolve soda in sour milk; add to creamed mixture. Sift cocoa, flour and salt together; add to batter, mixing well. Stir in vanilla. Beat on Low speed of electric mixer for 1 minute. Pour into greased 9 × 9-inch pan. Bake at 350 degrees for 45 to 50 minutes. Sprinkle with confectioners' sugar. Serve warm. Yield: 12 servings.

> *April Felts, Pres.*
> *Xi Epsilon Alpha X5279*
> *Muskogee, Oklahoma*

Sour Cream-Cocoa Cake
(1940)

¾ c. cocoa
¾ c. shortening
2⅓ c. sugar
3 c. cake flour
¾ tsp. salt
¾ tsp. soda
¾ c. evaporated milk
1 tbsp. vinegar
1½ tsp. vanilla extract
4 eggs whites, stiffly beaten

Combine cocoa and 1⅛ cups boiling water; stir until smooth. Cool. Cream shortening and sugar until light and fluffy. Add cocoa mixture; mix well. Sift flour, soda and salt together. Combine evaporated milk and vinegar; mix well. Add to creamed mixture alternately with dry ingredients, beating well after each addition. Add vanilla. Fold in egg whites. Pour into 3 waxed paper-lined 9-inch cake pans. Bake at 325 degrees for 30 minutes or until cake tests done. Frost as desired.

> *Mary N. Norris*
> *Laureate Lambda XP279*
> *Kansas City, Missouri*

Sugarless Chocolate Cake
(1943)

1½ c. chocolate malted milk
1 tsp. soda
1 c. flour
¼ tsp. salt
1 egg, beaten
1 c. sour cream
1 tsp. vanilla extract

Combine dry ingredients in mixer bowl; stir to mix. Add remaining ingredients. Stir until blended. Pour into 9 × 13-inch pan. Bake at 350 degrees for 30 minutes.

> *Cheryl Beckins, Pres.*
> *Gamma Tau No. 8948*
> *Ogallala, Nebraska*

White Chocolate Cake

½ lb. white chocolate
1 c. butter or margarine, softened
4 eggs, separated
2 c. sugar
2½ c. cake flour
1 tsp. baking powder
¼ tsp. salt
1 c. buttermilk
1 c. chopped pecans
1 c. flaked coconut
1 tsp. vanilla extract

Melt chocolate in top of double boiler. Combine butter and sugar; cream until smooth. Add egg yolks; mix well. Add melted chocolate; mix well. Sift dry ingredients together; add to creamed mixture alternately with buttermilk. Stir in pecans, coconut and vanilla. Beat egg whites until stiff peaks form; fold into batter. Pour into greased 13 × 9 × 2-inch pan or 3 layer pans. Bake at 350 degrees for 30 minutes. Frost as desired.

> *Peggy Hall, Treas.*
> *Preceptor Alpha Sigma XP996*
> *Marion, Ohio*

Gumdrop Cake
(1938)

1 c. sugar
1 c. butter, softened
2 eggs, beaten
1½ c. sweetened applesauce
4 c. flour
1 tsp. cinnamon
1 tsp. ground cloves
1 tsp. salt
1 tsp. soda
2 lb. gumdrops, halved
1 lb. white raisins
1½ c. chopped nuts

Cream sugar and butter until smooth. Add eggs and applesauce; beat well. Sift 2 cups flour, cinnamon, cloves and salt together. Add to creamed mixture gradually, mixing well. Dissolve soda in 1 teaspoon hot water; add to batter. Combine gumdrops, raisins, nuts and remaining flour; toss to coat well. Add gumdrop mixture to batter; blend well. Pour into greased and floured angel food cake pan. Bake at 350 degrees for 2 hours. Yield: 12 servings.

> *Julia Francis, Pres.*
> *Gamma Omicron No. 1163*
> *Dallas, Texas*

Cream of Coconut Cake

1 18½-oz. package white cake mix
3 eggs
¼ c. cooking oil
1 8-oz. carton sour cream
1 14½-oz. can cream of coconut
1 8-oz. package cream cheese, softened
2 c. confectioners' sugar
1 tsp. vanilla extract
2 tbsp. milk
Flaked coconut

Combine first 5 ingredients; mix well. Pour into 9 × 13-inch baking pan. Bake at 350 degrees for 45 minutes. Combine cream cheese, confectioners' sugar, vanilla and milk; mix until of spreading consistency. Spread over cake. Top with coconut. Yield: 15-20 servings.

Mary Lawrence, Treas.
Xi Alpha Iota No. 1953
Okmulgee, Oklahoma

Heavenly Fruit Cocktail Cake

2 c. flour
2 tsp. soda
Pinch of salt
1½ c. sugar
2 eggs
1 med. can fruit cocktail
½ c. butter
½ c. chopped nuts
1 can evaporated milk
1 7-oz. can coconut
1 c. (firmly packed) brown sugar
1 tsp. vanilla extract

Combine first 6 ingredients; mix well. Pour into greased and floured 9 × 13-inch pan. Bake at 325 degrees for 35 to 40 minutes. Combine remaining ingredients in medium saucepan; bring to a boil. Boil until thickened. Pour over hot cake. Cool.

Sharon P. Gisselman
Xi Chi X3130
Severn, Maryland

Grandma Vera's Waldorf Cake

1½ c. butter
2½ c. sugar
2 eggs, slightly beaten
¼ c. red food coloring
1 tsp. cocoa
1 tsp. salt
1 c. buttermilk
Cake flour

2 tsp. vanilla extract
1 tsp. soda
1 tsp. vinegar
1 c. milk

Combine ½ cup butter and 1½ cups sugar; cream until smooth. Add eggs; beat until light and fluffy. Combine food coloring and cocoa; stir to form paste. Add to creamed mixture; mix well. Combine salt and buttermilk; set aside. Sift 2¼ cups cake flour; add to creamed mixture alternately with buttermilk mixture. Add 1 teaspoon vanilla; mix well. Add soda; mix well. Add vinegar; mix well. Pour into two 8-inch layer pans. Bake at 350 degrees for 40 minutes. Combine 3 tablespoons flour and milk in saucepan; cook until smooth. Cool until thickened. Combine 1 cup sugar, 1 cup butter and 1 teaspoon vanilla; beat until light and fluffy. Add milk mixture; mix well. Spread over cake.

Deborah Mosbach, Pres.
Xi Zeta Xi X5460
Pella, Iowa

Italian Nut Cake
(1950)

1½ sticks butter
½ c. shortening
2 c. sugar
5 eggs, separated
2 c. flour
1 tsp. soda
1 c. buttermilk
2½ tsp. vanilla extract
1 c. chopped nuts
1 c. coconut
1 8-oz. package cream cheese, softened
1 box confectioners' sugar

Cream 1 stick butter and shortening. Add sugar; beat until smooth. Add egg yolks; beat well. Combine flour and soda. Add flour mixture to creamed mixture alternately with buttermilk. Stir in 1 teaspoon vanilla. Add nuts and coconut; mix well. Beat egg whites until stiff peaks form; fold into batter. Pour into 3 greased and floured 9-inch cake pans. Bake at 350 degrees for 30 minutes or until cake tests done. Combine cream cheese and ½ stick butter; beat until light. Add 1½ teaspoons vanilla and confectioners' sugar; beat until smooth. Spread on cake. Yield: 20 servings.

Ruth Gross, Pres.
Xi Zeta Pi X1815
Arcata, California

Lazy Daisy Cake

2 eggs
1 c. sugar
1 c. flour
¾ tsp. salt
1 tsp. baking powder
½ c. milk
4 tbsp. butter or margarine
1 tsp. vanilla extract
½ c. coconut
½ c. chopped pecans
5 tbsp. brown sugar
3 tbsp. cream

Place eggs in large mixer bowl; beat until light and fluffy. And sugar gradually; beat until fluffy. Sift flour, salt and baking powder together. Add dry ingredients to egg mixture; beat well. Combine milk and 1 tablespoon butter in saucepan; bring to boiling point. Add milk mixture to batter; mix well. Add vanilla; blend well. Pour into greased and floured 8×8-inch baking pan. Bake at 350 degrees for 30 minutes. Mix coconut, pecans, brown sugar, cream and 3 tablespoons butter in saucepan; cook until of spreading consistency. Spread on hot cake. Broil until browned. Yield: 9 servings.

Kathryn L. Crawford
Unionville, Missouri

Louisiana Pecan Praline Cake

4 c. flour
1 lb. pecans, broken
1½ lb. raisins
1 tbsp. baking powder
2 tsp. nutmeg
½ lb. butter
2 c. sugar
6 eggs, separated
1 c. Praline Liqueur

Sprinkle ½ cup flour over pecans and raisins. Add baking powder and nutmeg to remaining flour. Cream butter and sugar. Blend in egg yolks. Add flour and liqueur alternately; blend well. Pour over nuts and raisins; mix well. Fold in beaten egg whites. Pour into greased and floured tube pan. Bake at 250 degrees for 3 hours. Remove from oven. Let stand 1 hour. Turn out onto cake rack. Sift confectioners' sugar over cake.

Avis L. Lewis, V.P.
Preceptor Sigma XP1815
Slidell, Louisiana

Nana's Hot Water Cake
(1930)

2 tbsp. shortening
2 c. sugar
2 eggs
Dash of salt
2 c. flour
2 tsp. soda
2 tsp. baking powder
4 tbsp. (heaping) cocoa
2 tsp. vanilla extract

Combine all ingredients in order listed and 2 cups boiling water, mixing well after each addition. Pour into 2 greased and floured 8-inch round cake pans. Bake at 350 degrees for 35 to 45 minutes or until cake tests done. Cool. Frost with favorite fudge icing. Yield: 12-15 servings.

Judith C. Liscum, Pres.
Theta Pi No. 8716
Canton, New York

Lazy Day Cake
(1950)

1 c. quick-cooking oatmeal
Margarine
1 c. sugar
1½ c. (firmly packed) brown sugar
2 eggs
1⅓ c. flour
1 tsp. soda
1 tsp. cinnamon
½ tsp. salt
2 c. chopped walnuts
¼ c. evaporated milk
½ tsp. vanilla extract
1 c. coconut

Combine oatmeal, 1 stick margarine and 1¼ cups boiling water; let stand for 20 minutes. Add sugar, 1 cup brown sugar, eggs, flour, soda, cinnamon, salt and 1 cup walnuts; mix well. Pour into 9×12-inch baking pan. Bake at 350 degrees for 30 minutes. Combine evaporated milk, 2 tablespoons melted margarine, vanilla, 1 cup walnuts, ½ cup brown sugar and coconut in saucepan; cook until heated through, stirring. Pour over warm cake. Broil until topping is well-browned. Yield: 20 servings.

Bonnie J. McMillon, Pres.
Mu No. 1137
Tonopah, Nevada

Milkless-Eggless-Butterless Cake

1 c. (firmly packed) dark brown sugar
⅓ c. vegetable shortening
1 c. seedless raisins
1 tbsp. Angostura aromatic bitters
2 c. flour
½ tsp. baking powder
½ tsp. soda
½ tsp. salt
1 c. chopped walnuts
Confectioners' sugar

Combine brown sugar, shortening, raisins, bitters and 1 cup water in saucepan; mix well. Bring to a boil; boil for 1 minute. Cool to lukewarm. Stir in remaining ingredients; blend well. Pour into greased and floured 9-inch square baking pan. Bake at 350 degrees for 35 minutes or until center is firm. Cut into squares. Dust with confectioners' sugar.

Photograph for this recipe on page 169.

Oatmeal Cake

1 c. quick-cooking oats
½ c. shortening
1 tsp. cinnamon
¼ tsp. nutmeg
½ tsp. salt
2 c. (firmly packed) brown sugar
1 c. sugar
2 eggs
1⅓ c. flour, sifted
1 tsp. soda
3 tbsp. butter
⅔ c. coconut
¼ c. cream
½ c. chopped nuts (opt.)
1 tsp. vanilla extract

Pour 1¼ cups boiling water over oats; let stand for 20 minutes. Combine shortening, cinnamon, nutmeg, salt, 1 cup brown sugar, sugar and eggs; mix well. Stir into oatmeal mixture. Sift flour and soda together; add to batter, mixing well. Pour into 9 × 13-inch baking pan. Bake at 350 degrees for 35 to 40 minutes. Combine butter, 1 cup brown sugar, coconut, cream, nuts and vanilla in saucepan; cook until heated through, stirring. Spread on cake. Broil for 3 to 5 minutes.

Mary Johnson, Pres.
Preceptor Sigma XP637
Rockford, Illinois

Orange and Raisin Cake
(1930)

1 c. sugar
½ c. shortening
2 eggs
½ tsp. soda
⅔ c. sour milk or buttermilk
2 c. flour
1 tsp. baking powder
½ tsp. salt
1 orange
1 c. raisins

Cream sugar and shortening; add eggs. Combine soda and sour milk. Sift dry ingredients together; add to creamed mixture alternately with sour milk, beginning and ending with flour mixture. Grind orange and raisins together. Add to batter. Pour into greased and floured tube pan. Bake at 250 degrees for 45 minutes. Frost with butter cream or cream cheese frosting.

Margaret Liles
Preceptor Kappa XP1284
Las Vegas, Nevada

Pig'n Whistle Cake

4 eggs
2 c. sugar
2 c. sifted flour
2 tsp. baking powder
1¼ tsp. salt
1 c. scalded milk
1 tsp. vanilla
¼ c. butter
½ c. coconut
1 c. chopped nuts
6 tbsp. cream
1 c. (firmly packed) brown sugar

Cream eggs and sugar until fluffy. Sift dry ingredients together; add to creamed mixture alternately with milk beginning and ending with flour mixture. Add vanilla. Pour into greased baking pan. Bake at 375 degrees for 15 minutes. Reduce heat to 350 degrees. Bake for 15 minutes longer or until cake tests done. Melt butter in medium saucepan. Add remaining ingredients; mix well. Spread on top of hot cake.

Emma Lee Bahr, Rec. Sec.
Preceptor Beta Iota XP1627
Tacoma, Washington

Pineapple Upside-Down Cake (1953)

1 c. sugar
3 eggs
1 c. flour
2 tsp. baking powder
¼ tsp. salt
1 tsp. vanilla extract
1 stick margarine, melted
1 c. (firmly packed) brown sugar
7 slices pineapple, drained
7 maraschino cherries
½ c. pecan halves

Combine margarine and brown sugar in 10-inch skillet. Arrange pineapple slices in skillet with cherry in center of each. Arrange pecan halves between pineapple slices. Set aside. Place sugar in large mixer bowl; add eggs one at a time, beating well after each addition. Sift flour, baking powder and salt together; add to creamed mixture. Add vanilla and ¼ cup cold water; mix well. Pour batter over pineapple. Bake at 325 degrees for 25 minutes. Cool for 10 minutes. Invert onto cake plate. Yield: 8 servings.

Dora Smith, Pres.
Alpha Rhu Zeta No 10482
Cross Plains, Texas

Swedish Pineapple Cake

2 tsp. soda
¼ tsp. salt
2 c. flour
2 c. sugar
1 16-oz. can crushed pineapple
½ c. (firmly packed) brown sugar
½ c. chopped nuts
¾ stick margarine
1 sm. can evaporated milk

Sift soda, salt and flour together. Add 1¼ cups sugar and pineapple; mix well with wooden spoon. Pour into greased 9 x 13-inch baking pan. Sprinkle with brown sugar and nuts. Bake at 350 degrees for 30 minutes. Combine ¾ cup sugar, margarine and evaporated milk in saucepan; mix well. Bring to a boil; boil for 10 minutes, stirring. Pour hot icing over cake. Yield: 10-12 servings.

Rita C. Watson
Alpha Kappa XP820
Joplin, Missouri

Pineapple Icebox Cake
(1948)

½ lb. vanilla wafers, crushed
½ c. butter, softened
1½ c. confectioners' sugar
2 eggs
½ pt. whipping cream
1 8-oz. can crushed pineapple, drained

Press ½ of the crumbs into 7-inch square pan. Cream butter and sugar. Add eggs one at a time, beating well after each addition. Pour over crumbs. Whip cream until stiff peaks form; fold in pineapple. Spread over egg mixture. Sprinkle with remaining crumbs. Refrigerate overnight. Yield: 9 servings.

Alice C. Galbraith, Sec.
Laureate Beta PL123
Waukegan, Illinois

Aunt Eva's Pound Cake
(1940)

2 c. sugar
2 sticks butter, softened
4 eggs
½ tsp. salt
1 sm. can evaporated milk
2 c. flour
1 tsp. vanilla flavoring
1 tsp. lemon flavoring
½ tsp. baking powder

Combine all ingredients in mixer bowl; beat at High speed of electric mixer for 5 minutes. Pour into greased and floured tube pan. Bake at 300 degrees for 1 hour and 30 minutes. Yield: 14 servings.

Ruth W. Winde, Pres.
Xi Epsilon X795
Columbia, South Carolina

Buttermilk Pound Cake
(1930)

1 c. butter or margarine
2 c. sugar
4 lg. eggs
1 tsp. vanilla extract
¼ tsp. mace
3 c. flour
⅓ tsp. salt
⅓ tsp. soda
½ tsp. baking powder
1 c. buttermilk

Cream butter and sugar until fluffy. Add eggs one at a time, beating well after each addition. Add vanilla and mace; blend. Sift dry ingredients together; add to creamed mixture alternately with buttermilk, beginning and ending with flour. Pour batter into 10-inch greased, brown paper-lined pan. Bake at 350 degrees for 1 hour or until cake tests done. Cool for 10 minutes. Remove from pan. Dust with confectioners' sugar. Yield: 1 5-lb. cake.

Thelma Fisher
Preceptor Nu XP1498
Frederick, Maryland

Chocolate Pound Cake
(1930)

3 c. sugar
½ lb. butter, softened
½ c. oil
5 eggs, room temperature
3 c. flour
6 tbsp. cocoa
½ tsp. salt
½ tsp. baking powder
1 c. milk
2 tsp. vanilla extract

Combine sugar, butter and oil; beat until well-blended. Add eggs, one at a time, beating well after each addition. Sift dry ingredients together. Add to egg mixture alternately with milk. Beat with electric mixer for 5 minutes. Add vanilla. Pour into greased and floured tube pan. Bake at 300 degrees for 1 hour and 30 minutes or until cake tests done. Yield: 18-24 servings.

Gene Hollamon
Xi Beta Epsilon X4291
Camp Varde, Arizona

Lemon Yogurt Pound Cake

3½ c. flour
1 tsp. soda
1 tsp. salt
5 eggs, separated
1 c. margarine
2½ c. sugar or 1 c. honey
1 c. unflavored yogurt, room temperature
Juice and grated rind of 1 lemon

Sift flour, soda and salt together. Beat egg whites until stiff peaks form; set aside. Cream margarine until light and fluffy. Beat egg yolks until thickened; add to margarine, beating until smooth. Stir yogurt until creamy; add to egg yolk mixture. Add flour mixture; mix well. Stir in lemon juice and rind. Fold in egg whites. Pour into greased 10-inch tube pan. Bake at 325 degrees for 20 minutes. Increase heat to

350 degrees. Bake at 350 degrees for 45 to 50 minutes longer. Cool in pan on wire rack.

Carol Callas, Pres.
Delta Omicron No. 9608
Merville, British Columbia, Canada

Caramel-Nut Pound Cake

1 c. butter or margarine
½ c. shortening
1 1-lb. package light brown sugar
1 c. sugar
5 eggs
½ tsp. baking powder
½ tsp. salt
3 c. flour
1 c. milk
1 tbsp. vanilla extract
1 c. finely chopped nuts
Confectioners' sugar (opt.)

Cream butter, shortening and brown sugar. Add sugar gradually; cream until smooth. Add eggs, one at a time, beating well after each addition. Combine baking powder, salt and flour; add alternately with milk to creamed mixture, beginning and ending with flour mixture. Add vanilla and nuts; blend well. Pour into greased and floured 10-inch tube pan. Bake at 325 degrees for 1 hour and 30 minutes or until cake tests done. Cool for 15 minutes. Remove from pan. Dust with confectioners' sugar. I won first place with this cake in the 1977 Taylor County Pecan Festival.

Mamie W. Steck, Rec. Sec.
Xi Nu Chi X4005
Merkel, Texas

Sour Cream Pound Cake

3 c. sugar
2 sticks butter, softened
6 lg. eggs, room temperature
8 oz. sour cream
3 c. flour
1 tsp. vanilla extract

Combine sugar and butter in mixer bowl; mix on Medium speed of electric mixer. Add eggs, one at a time, beating well after each addition. Add vanilla; blend well. Add flour and sour cream alternately to batter, mixing on Low speed of electric mixer. Pour into buttered tube pan. Bake at 325 degrees for 1 hour and 15 to 30 minutes or until sides are golden brown. Cool for 5 to 10 minutes. Remove from pan.

Frost with favorite seven-minute icing recipe. Store at room temperature.

June Dusenbury, Pres.
Gamma Omicron No. 9881
Myrtle Beach, South Carolina

Super-Simple Pound Cake

2 sticks butter or margarine, melted
½ c. vegetable oil
3 c. sugar
5 eggs
3 c. flour
1 c. milk
½ tsp. baking powder
2 tsp. vanilla extract

Combine all ingredients in large mixer bowl. Beat with electric mixer until smooth. Pour into greased and floured bundt pan. Place in cold oven. Turn temperature setting to 300 degrees. Bake for 1 hour and 30 minutes to 2 hours or until cake tests done.

Judy J. Crump, Rec. Sec.
Epsilon Pi
Church Road, Virginia

Rum Cakes

1 c. sifted cake flour
¼ tsp. baking powder
½ tsp. soda
¼ tsp. salt
¼ c. butter or margarine
1 tbsp. grated orange rind
Sugar
1 egg, well beaten
½ c. sour cream
½ c. chopped nuts
⅔ c. chopped maraschino cherries
½ c. orange juice
2 tbsp. rum or 1 tsp. rum extract

Sift flour, baking powder, soda and salt together. Cream butter, orange rind and ½ cup sugar until fluffy. Add egg, beating well. Add sour cream alternately with flour mixture; beat until smooth. Fold in nuts and cherries. Spoon ¼ cup batter into greased individual pans, filling half full. Bake at 350 degrees for 30 minutes or until cakes test done. Combine ⅔ cup sugar, orange juice and rum; mix well. Pour over hot cakes. Cool in pans. Serve with whipped cream or sour cream. Garnish with stemmed maraschino cherries. Yield: 10 servings.

Grace Autry, Treas.
Preceptor Delta Delta XP932
Arroyo Grande, California

Pumpkin Roll

3 eggs
1 c. sugar
⅔ c. pumpkin
1 tsp. lemon juice
¾ c. flour
2 tsp. cinnamon
1 tsp. baking powder
½ tsp. salt
1 tsp. ginger
1 tsp. nutmeg
1¼ c. confectioners' sugar
1 8-oz. package cream cheese, softened
¼ c. butter, softened
½ tsp. vanilla extract

Place eggs in mixer bowl; beat at High speed of electric mixer for 5 minutes. Add sugar gradually, beating well. Stir in pumpkin and lemon juice. Combine flour, cinnamon, baking powder, salt, ginger, and nutmeg; mix well. Add flour mixture to pumpkin mixture, blending well. Spoon into 15 x 10 x 1-inch jelly roll pan; spread evenly. Bake at 375 degrees for 15 minutes. Turn cake out on towel sprinkled with ¼ cup confectioners' sugar. Roll cake and towel as for jelly roll. Cool. Combine 1 cup confectioners' sugar, cream cheese, butter and vanilla; beat until smooth and creamy. Unroll cake; spread with cream cheese mixture. Reroll, seam side down. Chill. Cut into slices.

Deborah Goldy
Gamma Delta No. 6896
Mt. Sterling, Kentucky

Mother's Rhubarb Cake
(1950)

½ c. margarine, softened
1½ c. (firmly packed) brown sugar
2 eggs
1 c. buttermilk
1 tsp. vanilla extract
2 c. sifted flour
1 tsp. soda
Dash of salt
1½ c. diced rhubarb
½ c. sugar
1 tsp. cinnamon
½ c. chopped nuts

Cream margarine and brown sugar. Add eggs, buttermilk and vanilla; blend well. Sift flour, soda and salt together; add to creamed mixture gradually. Fold in rhubarb. Pour into greased 9 x 12-inch pan. Combine sugar, cinnamon and nuts in small bowl. Sprinkle over batter. Bake at 350 degrees for 45 to 50 minutes or until cake tests done. Serve with whipped cream.

Annelle Mizell
XI Epsilon Gamma X2317
Petersburg, Illinois

Quick Tomato-Spice Cake

1 pkg. spice cake mix
1 10¾-oz. can Campbell's tomato soup
2 eggs, slightly beaten
1 c. chopped walnuts

Combine cake mix, soup, eggs and ½ cup water; mix according to package directions. Fold in walnuts. Bake according to package directions. Frost with favorite white icing.

Photograph for this recipe on page 173.

Toasted Spice Cake
(1930)

¾ c. vegetable shortening
3 c. (firmly packed) brown sugar, sifted
2 eggs, separated
1 tsp. soda
1¼ c. sour milk
2⅓ c. sifted flour
1 tsp. baking powder
1 tsp. cloves
1 tsp. cinnamon
¾ tsp. salt
1 tsp. vanilla extract
½ c. chopped nuts (opt.)

Combine shortening, 2 cups brown sugar and egg yolks; beat until well blended. Dissolve soda in sour milk. Sift dry ingredients together. Add sour milk mixture to shortening mixture alternately with dry ingredients, mixing well. Stir in vanilla; mix until smooth. Pour into greased and floured 8 x 12-inch pan. Beat egg whites until soft peaks form. Add 1 cup brown sugar gradually; beat until smooth. Spread over batter. Sprinkle with nuts. Bake at 350 degrees for 45 minutes.

Doris Holroyd, Rec. Sec.
Preceptor Alpha Epsilon XP1343
Albion, Iowa

Squash Cake

3 eggs, slightly beaten
2 c. sugar
1 c. oil
2 c. flour
2 c. grated squash
1 tsp. salt
1 tsp. baking powder
2 tsp. soda
2 tsp. cinnamon
2 tsp. vanilla extract
1 c. chopped nuts

1 c. chopped dates
1 c. raisins

Combine all ingredients in order listed; mix well. Pour into floured 13½ x 9-inch baking pan. Bake at 300 degrees for 1 hour or until cake tests done. This recipe freezes well. Yield: 16 servings.

Kathie Utt, Pres.
Delta Omega No. 1892
Alturas, California

Sunshine Cake
(1955)

6 eggs, separated
⅓ tsp. cream of tartar
1 c. sugar
1 tsp. vanilla extract
½ c. orange juice
½ tsp. salt
1 c. flour

Combine egg whites and cream of tartar; beat until stiff peaks form. Set aside. Beat egg yolks until light. Add sugar; beat well. Combine vanilla and orange juice; mix well. Sift salt and flour together. Add dry ingredients alternately with orange juice mixture to egg yolk mixture, beating well after each addition.

Fold in egg whites. Pour into 10-inch tube pan; spread evenly. Place in cold oven. Set oven temperature at 350 degrees; bake for 1 hour or until cake tests done. Invert pan until cake is cooled. Remove from pan.

Lucy Bates, V.P.
Preceptor Laureate Alpha Kappa PL409
Escondido, California

Donna's Tomato Soup Cake

1 c. sugar
⅓ c. shortening
1 tsp. soda
1 can tomato soup
1½ c. flour
1 tsp. cinnamon
½ tsp. cloves
1 c. raisins

Combine sugar and shortening; cream until smooth. Dissolve soda in tomato soup; add to creamed mixture. Add flour and spices; mix well. Fold in raisins. Spoon into 8 x 8-inch baking pan. Bake at 325 degrees for 1 hour.

Donna Scott, Pres.
Xi Beta Omicron X4658
Squamish, British Columbia, Canada

Angostura Walnut Cake

5 egg yolks
Sugar
¼ c. fine dry bread crumbs
Angostura aromatic bitters
1 c. finely ground walnuts
5 egg whites, stiffly beaten
Juice of ½ lemon

Combine egg yolks and 6 tablespoons sugar; beat until thickened. Stir in crumbs, 1 teaspoon bitters and walnuts. Fold in egg whites. Pour into greased and floured 8-inch fluted pan. Bake at 350 degrees for 1 hour or until cake tests done. Remove from pan; cool on rack. Combine 1½ cups sugar, ½ cup water, lemon juice and 2 tablespoons bitters in saucepan; mix well. Bring to a boil; boil for 2 minutes. Place cake on serving platter. Spoon hot syrup slowly over cake. Garnish with rosettes of whipped cream and walnut halves.

Photograph for this recipe on page 124.

Athenian Nut Cake

1 c. chopped walnuts
2 c. Bisquick
1 tbsp. grated orange rind
2 tsp. baking powder
2½ c. sugar
1 tsp. cinnamon
¼ tsp. cloves
½ tsp. nutmeg
4 eggs, slightly beaten

Combine first 8 ingredients and 1 cup sugar in large mixer bowl; blend well. Pour into greased and floured 9 x 13-inch pan. Bake at 350 degrees for 30 minutes. Combine remaining 1½ cups sugar and 1¼ cups water in small saucepan; bring to a boil. Cool. Pour over hot cake.

Patricia Benos, V.P.
Xi Iota Chi X4711
Richmond, Ohio

5¢ Walnut Cake
(1930)

1⅓ c. sugar
½ c. Crisco
2 c. sifted flour
1 tsp. salt
1 c. milk
3 tsp. baking powder
2 eggs

1 tsp. vanilla extract
½ c. walnuts, chopped

Cream sugar and Crisco. Add flour and salt; blend well. Add ⅔ cup milk; beat well. Add baking powder, eggs, vanilla, walnuts and remaining ⅓ cup milk; beat for 2 minutes. Pour batter into greased and floured bundt pan. Bake at 350 degrees for 50 to 60 minutes or until cake tests done. Cool for 5 minutes. Remove from pan.

Sandra Phyllis Polsky
Xi Zeta Epsilon X2827
Hoffman Estates, Illinois

War Cake
(1942)

2 c. (firmly packed) brown sugar
2 tsp. shortening
½ to ¾ c. raisins
1 tsp. salt
1 tsp. cinnamon
1 tsp. cloves
1 tsp. soda
3 c. flour

Combine brown sugar, shortening, raisins, salt, cinnamon, cloves and 2 cups hot water in medium saucepan; mix well. Bring to a boil; boil for 5 minutes. Cool thoroughly. Dissolve soda in 2 teaspoons hot water. Add soda mixture to cooled mixture alternately with flour, mixing well after each addition. Pour into greased tube pan. Bake at 350 degrees for 1 hour or until cake tests done. Yield: 16 servings.

Mary Greenwalt, Pres.
Laureate Lambda PL461
Anderson, Indiana

Yahyah's Ravani

½ lb. butter
3 c. sugar
6 lg. eggs, beaten
1 c. flour
2 tsp. baking powder
1 c. quick-cooking cream of wheat
1 c. blanched ground almonds
¼ c. milk
½ tsp. grated lemon rind
1 tsp. honey
1 tsp. lemon juice

Cream butter. Add 1 cup sugar; continue beating until light and fluffy. Add eggs gradually. Add flour, baking powder, cream of wheat, almonds, milk and lemon rind; mix well. Pour into greased 9 x 13-inch pan. Bake at 350 degrees for 25 to 30 minutes. Combine 2 cups sugar, honey and 1½ cups water in saucepan. Boil for 10 minutes until a thin syrup is formed. Stir in lemon juice. Cool. Pour over hot cake. Cover with towel; let stand until thoroughly cooled. Cut into diamond-shaped pieces. This recipe won third place in the Gainesville, Texas Daily Register cooking contest October 22, 1976.

Elizabeth A. Boyd
Omicron Chi
McKinney, Texas

Versatile White Cake

3 c. sifted self-rising cake flour
1½ c. sugar
¾ c. margarine, softened
¾ c. milk
4 egg whites
1½ tsp. vanilla extract

Sift flour and sugar together in mixer bowl. Add margarine and ½ cup milk; beat for 2 minutes at Medium speed of electric mixer. Add egg whites, vanilla and ¼ cup milk; beat for 1 minute. Pour into greased and floured cake pans. Bake at 375 degrees for 30 minutes or until cake tests done. Decorate as desired.

Photograph for this recipe on page 175.

Fudge Cupcakes

2 sticks butter or margarine
4 sq. semisweet chocolate
1½ c. chopped pecans
1¾ c. sugar
1 c. flour
4 lg. eggs, beaten
1 tsp. vanilla extract

Melt butter and chocolate in top of double boiler. Add pecans; stir. Set aside. Cream sugar and flour. Add eggs and vanilla; blend. Fold in chocolate mixture. Fill paper-lined cupcake cups ⅔ full. Bake at 325 degrees for 25 minutes. Yield: 18-24 cupcakes.

Sue Starkey, Pres.
Alpha Sigma, Zeta No. 10660
Georgetown, Texas

Jiffy Chocolate Cupcakes
(1950)

1 egg
½ c. cocoa
½ c. shortening
1½ c. sifted flour
½ c. sour milk or buttermilk
1 tsp. vanilla extract
1 tsp. soda
1 c. sugar
½ tsp. salt

Combine all ingredients and ½ cup hot water in large mixer bowl. Beat for 4 minutes at medium speed of electric mixer. Pour into baking cups, filling ½ full. Bake at 375 degrees for 15 to 20 minutes.

Sharon J. De Shazer, Pres. City Coun.
Xi Beta Sigma X2239
Hutchinson, Kansas

Pasta Frolla
(1940)

4 egg yolks
1 c. sugar
½ lb. margarine or butter, softened
3 c. flour
Jelly or jam

Combine egg yolks and sugar in mixer bowl; mix well. Cream margarine; add egg mixture. Add flour gradually, mixing well. Place paper muffin cups into muffin pans. Press dough into papers until ⅓ full. Make slight depression in center of dough; fill with jelly or jam. Bake at 350 degrees for 20 minutes. Remove from paper cups while warm to prevent sticking. Yield: 12-24 servings.

Lesley Sharer Evans
Beta Psi No. 9037
Gaithersburg, Maryland

Poor Man Cupcakes
(1930)

2 tsp. soda
1 lb. seedless raisins
4 c. flour
½ tsp. salt
1½ tsp. cloves
1½ tsp. cinnamon
½ tsp. baking power
½ c. shortening
2 c. sugar

Dissolve soda in 2 cups hot water in medium saucepan. Add raisins; cook until tender. Do not drain. Sift dry ingredients together. Combine sifted ingredients, raisin mixture, shortening, sugar and 1 cup cold water; mix well. Pour into muffin pans, filling ½ full. Bake at 350 degrees for 20 to 25 minutes.Yield: 3½ dozen.

Kandee K. Graham, Treas.
Xi Epsilon Phi X4353
Campbelltown, Pennsylvania

Chicago Cake

1 pkg. Duncan Hines white cake mix
1 3¾-oz. package lemon instant pudding mix
1 3¾-oz. package vanilla instant pudding mix
5 eggs, slightly beaten
½ c. milk
½ c. oil
1 stick butter
1 c. sugar
½ tsp. soda
½ c. buttermilk

Combine first 6 ingredients in order listed; mix well. Pour into baking pan. Bake at 350 degrees for 1 hour. Melt butter in saucepan. Add sugar; mix well. Combine soda and buttermilk; add to butter mixture, mixing well. Bring to a boil; boil for 1 minute. Pour on hot cake. Yield: 12 servings.

Alice Montgomery, Pres.
Preceptor Alpha Zeta No. 1167
Shelbyville, Indiana

Almost-No-Time Cake

1 pkg. yellow cake mix
1 pkg. vanilla instant pudding mix
1 c. sour cream
4 eggs
½ c. corn oil
1 12-oz. package chocolate chips

Combine first 5 ingredients in mixer bowl; blend well. Fold in chocolate chips. Pour into greased and floured tube pan. Bake at 350 degrees for 45 to 60 minutes.

Mary Ann Simmons, Pres.
Maryland Xi Alpha Omicron X4628
Upper Marlboro, Maryland

Karen's Mississippi Mud

1½ c. margarine
1¼ c. flour
¼ c. chopped pecans or walnuts
2 env. Dream Whip
1 8-oz. package cream cheese

2 tsp. vanilla extract
1 c. confectioners' sugar
2 4-oz. packages instant chocolate pudding mix
3 c. milk

Combine margarine, flour, pecans and 2 teaspoons ice water in mixer bowl; beat well. Press into 12 x 9-inch oblong baking pan. Bake at 350 degrees for 25 minutes or until lightly browned. Cool. Prepare Dream Whip according to package directions. Blend cream cheese until soft. Combine ½ of the Dream Whip, cream cheese, 1 teaspoon vanilla and confectioners' sugar; mix well. Spread over cooled layer. Combine pudding mix, milk and 1 teaspoon vanilla; beat well. Let stand for 5 minutes or until mixture thickens. Pour over cream cheese mixture. Cover with remaining Dream Whip. Decorate with grated chocolate. Chill until firm. Yield: 15 servings.

Karen MacKay
Alpha Rho No. 2783
Cambridge, Ontario, Canada

Hawaiian Wedding Cake

1 1-lb 2½-oz. package yellow cake mix
1½ c. milk
1 3¾-oz. package instant vanilla pudding mix
1 8-oz. package cream cheese, softened
1 20-oz. can crushed pineapple, drained
1 lg. package Dream Whip
½ tsp. vanilla extract
1 med. can flaked coconut

Prepare cake according to package directions. Bake in 13 x 9-inch pan. Cool. Combine 1 cup milk, pudding mix and cream cheese; mix well. Spread on cooled cake. Cover with pineapple. Prepare Dream Whip according to package directions, using ½ cup milk and ½ teaspoon vanilla. Spread over pineapple. Sprinkle with coconut. Yield: 20-24 servings.

Pat A. Miller
Preceptor Beta Zeta X1793
Chambersburg, Pennsylvania

Pig Pickin Cake

1 pkg. Duncan Hines yellow cake mix
4 eggs
½ c. Crisco oil
1 11-oz. can mandarin oranges
1 20-oz. can crushed pineapple
1 3-oz. package instant vanilla pudding mix
1 lg. carton Cool Whip

Combine cake mix, eggs, oil and mandarin oranges; mix well. Pour into 2 greased and floured 9-inch round cake pans. Bake at 350 degrees for 30 to 35

minutes. Combine pineapple, pudding mix and Cool Whip; mix well. Frost sides and top of cake. Keep refrigerated. Yield: 15 servings.

Ginger McWilliams, Pres.
Xi Epsilon Delta No. 4452
Mt. Pleasant, Iowa

Pina Colada Cake

1 pkg. white cake mix
2 sm. packages instant coconut cream or vanilla pudding mix
4 eggs
⅔ c. dark rum
½ c. Wesson oil
1 8-oz. can crushed pineapple in juice
1 9-oz. carton frozen whipped topping, thawed
1 c. flaked coconut

Combine cake mix, 1 package pudding mix, eggs, ⅓ cup rum, oil and ½ cup water in large mixer bowl; beat at Medium speed of electric mixer for 4 minutes. Pour into 2 greased and floured 9-inch layer cake pans. Bake at 350 degrees for 25 to 30 minutes or until cake tests done. Cool for 15 minutes. Remove from pans; cool on wire rack. Combine pineapple, remaining pudding mix and ⅓ cup rum; beat until well blended. Fold in whipped topping. Fill and frost cake. Sprinkle with coconut. Chill until serving time. If using vanilla pudding mix, increase water to ¾ cup and add 1 cup flaked coconut to batter.

Patricia C. Blinn, Pres.
Xi Theta Phi X4149
Perrysburg, Ohio

Watergate Cake

1 pkg. white cake mix
2 pkg. pistachio pudding mix
3 eggs, slightly beaten
1 c. Crisco oil
1 c. 7-Up
1½ c. milk
9 oz. Cool Whip

Combine cake mix, 1 package pudding mix, eggs, oil and 7-Up; beat for 4 minutes. Pour into greased and floured 9 x 13-inch baking pan. Bake at 350 degrees for 35 to 40 minutes. Cool completely. Combine remaining package pudding mix and milk; beat for 2 minutes. Fold in Cool Whip. Spread on cooled cake. Keeps well in refrigerator.

Sheri Duerst, Pres.
Preceptor Theta Delta XP1720
San Marcos, California

Punkin' Delight

1 pkg. yellow cake mix
Margarine
4 eggs
2 1-lb. cans pumpkin
½ c. (firmly packed) brown sugar
¾ c. sugar
⅔ c. milk
½ tsp. cinnamon
½ c. chopped nuts
Whipped cream

Reserve 1 cup dry cake mix. Combine remaining cake mix, ½ cup melted margarine and 1 beaten egg; mix well. Press into greased and floured 9 x 13-inch pan. Combine pumpkin, 3 eggs, brown sugar, ¼ cup sugar, milk and cinnamon; mix well. Spread over batter. Combine reserved 1 cup cake mix, pecans, ½ cup sugar and ¼ cup margarine; mix until crumbly. Sprinkle over pumpkin mixture. Bake at 350 degrees for 50 to 60 minutes or until cake tests done. Cool. Top with whipped cream.

Diana L. Beck, Pres.
Beta Eta No. 4572
Lafayette, Louisiana

Aunt Mabel's Strawberry Cake

1 pkg. white cake mix
⅔ c. salad oil
1 3-oz. package strawberry Jell-O
4 eggs
1 10-oz. package frozen strawberries
1 box confectioners' sugar
¼ lb. butter or margarine, softened

Combine cake mix, salad oil, Jell-O, eggs, ½ cup water and half the strawberries in a large mixer bowl. Beat at Medium speed of electric mixer until smooth. Pour into greased and floured 9 x 13-inch pan. Bake at 350 degrees for 45 minutes. Cool. Combine confectioners' sugar, butter and remaining strawberries in mixer bowl. Beat until light and fluffy. Spread on cold cake.

Gayle E. Swanson
Xi Theta Nu No. 3738
Wheaton, Illinois

Angostura Cake

2 c. flour
1½ c. sugar
½ c. cocoa
2 tsp. baking powder
½ tsp. salt
½ c. vegetable shortening
1½ c. milk
1 tsp. vanilla extract
2 eggs
1 c. light cream, chilled
½ c. cold coffee
1 tsp. Angostura bitters
1 pkg. instant chocolate pudding mix

Sift flour, sugar, cocoa, baking powder and salt together in large mixer bowl. Add shortening, milk and vanilla; beat for 2 minutes with electric mixer. Add eggs; beat for 1 minute. Pour into 2 greased layer pans. Bake at 350 degrees for 20 minutes. Cool thoroughly. Combine cream and coffee. Add bitters and pudding mix; beat with egg beater for 1 minute or until well blended. Let stand for 5 minutes. Frost cake. Decorate with walnut halves.

Photograph for this recipe on page 179.

Apple Bundt Cake

3 c. flour
2 tsp. soda
½ tsp. salt
2 tsp. cinnamon
1½ c. cooking oil
1½ c. sugar
2 c. grated Golden Delicious apples
1 8-oz. can crushed pineapple
Chopped walnuts
½ c. coconut
1½ tsp. vanilla extract
3 eggs
1½ c. confectioners' sugar
3 tsp. butter, softened
½ tsp. grated lemon rind
2 tsp. lemon juice

Sift flour, soda, salt and cinnamon together. Combine oil and sugar; add half the dry ingredients, mixing well. Blend in apples, pineapple, ½ cup walnuts, coconut and vanilla. Add remaining dry ingredients. Add eggs, one at a time, beating well after each addition. Pour into greased 3-quart bundt pan. Bake at 350 degrees for 1 hour or until cake tests done. Cool in pan for 15 minutes. Remove from pan. Cool on wire rack. Combine confectioners' sugar, butter, lemon rind, lemon juice and 1½ teaspoons hot water. Stir until smooth. Drizzle on cake. Sprinkle with 2 tablespoons walnuts.

Helen J. Karn, Prog. Chm.
Preceptor Gamma XP284
Boise, Idaho

Butterscotch Cake

½ c. shortening
2 c. (firmly packed) brown sugar
2 eggs
¼ c. vinegar
¼ c. cocoa
Salt
1 tsp. soda
2½ c. cake flour
3 tsp. vanilla extract
½ c. chopped nuts
1½ c. sugar
⅛ tsp. cream of tartar
2 egg whites, stiffly beaten
1 sm. can crushed pineapple, drained

Cream shortening and brown sugar. Add eggs, one at a time, beating well after each addition. Add vinegar and ¾ cup cold water; mix well. Sift cocoa, ¼ teaspoon salt, soda and flour together. Add to creamed mixture, mixing well. Add 2 teaspoons vanilla and nuts; beat until fluffy. Pour into 3 greased and floured cake pans. Bake at 350 degrees for 30 minutes or until cake tests done. Combine sugar, ¾ cup boiling water, pinch of salt and cream of tartar in saucepan. Stir until sugar is dissolved. Boil until soft-ball stage. Pour slowly over egg whites, beating constantly. Add 1 teaspoon vanilla. Spread pineapple on cake layers; cover with icing. Stack layers. Frost top and sides.

Juanita Mattice, Corr. Sec.
Preceptor Alpha Mu XP672
Amarillo, Texas

Butter Sponge Cake

2 eggs
¼ tsp. salt
1 c. sugar
1 tsp. vanilla or lemon flavoring
½ c. milk
1 tsp. butter
1 c. flour
1 tsp. baking powder

Beat eggs until light. Add salt, sugar and flavoring; beat well. Combine milk and butter in saucepan; bring to a boil. Add milk mixture to egg mixture, beating well. Sift flour and baking powder together. Add flour mixture to egg mixture; beat well. Pour into greased and floured 9-inch cake pan. Bake at 350 degrees until cake tests done.

Teri Bateman, Sec.
Xi Epsilon Gamma X1742
Denison, Texas

Baby Food Cake

Flour
2 c. sugar
2 tsp. cinnamon
2 tsp. baking powder
1 c. chopped pecans
1 c. oil
3 eggs
1/3 tsp. cloves
1 tsp. salt
2 jars plum baby food

Combine 2 cups plus 2 tablespoons flour and remaining ingredients in order listed; mix well. Pour into greased and floured tube or bundt pan. Bake at 350 degrees for 1 hour and 15 minutes or until cake tests done. Cool for 10 minutes. Remove from pan. Frost as desired.

Freddie Holland, Rec. Sec.
Xi Rho Nu X4693
San Antonio, Texas

Creme de Menthe Cake

1 pkg. white cake mix
1/2 c. Creme de Menthe
1 16-oz. can Hershey Fudge Topping
1 9-oz. carton Cool Whip

Prepare cake mix according to package directions. Stir in 1/4 cup Creme de Menthe. Spread in 9x13-inch cake pan. Bake at 350 degrees for 30 minutes or until cake tests done. Cool thoroughly. Spread with fudge topping. Combine Cool Whip and 1/4 cup Creme de Menthe; mix well. Spread over fudge topping. Chill until serving time. Yield: 20 servings.

Debra K. Denowh, Pres.
Alpha Rho No. 8266
Sidney, Montana

Dark Fruitcake
(1930)

2 c. sugar
3 c. grape juice
1 lb. raisins
1 tbsp. cinnamon
1 c. shortening
1 tsp. soda
1/2 tsp. salt
1/2 tsp. cloves
2 tsp. baking powder
2 tbsp. cocoa
1 c. nuts
1 c. mixed candied citrus fruits
4 c. flour

Combine sugar, grape juice, raisins and cinnamon in large saucepan. Boil over low heat for 30 minutes.

Remove from heat. Add shortening, stirring until melted. Add soda; stir until mixture bubbles. Batter will turn green. Add remaining ingredients; mix well. Pour into 10-inch tube pan. Bake at 350 degrees for 1 hour and 15 minutes or until cake tests done. Cool in pan.

Carol M. Beeson, Pres.
Omega No. 3422
Buhl, Idaho

Eleven Minute Cake

1 1/2 c. milk
1 1/2 c. sugar
2 c. flour
3 tsp. baking powder
1/2 tsp. salt
4 egg whites, stiffly beaten
1/2 tsp. vanilla extract

Combine milk and sugar in saucepan. Bring to a boil; boil for 1 minute. Combine flour, baking powder and salt. Add milk mixture; mix well. Fold in egg whites and vanilla. Pour into tube pan. Bake at 425 degrees for 11 minutes.

Flo Leetch
Xi Gamma Eta
Lee's Summit, Missouri

Farina Cake

1/2 lb. butter, softened
4 c. sugar
6 eggs
1 c. Farina
1 c. flour
2 tsp. baking powder
3 tbsp. milk

Cream butter and 1 cup sugar until smooth. Add eggs, Farina, flour, baking powder and milk; beat until well blended. Pour into 9x14-inch pan. Bake at 350 degrees for 30 minutes or until cake tests done. Combine 3 cups sugar and 4 cups water in saucepan; mix well. Cook until heated through. Pour over cake slowly. Decorate with cinnamon and chopped walnuts. Yield: 10-12 servings.

Georgia Carter
Theta Iota No. 10732
Pineville, Louisiana

Grandma's Eggless Fruitcake

2 c. raisins
1 c. sugar
¼ c. Crisco
1 c. buttermilk or sour milk
1 tsp. soda
2 tsp. cinnamon
1 tsp. ground cloves
½ tsp. nutmeg
2¼ c. flour
½ c. wine (opt.)
1 c. chopped dates
2 lb. mixed fruit, chopped
1 c. chopped nuts

Soak raisins in hot water until softened. Cream sugar and Crisco until smooth. Add buttermilk, mixing well. Sift dry ingredients together. Add dry ingredients to creamed mixture; mix well. Add wine; mix until well blended. Drain raisins. Add raisins, dates, mixed fruit and nuts; mix well. Batter will be thick. Pour into 2 waxed paper-lined 2-quart loaf pans. Bake at 350 degrees for 1 hour or until cake tests done. Cool on racks for 10 minutes. Remove from pans. Remove waxed paper while still warm. Will keep refrigerated for several weeks.

Linda L. Frederick, Pres.
Xi Alpha Mu No. 2675
Omaha, Nebraska

Grandmother's Burnt Sugar Cake

2 c. sugar
Butter
3 eggs, beaten
2½ c. flour
2 tsp. baking powder
1 tsp. vanilla extract
2½ to 3 c. confectioners' sugar
Milk

Melt ½ cup sugar until it is very dark; add ¼ cup hot water. Cook until thick. Cream 1½ cups sugar and ½ cup butter. Add eggs, mixing well. Sift flour and baking powder together. Add 1 cup water and flour mixture to creamed mixture; beat well. Add vanilla and 3 tablespoons burnt sugar syrup; mix well. Pour into 2 greased and floured 9-inch cake pans. Bake at 350 degrees until cake tests done. Cool. Cream confectioners' sugar and 3 tablespoons butter. Add 1 tablespoon burnt sugar syrup and enough milk to thicken to spreading consistency. Frost cake.

Betty Behrend, Treas.
Xi Alpha Eta X1095
Atchison, Kansas

Leprechaun Cake

2 eggs
⅔ c. sugar
1 tsp. vanilla extract
½ c. milk
1 c. Bisquick baking mix
Confectioners' sugar
1½ c. miniature mashmallows
2 tbsp. green Creme de Menthe
4 tsp. Creme de Cacao
1 2-oz. envelope dessert topping mix

Beat eggs in small mixer bowl for 5 minutes or until thick and lemon colored. Add sugar gradually, beating well after each addition. Add vanilla and ¼ cup milk; beat on Low until well blended. Add baking mix gradually, beating just until batter is smooth. Pour into aluminum foil-lined 15x10x1-inch jelly roll pan. Bake at 375 degrees for 12 to 15 minutes or until cake tests done. Invert on towel sprinkled with confectioners' sugar. Remove foil carefully; trim edges of cake. Roll cake and towel from narrow end immediately. Cool on wire rack. Combine marshmallows and ¼ cup milk in saucepan. Cook over Medium heat until marshmallows are melted, stirring constantly. Chill until thickened. Add liqueurs; blend well. Prepare topping mix according to package directions. Fold in marshmallow mixture. Unroll cake; spread with marshmallow mixture. Reroll. Frost as desired. Chill for several hours or overnight.

Martha W. Gould
City Council Alternate
Preceptor Theta XP819
Beatrice, Nebraska

Marigold Cake

6 egg whites, stiffly beaten
1½ c. sugar, sifted 3 times
1 tsp. vanilla extract
1½ tbsp. vinegar
6 egg yolks, slightly beaten
1½ c. flour, sifted 3 times

Combine egg whites and sugar; beat well. Add vanilla, vinegar and egg yolks; mix well. Add flour; mix until well blended. Pour into funnel pan. Bake at 350 degrees until cake tests done.

Gertrude M. Jarvis
Preceptor Iota XP413
Eugene, Oregon

Matrimonial Cake

2 c. flour
½ tsp. salt
½ tsp. soda
2 c. oatmeal
1½ c. (firmly packed) brown sugar
1 c. butter, softened
½ lb. dates, chopped
1 tbsp. lemon juice

Combine flour, salt, soda, oatmeal and 1 cup brown sugar in large bowl; mix well. Cut in butter with pastry blender until well blended. Press half the mixture into 9-inch square pan. Set aside. Combine dates, lemon juice, ½ cup brown sugar and ¾ cup water in saucepan; mix well. Cook over Medium heat for 8 minutes or until mixture boils and dates are well blended, stirring frequently. Spread evenly over crumb mixture in pan. Top with remaining crumb mixture, pressing gently. Bake at 350 degrees for 30 minutes or until browned. Cut into squares while warm.

Karen Scanlan, Pres.
Xi Eta X3393
Don Mills, Ontario, Canada

Milky Way Cake

6 Milky Way candy bars
1 c. butter
2 c. sugar
4 eggs
2½ c. sifted flour
½ tsp. soda
1¼ c. buttermilk
1 tsp. vanilla extract
1 c. chopped nuts

Melt candy bars and ½ cup butter over Low heat. Cream remaining butter and sugar until fluffy. Add eggs, one at a time, beating well after each addition. Sift flour and soda together. Add flour mixture to creamed mixture alternately with buttermilk, beginning and ending with flour mixture. Beat until smooth. Add melted candy; stir well. Stir in vanilla and nuts. Pour into greased and floured 10-inch tube or bundt pan. Bake at 350 degrees for 1 hour and 20 minutes.

Olga B. Clarke, Pres.
Xi Theta Eta
Satellite Beach, Florida

Milk Chocolate Cake

½ c. butter, softened
1½ c. sugar
2 eggs
2 c. flour
¾ tsp. salt
1 c. sour milk
5 sq. chocolate
2 tsp. vanilla extract
1 tsp. soda
1 tbsp. vinegar
4 tbsp. Crisco
3 c. sifted confectioners' sugar
6 tbsp. hot milk

Cream butter. Add sugar gradually, beating well after each addition. Add eggs, one at a time, beating well after each addition. Sift flour and ½ teaspoon salt together. Add to creamed mixture alternately with sour milk, beginning and ending with flour mixture. Add 2 squares melted chocolate and 1 teaspoon vanilla. Dissolve soda in vinegar; add to chocolate mixture, mixing well. Pour into greased and floured round cake pans. Bake at 375 degrees for 25 minutes. Cool. Cream Crisco and 1 cup confectioners' sugar. Add 3 squares melted chocolate, 1 teaspoon vanilla and ¼ teaspoon salt. Add remaining confectioners' sugar alternately with hot milk, beating until smooth. Frost top and sides of cake.

Jacqueline Wires, Pres.
Alpha Iota X3926
Walbridge, Ohio

Prune Cake

1 c. Wesson oil
3½ c. sugar
2 c. self-rising flour
3 eggs
1 8-oz. jar prunes and apples junior baby food
1 c. chopped pecans
3 tbsp. allspice
Vanilla extract
¾ c. buttermilk
1½ sticks margarine
2 tbsp. light corn syrup
¾ tsp. soda

Combine oil, 2 cups sugar, flour, eggs, baby food, pecans, allspice and 1 tablespoon vanilla in order listed; mix lightly. Pour into greased and floured tube pan. Bake at 350 degrees for 1 hour. Combine buttermilk, margarine, corn syrup, soda, 1½ cups sugar and ¾ teaspoon vanilla in saucepan. Cook over Medium heat until soft-ball stage, stirring constantly. Pour over hot cake.

Linda Lyons
Alpha Theta No. 2871
Maggie Valley, North Carolina

Monkey Cake

4 pkg. Pillsbury biscuits
1½ c. sugar
1½ tbsp. cinnamon
1 stick margarine

Separate biscuits; cut each biscuit into 4 pieces. Combine sugar and cinnamon in plastic bag. Place biscuits, 10 at a time, in bag. Shake to coat well. Place biscuits in greased tube pan. Melt margarine in saucepan; add unused sugar and cinnamon from plastic bag. Bring to a boil; boil until sugar is dissolved. Pour over biscuits. Bake at 350 degrees for 45 minutes. Invert onto serving plate.

Virginia L. Burns, Rec. Sec.
Xi Nu X270
York, Pennsylvania

Mother's Spice Cake
(1945)

1¾ c. Bisquick
¾ c. sugar
1½ tsp. cinnamon
1 egg, slightly beaten
½ c. milk

Combine Bisquick, sugar and cinnamon; mix well. Stir in egg and milk. Pour into greased and floured loaf pan. Bake at 350 degrees for 35 to 40 minutes or until cake tests done.

Barbara Albright, Pres.
Xi Tau X1104
Lawton, Oklahoma

Peaches And Cream Cake

1 pkg. yellow cake mix
1 sm. package instant vanilla pudding mix
4 eggs
⅓ c. oil
1 lg. can sliced peaches
1 8-oz. package cream cheese
½ c. sugar

Combine cake mix, pudding mix, eggs, oil and 1 cup water; mix well. Pour into greased and floured 9x13-inch pan. Drain peaches, reserving 4 tablespoons juice. Arrange peaches over batter. Combine cream cheese, sugar and reserved juice; mix well. Spread over peaches. Bake at 350 degrees for 40 to 50 minutes.

Mary Ann Mietty, Corr. Sec.
Iota Rho No. 4388
Painesville, Ohio

Peanut Butter-Chocolate Cake

1¾ c. flour, sifted
¾ tsp. soda
¾ tsp. salt
1 c. sugar
2 tbsp. shortening
2 tbsp. peanut butter
¼ c. cocoa
1 c. milk
1 tsp. vanilla extract

Combine flour, soda and salt; set aside. Cream sugar, shortening and peanut butter until smooth. Add to flour mixture; mix well. Stir in cocoa, milk and vanilla. Pour into tube pan. Bake at 350 degrees for 1 hour or until cake tests done. Frost with favorite chocolate icing.

Barbara B. Reese, Corr. Sec.
Xi Beta Zeta X4098
Hickory, North Carolina

Queen Elizabeth Cake
(1935)

1 c. dates, chopped
Butter
1 c. sugar
1 egg, beaten
1½ c. flour
¼ tsp. salt
1 tsp. baking powder
1 tsp. soda
½ c. chopped nuts
1 tsp. vanilla extract
5 tbsp. brown sugar
2 tbsp. milk
½ c. coconut

Pour 1 cup boiling water over dates; cool. Cream ¼ cup butter. Add sugar; mix well. Add egg; mix well. Sift flour, salt, baking powder and soda together. Add to creamed mixture; mix well. Add date mixture; mix thoroughly. Fold in nuts and vanilla. Pour into 9-inch square pan. Bake at 350 degrees for 45 minutes. Combine 3 tablespoons butter, brown sugar, milk and coconut in saucepan. Boil for 3 minutes. Spread over warm cake. Return to oven to brown. Yield: 8 servings.

Joane Hepton
Iota Beta No. 10559
Richmond, Ontario, Canada

Poppy Seed Cake

½ lb. butter, softened
1½ c. sugar
1 bottle of poppy seed
1 c. sour cream
4 egg yolks, beaten
2 c. flour
1 tsp. soda
2 tsp. vanilla extract
4 egg whites, stiffy beaten

Cream butter and sugar until smooth. Add poppy seed; mix well. Add sour cream and egg yolks, mixing well. Add flour and soda; mix until well blended. Stir in vanilla. Fold in egg whites. Pour into greased and lightly floured tube pan. Bake at 350 degrees for 55 to 60 minutes or until cake tests done. Serve warm.

Debora Kukuk
Gamma Delta No. 8651
Shaw AFB, South Carolina

7-Up Cake

1½ c. butter, softened
3 c. sugar
5 eggs
3 c. flour
2 tbsp. lemon extract
¾ c. 7-Up
Confectioners' sugar

Cream butter and sugar until smooth. Add eggs, one at a time, beating well after each addition. Add flour, lemon extract and 7-Up; mix well. Pour into greased angel food cake pan. Bake at 325 degrees for 1 hour and 15 minutes or until cake tests done. Sprinkle with confectioners' sugar.

Donna Baughman, Treas.
Iota Theta
Valparaiso, Indiana

Sour Cream-Prune Cake
(1946)

1 c. diced prunes
2 eggs, well beaten
1½ c. (firmly packed) brown sugar
1 tsp. vanilla extract
1 c. sour cream
1½ c. cake flour
2 tsp. baking powder
½ tsp. soda
½ tsp. salt
1½ tsp. cinnamon
½ tsp. nutmeg
1½ tsp. cloves

Soak prunes until softened; drain. Combine eggs, brown sugar, vanilla, sour cream and ¼ cup cold water; mix well. Sift 1¼ cups flour, baking powder, soda, salt, cinnamon, nutmeg and cloves together. Add to sour cream mixture; beat well. Dredge prunes in ¼ cup flour. Stir prunes into batter. Pour into greased 4x8x2-inch loaf pan. Bake at 375 degrees for 45 minutes.

Sherry Sorenson
Beta Lambda XP1788
Garden City, Kansas

Swedish Cake

2 c. flour
2 c. sugar
2 eggs
2 tsp. soda
2 tsp. vanilla extract
1 20-oz. can crushed pineapple
1 c. chopped walnuts
1 8-oz. package cream cheese
1 stick butter, softened
1¾ c. confectioners' sugar

Combine flour, sugar, eggs, soda, 1 teaspoon vanilla, pineapple and ½ cup walnuts, mixing well after each addition. Pour into 9x13-inch baking pan. Bake at 350 degrees for 35 to 40 minutes or until cake tests done. Combine cream cheese, butter, confectioners' sugar, 1 teaspoon vanilla and ½ c. walnuts; mix until of spreading consistency. Spread on hot cake.

Sue Cherry, Corr. Sec.
Lamba Tau No. 10495
Anderson, Indiana

Vanilla Wafer Cake
(1959)

2 sticks margarine, softened
2 c. sugar
6 eggs
1 12-oz. package vanilla wafers, crushed
½ c. milk
1 7-oz. package coconut
1 c. chopped nuts

Cream margarine and sugar until smooth. Add eggs, one at a time, beating well after each addition. Add vanilla wafer crumbs and milk; mix well. Add coconut; mix until well blended. Fold in nuts. Pour into greased and floured tube pan. Bake at 300 degrees for 1 hour and 30 minutes.

Marilyn Tiffault
Gamma Delta No. 8651
Sumter, South Carolina

CAN SIZE CHART

8 oz. can or jar	1 c.	1 lb. 13 oz. can or jar	
10½ oz. can (picnic can)	1¼ c.	or No. 2½ can or jar	3½ c.
12 oz. can (vacuum)	1½ c.	1 qt. 14 fl. oz. or 3 lb. 3 oz.	
14-16 oz. or No. 300 can	1¼ c.	or 46 oz. can	5¾ c.
16-17 oz. can or jar		6½ to 7½ lb.	
or No. 303 can or jar	2 c.	or No. 10 can	12-13 c.
1 lb. 4 oz. or 1 pt. 2 fl. oz.			
or No. 2 can or jar	2½ c.		

EQUIVALENT CHART

3 tsp.	1 tbsp.	2 pt.	1 qt.
2 tbsp.	⅛ c.	1 qt.	4 c.
4 tbsp.	¼ c.	⅝ c.	½ c. + 2 tbsp.
8 tbsp.	½ c.	⅞ c.	¾ c. + 2 tbsp.
16 tbsp.	1 c.	1 jigger	1½ fl. oz. (3 tbsp.)
5 tbsp. + 1 tsp.	⅓ c.	2 c. fat	1 lb.
12 tbsp.	¾ c.	1 lb. butter	2 c. or 4 sticks
4 oz.	½ c.	2 c. sugar	1 lb.
8 oz.	1 c.	2⅔ c. powdered sugar	1 lb.
16 oz.	1 lb.	2⅔ c. brown sugar	1 lb.
1 oz.	2 tbsp. fat or liquid	4 c. sifted flour	1 lb.
2 c.	1 pt.	4½ c. cake flour	1 lb.

3½ c. unsifted whole wheat flour.. 1 lb.
8 to 10 egg whites.. 1 c.
12 to 14 egg yolks.. 1 c.
1 c. unwhipped cream.. 2 c. whipped
1 lb. shredded American cheese.................................... 4 c.
¼ lb. crumbled blue cheese.. 1 c.
1 chopped med. onion.................................... ½ c. pieces
1 lemon.. 3 tbsp. juice
1 lemon.. 1 tsp. grated peel
1 orange.. ⅓ c. juice
1 orange.................................... about 2 tsp. grated peel
1 lb. unshelled walnuts.............................. 1½ to 1¾ c. shelled
1 lb. unshelled almonds.................................... ¾ to 1 c. shelled
4 oz. (1 to 1¼ c.) uncooked macaroni................. 2¼ c. cooked
7 oz. spaghetti.. 4 c. cooked
4 oz. (1½ to 2 c.) uncooked noodles........................ 2 c. cooked
28 saltine crackers.. 1 c. crumbs
4 slices bread.................................... 1 c. crumbs
14 square graham crackers............................ 1 c. crumbs
22 vanilla wafers.. 1 c. crumbs

SUBSTITUTIONS FOR A MISSING INGREDIENT

1 square *chocolate* (1 ounce) = 3 or 4 tablespoons cocoa plus ½ tablespoon fat.
1 tablespoon *cornstarch* (for thickening) = 2 tablespoons flour.
1 cup sifted *all-purpose flour* = 1 cup plus 2 tablespoons sifted cake flour.
1 cup sifted *cake flour* = 1 cup minus 2 tablespoons sifted all-purpose flour.
1 teaspoon *baking* powder = ¼ teaspoon baking soda plus ½ teaspoon cream of tartar.
1 cup *sour milk* = 1 cup sweet milk into which 1 tablespoon vinegar or lemon juice has been stirred; or 1 cup buttermilk (let stand for 5 minutes).

SUBSTITUTIONS FOR A MISSING INGREDIENT

1 cup *sweet milk* = 1 cup sour milk or buttermilk plus ½ teaspoon baking soda.
1 cup *canned tomatoes* = about 1⅓ cups cut-up fresh tomatoes, simmered 10 minutes.
¾ cup *cracker crumbs* = 1 cup bread crumbs.
1 cup *cream, sour, heavy* = ⅓ cup butter and ⅔ cups milk in any sour milk recipe.
1 cup *cream, sour, thin* = 3 tablespoons butter and ¾ cup milk in sour milk recipe.
1 cup *molasses* = 1 cup honey.
1 teaspoon *dried herbs* = 1 tablespoon fresh herbs.
1 *whole egg* = 2 egg yolks for custards.
½ cup *evaporated milk* and ½ cup *water* or 1 cup *reconstituted nonfat dry milk* and 1 tablespoon
          butter = 1 cup whole milk.
1 package *active dry yeast* = 1 cake compressed yeast.
1 tablespoon *instant minced onion, rehydrated* = 1 small fresh onion.
1 tablespoon *prepared mustard* = 1 teaspoon dry mustard.
⅛ teaspoon *garlic powder* = 1 small pressed clove of garlic.

METRIC CONVERSION CHARTS FOR THE KITCHEN

VOLUME

1 tsp.	4.9 cc	2 c.	473.4 cc
1 tbsp.	14.7 cc	1 fl. oz.	29.5 cc
⅓ c.	28.9 cc	4 oz.	118.3 cc
⅛ c.	29.5 cc	8 oz.	236.7 cc
¼ c.	59.1 cc	1 pt.	473.4 cc
½ c.	118.3 cc	1 qt.	.946 liters
¾ c.	177.5 cc	1 gal.	3.7 liters
1 c.	236.7 cc		

CONVERSION FACTORS:

Liters	X	1.056	=	Liquid Quarts
Quarts	X	0.946	=	Liters
Liters	X	0.264	=	Gallons
Gallons	X	3.785	=	Liters
Fluid Ounces	X	29.563	=	Cubic Centimeters
Cubic Centimeters	X	0.034	=	Fluid Ounces
Cups	X	236.575	=	Cubic Centimeters
Tablespoons	X	14.797	=	Cubic Centimeters
Teaspoons	X	4.932	=	Cubic Centimeters
Bushels	X	0.352	=	Hectoliters
Hectoliters	X	2.837	=	Bushels
Ounces (Avoir.)	X	28.349	=	Grams
Grams	X	0.035	=	Ounces
Pounds	X	0.454	=	Kilograms
Kilograms	X	2.205	=	Pounds

WEIGHT

1 dry oz.	28.3 Grams
1 lb.	454 Kilograms

LIQUID MEASURE AND METRIC EQUIVALENT

(NEAREST CONVENIENT EQUIVALENTS)

CUPS SPOONS	QUARTS OUNCES	METRIC EQUIVALENTS
1 teaspoon	⅙ ounce	5 milliliters 5 grams
2 teaspoons	⅓ ounce	10 milliliters 10 grams
1 tablespoon	½ ounce	15 milliliters 15 grams
3⅓ tablespoons	1¾ ounces	50 milliliters
¼ cup (4 tablespoons)	2 ounces	60 milliliters
⅓ cup (5⅓ tablespoons)	2⅔ ounces	79 milliliters
⅓ cup plus 1 tablespoon	3½ ounces	100 milliliters
½ cup (8 tablespoons)	4 ounces	118 milliliters
1 cup (16 tablespoons)	8 ounces	¼ liter 236 milliliters
2 cups	1 pint 16 ounces	½ liter less 1½ tablespoons 473 milliliters
2 cups plus 2½ tablespoons	17 ounces	½ liter
4 cups	1 quart 32 ounces	946 milliliters
4⅓ cups	1 quart, 2 ounces	1 liter 1000 milliliters

CONVERSION FORMULAS:

To convert Centigrade to Fahrenheit: multiply by 9, divide by 5, add 32.
To convert Fahrenheit to Centigrade: subract 32, multiply by 5, divide by 9.

DRY MEASURE AND METRIC EQUIVALENT

(MOST CONVENIENT APPROXIMATION)

POUNDS AND OUNCES	METRIC	POUNDS AND OUNCES	METRIC
⅙ ounce	5 grams	¼ pound (4 ounces)	114 grams
⅓ ounce	10 grams	4⅛ ounces	125 grams
½ ounce	15 grams	½ pound (8 ounces)	227 grams
1 ounce	30 grams (28.35)	¾ pound (12 ounces)	250 grams
1¾ ounces	50 grams	1 pound (16 ounces)	454 grams
2⅔ ounces	75 grams	1.1 pounds	500 grams
3½ ounces	100 grams	2.2 pounds	1 kilogram 1000 grams

Regal Cheesecake Pie

2 c. fine vanilla wafer or graham cracker
  crumbs
6 tbsp. butter or margarine, melted
Sugar
4 3-oz. packages cream cheese, softened
3 eggs
1 11-oz. can Cheddar cheese soup
2 tbsp. lemon juice
2 tsp. grated lemon rind
2 tsp. vanilla extract
¼ tsp. almond extract
1 c. sour cream

Combine crumbs, butter and ¼ cup sugar; mix well.
Press into 10-inch pie plate to form crust. Chill for 1
hour. Place cream cheese in mixer bowl; cream until
smooth. Add ⅔ cup sugar and eggs alternately to
cream cheese, mixing at Medium speed of electric
mixer. Add 1 cup soup, lemon juice, 1 teaspoon
grated rind, 1 teaspoon vanilla and almond extract;
mix well. Pour into chilled pie crust. Bake at 350
degrees for 50 minutes. Combine sour cream,
remaining soup, ¼ cup sugar, 1 teaspoon grated rind
and 1 teaspoon vanilla; mix well. Spread on pie. Bake
at 350 degrees for 5 minutes longer. Chill until set.
Garnish with cherry pie filling or sliced peaches.

Photograph for this recipe on page 1.

Mushroom Soup With Whipped Cream

1 lb. mushrooms, chopped
¼ lb. butter
3 tbsp. flour
Pinch of salt
1 qt. milk, warmed
1 bay leaf
½ pt. heavy cream, whipped

Saute mushrooms in butter over Low heat until
tender and golden brown. Add flour and salt; stir
until smooth. Stir in milk. Add bay leaf. Simmer until
thickened, stirring constantly. Remove bay leaf. Pour
into tureen. Top with whipped cream.

Photograph for this recipe on page 2.

Lamb Shoulder With Orange Mint Sauce

1 6-oz. can frozen orange juice
¼ c. lemon juice
¼ c. butter or margarine
½ tsp. salt
1 4-lb. lamb shoulder
½ c. finely chopped celery
½ c. blanched almonds, slivered
1 tbsp. mint flakes

Combine orange juice, lemon juice, butter and salt in
1-quart glass casserole. Microwave on High for 3
minutes. Place shoulder in 9-inch glass cake dish;
brush with small amount of orange juice mixture.
Microwave on High for 35 minutes or until of desired
doneness, brushing with orange juice mixture and
rotating dish frequently. Add celery, almonds and
mint flakes to remaining orange juice mixture.
Microwave on High for 5 minutes. Garnish lamb with
orange slices and parsley. Serve with orange-mint
sauce.

Photograph for this recipe on page 35.

Melba Ice Cream Cake

1 10-oz. package frozen raspberries, thawed
1 tbsp. cornstarch
½ c. red currant jelly
16 to 18 ladyfingers, split
3 pt. vanilla ice cream, slightly softened
1 c. sliced peaches, sweetened

Drain raspberries, reserving juice. Dissolve cornstarch in 2 tablespoons reserved juice. Combine
raspberries, remaining reserved juice and jelly in
saucepan; bring to a boil. Add cornstarch gradually;
cook until thickened and clear, stirring constantly.
Cook for 2 minutes longer; cover. Chill. Cut tips off
10 to 11 ladyfingers. Stand ladyfingers upright
around sides of 9-inch springform pan. Line bottom
of pan with remaining ladyfingers and pieces.
Spread ½ of the ice cream over ladyfingers. Drizzle
with ¼ cup raspberry mixture. Cover with remaining
ice cream. Drizzle with ¼ cup raspberry mixture;
cover. Freeze overnight or until firm. Top with
peaches. Cut into wedges. Serve with remaining
raspberry sauce. Yield: 12 servings.

Photograph for this recipe on page 36.

Lobster Casseroles

Butter or margarine
3 tbsp. flour
2 c. heavy cream
1 10½-oz. can golden mushroom soup
Salt and pepper to taste
5 5-oz. frozen South African rock lobster tails
2 tbsp. instant minced onion

2 tbsp. finely chopped parsley
½ c. corn flake crumbs

Melt 3 tablespoons butter in saucepan. Stir in flour until smooth. Add cream and soup gradually, beating well after each addition. Cook over Low heat until thickened and bubbly. Add seasonings. Drop lobster tails into boiling salted water; boil for 4 minutes. Drain; rinse with cold water. Remove underside membrane with scissors; pull meat out in one piece. Cut meat into 1-inch crosswise slices. Stir into soup mixture. Add onion and parsley, mixing well. Pour into shallow individual casseroles. Combine crumbs and ¼ cup melted butter; mix well. Sprinkle over lobster mixture. Bake at 350 degrees for 30 to 35 minutes.

Photograph for this recipe on page 69.

Rosy Butter

½ c. butter or margarine
¼ c. catsup
1 tbsp. lemon juice
Dash of tabasco

Combine all ingredients in small saucepan; mix well. Cook over Low heat until smooth and melted. Serve warm.

Photograph for this recipe on page 69.

Green Mayonnaise

1½ c. mayonnaise
¾ c. chopped watercress
¼ c. chopped parsley
2 tbsp. chopped chives
2 tsp. prepared mustard
2 tbsp. lemon juice
Salt to taste

Combine all ingredients in blender container; mix until smooth. Serve warm or cold.

Photograph for this recipe on page 69.

Lobster Kabobs

4 5-oz. frozen South African rock lobster tails, thawed
1 1-lb. can boiled potatoes, drained
1 6-oz. can button mushrooms, drained
1 1-lb. can boiled onions, drained
½ c. oil
¼ c. dry white wine
1 clove of garlic, mashed
2 tbsp. minced chives
¼ tsp. each oregano and thyme
1 tsp. salt

Remove underside membrane of lobster tails using kitchen shears; pull meat out in one piece. Cut each piece into 3 or 4 crosswise slices. Alternately spear rock lobster slices, potatoes, mushrooms and onions on 4 heatproof skewers. Place filled skewers, side by side, in shallow baking pan. Combine remaining ingredients; beat until blended. Pour over skewers; refrigerate for 1 hour, turning skewers occasionally. Broil for 10 to 12 minutes, turning skewers.

Photograph for this recipe on page 69.

Mini Quiches Florentine

1 10¾-oz. can cream of mushroom soup
1 8-oz. package cream cheese, softened
4 eggs, slightly beaten
1 c. finely chopped fresh spinach
⅔ c. shredded Swiss cheese
½ c. finely chopped ham
¼ c. finely chopped green onions
½ tsp. hot pepper sauce
24 6-in. crepes

Combine soup and cream cheese; blend until smooth. Stir in remaining ingredients except crepes; mix well. Fold crepes, browned-side down, to form 3½-inch square. Place each square in lightly oiled muffin cups, pressing to line bottom and sides. Corners of folded crepes will extend above muffin cups. Spoon 3 tablespoons spinach mixture into each crepe-lined cup. Bake at 375 degrees for 10 minutes. Cover with aluminum foil. Bake for 20 minutes longer or until done. Remove from muffin cups. Cool. Yield: 24 servings.

Photograph for this recipe on page 70.

Lifesaver Rice

1 c. chopped onions
1 c. sliced celery
½ c. diced green pepper
2 tbsp. butter or margarine
3 c. cooked rice
2 c. diced cooked ham
1 tbsp. grated orange rind
Salt and pepper to taste
⅔ c. mayonnaise
2 c. orange segments

Saute onions, celery and green pepper in butter until tender-crisp. Add rice, ham, grated rind, salt, pepper and mayonnaise; toss lightly. Pour into buttered casserole. Bake at 350 degrees for 15 to 20 minutes. Garnish with orange segments. Yield: 6 servings.

Photograph for this recipe on page 103.

Old-Fashioned Blueberry-Sugar Cakes

1 c. sugar
½ c. vegetable shortening
½ tsp. salt
3 eggs, slightly beaten
2 c. flour
2 tsp. baking powder
½ tsp. cinnamon
1 c. milk
1 c. blueberries

Cream sugar and shortening until fluffy. Add salt; mix well. Stir in eggs. Sift flour and baking powder together. Add flour mixture to creamed mixture, mixing well. Add cinnamon; mix well. Add milk gradually, beating well after each addition until smooth and glossy. Dust blueberries lightly with additional flour. Fold blueberries into batter. Spoon into well-greased muffin cups, filling ⅔ full. Bake at 400 degrees for 20 to 25 minutes or until toothpick inserted into center comes out clean. Yield: 12 servings.

Photograph for this recipe on page 104.

Classic Blueberry Pie

1 pkg. pie crust mix
3 tbsp. cornstarch
1 qt. blueberries
1 c. sugar
2 tbsp. lemon juice
Milk

Prepare pie crust according to package directions. Dissolve cornstarch in ¼ cup cold water; set aside. Combine blueberries, sugar, ½ cup water and lemon juice in saucepan; bring to a boil. Stir in cornstarch mixture. Remove from heat; cool. Roll out ⅔ of the pie crust large enough to line bottom and sides of 8-inch pie plate. Pour blueberry mixture into pie crust. Roll out remaining crust; cover top of pie. Seal edges with small amount of milk; crimp. Make slits in top to vent. Bake at 450 degrees for 10 minutes. Reduce heat to 350 degrees. Bake for 20 minutes longer or until crust is lightly browned.

Photograph for this recipe on page 104.

Blueberry Parfait

2 c. heavy cream
⅓ c. sugar
1 tsp. vanilla extract
4 c. blueberries

Whip cream, adding sugar gradually until soft peaks form. Stir in vanilla. Spoon alternating layers of blueberries and whipped cream into tall parfait glasses, beginning and ending with blueberries. Top with dollop of whipped cream. Yield: 6 servings.

Photograph for this recipe on page 104.

Photography Credits

Cover Design—Lee Hamblen; Campbell Soup Company; American Lamb Council; United Dairy Industry Association; Ruth Lundgren, Ltd.; Rice Council; Florida Citrus Commission; American Dairy Association; California Avocado Advisory Board; National Kraut Packers; National Macaroni Institute; National Dairy Council; National Cherry Growers and Industries Foundation; National Live Stock and Meat Board; Evaporated Milk Association; California Apricot Advisory Board; Best Foods; Artichoke Advisory Board; United Fresh Fruit and Vegetable Association; Louisiana Yam Commission; California Raisin Advisory Board; Green Giant Company; Fleischmann's Yeast; The Quaker Oats Company; Wheat Flour Institute; The J. M. Smucker Company.

Index

FAVORITE RECIPES OF
BETA SIGMA PHI INTERNATIONAL
COOKBOOKS

Add to
Your Cookbook Collection
Select from These ALL-TIME
Favorites

BOOK TITLE	ITEM NUMBER
The Golden Anniversary Cookbook (1980) 200 Pages	11665
Dining Room (1979) 200 Pages	10006
Recipes From The World Of BSP (1978) 200 Pages	01341
Dieting To Stay Healthy (1977) 200 Pages	00949
Bicentennial Heritage Recipes (1976) 200 Pages	70262
Save and "Win" (1975) 200 Pages	70017
Money-Saving Casseroles (1974) 200 Pages	70009
Party Book (1973) 192 Pages	70378
Gourmet (1973) 200 Pages	70025
Fondue & Buffet (1972) 192 Pages	70033
Holiday (1971) 288 Pages	70041
Meats (1968) 384 Pages	70076

FOR ORDERING INFORMATION
Write to:

Favorite Recipes Press
P.O. Box 77
Nashville, Tennessee 37202

BOOKS OFFERED SUBJECT TO AVAILABILITY.